# MEN

# MEN

## 'THE MALE MYTH EXPOSED'

*Mary Ingham*

CENTURY PUBLISHING
LONDON

*To NMI*

Copyright © Mary Ingham 1984

*All rights reserved*

First published in Great Britain in 1984
by Century Publishing Co. Ltd,
Portland House,
12-13 Greek Street, London W1V 5LE

British Library Cataloguing in Publication Data

Ingham, Mary
  Men.
  1. Men——Psychology
  I. Title
  155.6'32     BF692.5

ISBN 0 7126 0190 2

Printed in Great Britain
by St Edmundsbury Press, Bury St Edmunds, Suffolk
and bound by Butler & Tanner Ltd, Frome, Somerset.

# CONTENTS

# ACKNOWLEDGEMENTS

FIRST AND foremost I should like to thank the 96 men who responded so patiently and obligingly to my interrogations and without whom this book would not have been possible. Where quoted, their names have been fictionalised.

I am grateful to Tom Crabtree, Steve Cropley, Neville Darby, Nick Hern, Tim Jeal, John Lahr and Bob Woodings for their helpful advice when the project was in its early stages; to Richard Carvalho, Drs Wyndol Furman and Howard Markman, University of Denver, Colorado, Dr David Hargreaves, University of Leicester, John Harris, Peter Moss, Thomas Coram Research Unit and Ken Roberts, University of Liverpool, for the information they provided; to Mike and Liz, Joan and John and Rachel and Peter for sheltering us when we were traipsing the country; to Mick Dunn, Dave Gee, John Goodier, Roy Greenslade, Gerry Popplestone, Fred Riley and Mike Wall for their invaluable help; and most of all to Dave, without whose untiring willingness to view nearly every provincial town centre in the country (or so it must have felt) the research could not have been completed. I should also like to take this opportunity of telling Debbie that I kept my promise.

Acknowledgement is gratefully made to the following for permission to quote extracts: to John Berger for the extract from *A Fortunate Man*, 1967, on page 15; to Gyles Brandreth for the extract from *Created in Captivity*, 1972, on page 13; to Andre Deutsch Ltd for the extract from Mervyn Jones, *Two Women and their Man*, 1981, on page 93; to Gerald Duckworth & Co Ltd, for the extracts from Charles Hampden-Turner, *Radical Man*, on pages 183 and 221; to the *Guardian* for extracts from an article by Martin Stone (19 April 1983) on pages 229 and 230 and an article by Mike Hales (2 December 1980) on pages 33 and 34; to Methuen London Ltd for an extract from Wallace Shawn, *My Dinner with André* and *Marie and Bruce*, 1983, on page 233; to Random House Inc for an extract from Charles A. Reich, *The Greening of America*, 1970, on page 159.

# PREFACE

THIS BOOK is dedicated to my father, who died just as I had begun writing it. The shock of his sudden illness and death inevitably set back the progress of the book, but also, unexpectedly, pinpointed the feelings that led me to want to write it.

My father was a kind, reticent, peaceable person, with a sort of quiet determination I only recently discovered. He was a stranger to me when I was growing up. My elder sister remembers him patiently helping her with her homework, but by the time I arrived on the scene my father was simply a function I took for granted, the provider, the one who supported us all, while my mother brought us up. When my father was not behind the paper, in front of current affairs programmes on the television, or eating his lunch on a tray with Wimbledon or the cricket in the summer, he was out at 'meetings' to do with his work or associations to which he belonged. I can picture him switching off electric fires or lights we had left burning, issuing the occasional reprimand, and driving us out in the car on Sunday afternoons. I have one very strong flash memory image of him, when I must have been very small, bouncing me on his knee and trying to make me smile, but otherwise nothing—whereas my mother seems to accompany every childhood memory I have.

He rarely spoke about himself in those days. I discovered more about him than I'd ever known in twenty years of living in the same house, when I interviewed him for a psychology course project while I was at university. I had chosen to analyse my father's attitude towards his imminent retirement, which I concluded was very unrealistic—he could not seem to see beyond it being a well-earned rest. He retired early, at sixty, and they moved to a bungalow by the sea. My father devoted himself to his garden for the first few years, until my mother became an invalid, when he devoted himself to her.

It was only after my mother died that I began to realise how much they had functioned as a symbiotic whole, of which my mother was the emotional, demonstratively affectionate half, the one who wrote letters, rang up. A letter from my father always meant that my mother was too ill to write, and he hardly ever rang *me* in his life. If financially my mother had always depended on my father, emotionally my father had always existed through her.

After my mother died, it was very hard to get close to him. He was lonely, but he couldn't seem to make friends or respond to invitations from old friends. Perhaps it was simply shyness, but it seemed as if something in him, some facility or skill for making relationships, had atrophied, like an unused muscle, years before. For me, he will always be a solitary figure in an old trilby hat and overcoat, standing waiting at the bottom of the station ramp on the days that I visited him. His constant question, whether I was 'all right financially', seemed to be the only way he knew of showing affection, and I think our independence of him robbed him of a role or a sense of relatedness to us. He would sometimes say how useless he felt, in comparison with the time when he held down a responsible job. 'What am I now?' he would say. 'Just an old age pensioner.'

His death left me with a terrible feeling, that we had had no common language, that he had worked all his life supporting us, leaving us his savings, and yet we had never been able to give him anything in return, because we couldn't get close to him. Superficially, my father's life had carried every masculine advantage—a good education, a good career, a career dominated by men, in which he made a reasonable mark for himself, waited on hand and foot by my mother, with the independent status and individual fulfilment she lacked—yet he ended his days in loneliness and lack of purpose, having decidedly missed out on something.

The week before my father died, my elder brother drove down to visit him in hospital. My brother confessed that on the long journey—a rare time of solitude for a married man with three teenage children—he had reflected how he hardly knew his father, that they were relative strangers. He saw this as being chiefly because our father had put all his energy into his job, and felt it was a warning for himself, not to go the same way. Yet he suddenly saw himself cast in the same mould: he'd gone into the same profession, had a similarly large family and a housewife wife. And he saw in himself the danger of a similar sort of diffidence towards people, detachment, neglect of relationships, and of himself.

Most men do not find themselves in the position my father was in; because most men do not outlive their wives (one lethal statistical symptom of the male role). This book is also dedicated to all men who have the courage to explore the inner part of their being, in which they feel separate from their fathers, distanced in their relationships and undisclosed to themselves.

# INTRODUCTION

*What motivates people? Ego and the money to buy things they and their families want.*
(The Regional Sales Manager of Data General[1])

*The male who feels he must prove his masculinity via occupational success and cannot find time for non-vocational and family pursuits is a rather common phenomenon.*
(Henry B. Biller[2])

IN THE course of researching this book I came up against one major drawback to writing about men. I had expected problems, and initially assumed they would centre around the insurmountable handicap of not being a man. This particular problem is not to be underestimated since the fact of our physiological make-up cuts us off, men from women and women from men, all through life in so many different ways, starting with our positions in relation to our parents, and then from the school playground onwards, so that when we each reach into our experience we are rummaging in a different store of memories. For the writer, it means one cannot *know* in a gut sense the truth of an obscure theory, confirm an insight because it reverberates within, or conjure up an instinctive image to express the reality of the opposite sex. But it is not the main problem of writing about men.

Nor is it the relative lack of reference books devoted to the subject, the missing catalogue entries, the lack of anything between 'meaning' and 'monogamy' in the indexes of relevant works. Since the early 1970s there has been a steady, if small, stream of titles on the subject of men published in the United States, some of which have managed to filter across the Atlantic. But otherwise, researchwise, it is a question of hacking through a forest of facts and figures, with only the narrowest of footpaths marked 'men' alongside the now broad motorway of works on women.

No, the really major problem of writing about men is that the majority of men do not think they have a problem. And this is a big problem if you want to delve into a subject and really get to grips with it. Of course, I did not realise this when I first set out to write about men.

I decided to write about men because I had just finished writing a book about the women of my generation, the final chapter of which threw up some questions about men. It was then that it struck me that although I had written about my generation, I had left half of it out. I had written about the changes my generation of women had lived through, in relation to the female role, and I began to wonder how much these changes had also affected men. Also, it seemed that women's experience in isolation had been done to death; there seemed something very stale and claustrophobic about all-women discussions. Writing about men offered the chance of letting some light in on the subject of sex roles. (Around this time Betty Friedan brought out *The Second Stage*,[3] in which she claimed that men would be at the cutting edge of the next stage in the emancipation of women.) But I also wanted to write about men themselves, for their own sake. It seemed to me that the women's movement was somehow shadow-boxing with stereotyped images of the opposite sex. I wanted to know what men were really like, what they really felt and believed in. But most of all I had what I now know to have been a very naive crusading spirit which impelled me to find out what made men tick, what was vulnerable about them. I imagined it would just take a sympathetic female ear and they would bare their souls, just like women do; which of course was my first fundamental error of judgement.

For *Now We Are Thirty*,[4] my first book, I traced and interviewed the women I had been at school with, around the time when we all reached thirty, a critical age for most women. The most logical next step would have been to contact all the men I was at school with, but here I encountered a slight drawback, since I went to a single sex school. I overcame that one by doing the next best thing, tracing people who were at school with various of my acquaintances, and there is one man to whom I am especially indebted, for providing me with the contact addresses from when he traced *his* year at school, for a book written about ten years previously.

Most of the men had attended grammar schools in different parts of the country, but I also spoke to men who had been to public or secondary modern schools. It all took some time. Tracing men who have been at school together is more difficult than tracing women, who seem to keep in touch with one or two old friends from school even though they invariably change their names. But men moved house without telling the neighbours, fell out or lost contact with their parents, went abroad, and, which was the most frustrating, failed to keep in touch with old friends from school even when they bumped into them in the street. They were also much more prone to put off or cancel interview appointments at a moment's notice, being invariably up to their eyes in work, although some men kindly made room for me on their official schedule; but it was usually after office hours, in the evenings or at weekends, none of the cosy afternoon chats I had with my old school friends, before the children arrived home at four. In the end, over a two-year period, I tracked down and interviewed nearly a hundred men, mainly from three schools, one of which was co-educational.

The trouble was that although I had achieved what I wanted and talked to ordinary men, I hadn't found what I was looking for. I had met a selection of agreeable, fairly normal family men, who had reached the age of thirty-five, who cut the lawn, washed the car, played the occasional game of squash, liked to watch television and go out for a meal with friends, and were fairly contented with where they had got in their work. Some were more ambitious than others. Many had exercised very little conscious choice over their career and suffered several changes in their late teens and early twenties before settling into something with reasonable prospects.

Talking about work, they showed satisfaction or frustration to varying degrees, but generally within the context of overall acceptance of the limitations within which they had made what they considered relatively free and responsible choices. None of them was unemployed, although a few had experienced redundancy. Hardly any of them would have entertained the idea of changing places with their wives.

In Betty Friedan's *The Second Stage*, one of the chapters is entitled 'The Quiet Movement of American Men'. It opens by describing men still apparently going about their normal lives, but at the same time struggling inside themselves, silently questioning the outward goals which dictate most men's lives, each wondering if this is what he really wants. But if there was a quiet movement of British men, they were keeping very quiet indeed, especially when it came to questioning the daily routine of their lives. Although a large number of men worked long hours, either because they needed the overtime pay or because the responsibilities of their job demanded it, few showed any real resentment of this intrusion into their personal lives. Most actively enjoyed their work; several claimed that they never really noticed they worked longer hours.

I couldn't understand. These men accepted the very real burden of supporting several people so willingly. One or two did live with the fantasy of dropping out, moving to the coast and getting a nice free and easy job as a postman, or retiring early, but there was none of the unrest and self-questioning which Friedan had led me to expect. There was of course one easy answer. They were doing all right, Jack. Betty had got it wrong. De Beauvoir was right in seeing men's sex roles as supportive of self-fulfilment. They had not been knitting their brows waiting for the likes of me to turn up with a tape recorder so they could amplify their doubts. My concern had been misplaced.

My concern *had* been misplaced, but not in the way I imagined. In the middle of wondering what I was going to be able to write about, it was beginning to strike me, rather forcefully, on the transcription side of numerous C90 tapes, that men seemed rather resistant to the idea of being identified with other men. Most were careful never to generalise, adding the disclaimer that what they were saying was simply their own personal experience, opinion, etc. Unlike women, they seemed to have no idea how men in general behave or respond, let alone whether they are changing.

The growing feeling of discomfort about the subject I had chosen wasn't helped by the comments of male acquaintances and friends, especially when I jokingly announced that I was 'feeling my way round the subject', which didn't go down well at all. The great conversation party piece I had always felt I lacked became more of a conversation stopper. I had assumed men would leap at the opportunity to at least get their spoke in and redress the balance against women, but at best I got a signal lack of response. At worst I found myself pinned down and under attack. Somehow I had stirred up a nest of hostility which I simply could not understand.

Male friends who in other circumstances (usually, I later realised, when they were on their own) had professed interest and enthusiasm and answered my questions on the subject turned tail, and leaning across the dinner table pronounced that you could not possibly generalise about men because they are all so different.

I would counter that of course men are all different; so are women, but that hasn't stopped the countless trees felled and reams of paper covered on the subject of women as a sex, and their sex role. Ah, but that's different. The traditional female role, I was told, involves certain activities stemming from women's sexual function with which women either do or don't conform, like housework, and childcare. Women's lives can therefore be analysed through their approach to these role expectations. Well, I said. The male role, they continued, apart from an overall tendency to watch football matches on Saturday afternoons and wash the car or tackle DIY on Sundays, simply consists of what you spend your money on and how you earn it, which is a highly individual thing (as I was beginning to learn, listening to the daily intricacies of and differences between the lives of salesmen, accountants, firemen and plumbers).

Perhaps I had simply caught the men I interviewed too early, although I had thought thirty-five to be the ideal age, the onset of the midlife crisis. Perhaps, though, Betty

Friedan had talked largely to her own generation, menopausal middle-aged men with regrets and adolescent
longings. Perhaps I had asked the wrong questions and
failed to ask the right ones, or simply not managed to
penetrate the wall of a stranger's wary platitudes. However
much I shook it, the liquid in the test-tube stayed cloudy.

Refusing to admit defeat, I cornered every man I came
across, even quizzing the gasman when he came to fix the
water heater. He had recently weathered a stormy patch in
his marriage and wasn't averse to reflecting about the
problems of being a man. Nevertheless, when I began to
query about men's relationship to their role, to their work,
he said very much the same as I had already heard from so
many other men, depicting men as practical realists who get
on with things and rarely contemplate the extent to which
they may be trapped by their responsibilities.

But, I protested, growing desperate, I'm looking for the
cracks. I had chosen the word to mean strain, stresses, but the
gasman took it a different way. 'The cracks in the plaster,
d'you mean?' was what he said. And that made me look at all
the material I had gathered in a very different light. What if
men were feeling all the strains and stresses, but plastering
them over, covering them up in a classic defensive way? I had
expected men to explain their dilemma, to *tell* me what was
wrong, to be consciously aware of it and able to articulate it,
give it a name. I had taken Betty Friedan too literally and
expected men to be staring ruminatively into their coffee
dregs at the end of a business lunch before the prospect of
another sales conference and thinking 'Is this all?', in the
same way that Betty Friedan described women's doubts
about the point of a life spent shopping for matching
pillow-slips.

Betty Friedan's women had been able to sense that
something was wrong because some of them, like Friedan
herself, had left satisfying jobs after the war ended. They had
a perspective on the traditional women's role. And the
female role itself was also changing rapidly during the late
1950s and early 1960s, because of technological advances
(aerosols, dehydrated foods and strong detergents) made
during the war and exploited for domestic consumption

after it. Housework was becoming streamlined and, in the process, less of a craft and more of a purely menial chore, the repetitive tasks of a factory robot. Suburbia and super-markets, social phenomena of the mid 1960s, increased women's social isolation, taking the heart out of the communities of which women were a part. And at the same time work beckoned, the man's world, bright, lively, centrally heated, luxurious, offering new opportunities for mobility and affluence, more stimulation, company, satisfy-ing work.

Ironically of course this questioning of the female role only served to bolster the idea that the male's existence was the more desirable. There does now exist a comparable threat to the male role, in fact two, one of which is the new demand within the women's movement for a change in men. The other is unemployment. However, the men I had chosen to interview, men in mid-career, were the ones least likely to suffer this. Unemployment has so far tended mainly to hit school-leavers and older men. A few of the men I interviewed had suffered redundancy, but found other work. Several men had moved 'sideways', expressing a certain amount of controlled anxiety, false optimism, and dubious rational-isation. One man who had voluntarily left his job and taken six weeks to find another had experienced enough of the reality of unemployment to understand why he needed to go out to work, but the majority of men in their mid-thirties seem to shrug it off, confident that there are jobs around if you are willing to knuckle under. Many of them were aware of the staggering numbers of applicants for new posts when they applied for promotion, but the reality of unemploy-ment had never touched them.

Perhaps this was the reason for the complacency I had uncovered, that I had unwittingly chosen men whose jobs weren't threatened and whose wives were too busy bringing up children to worry about women's rights. Certainly it did not seem at all the stuff that books are made of, as various of them cheerfully pointed out to me. And yet, and yet. Was it not possible that all this apparent stability was still a façade?

Meanwhile, where Betty Friedan had uncovered a problem which merely lacked a name, I had not even found doubt or uneasiness. The masculine mystique, the male dilemma, not only didn't appear to have a name, it didn't appear to exist. The integrity of the male role and its positive effects remained irritatingly and annoyingly intact, and not just intact but seemingly waterproof and shock-protected. All I was collecting, or so it seemed, were long, fascinatingly detailed but unproductive conversations with normal people leading normal lives. It seemed somehow wrong to hope that the stucco might be crumbling, that the plaster of complacency these men were cheerfully repainting actually covered up something nasty in the brickwork which would shortly begin to emerge...

And slowly but surely it did. It began to strike me that there was something odd about the way in which men centred their lives almost exclusively around work, without feeling they were missing out on anything. Life is, after all, the most precious possession we have. How we spend it determines how richly we can look back on it when we are older. Why then do so many men bury themselves up to the neck for the major part of their lives in accountancy, or polythene bags, or make the same trip, every day, to the same office in the same building? Most of my interviewees, inside this strait jacket, merely shrugged, and even if they had been doing the same job for twenty years, rationalised any object of moving away. One or two did express a hazy dark yearning for something different, like Dick, who had been in the same job for thirteen years:

> If I hadn't got to where I am now, I would have changed jobs completely. I would have liked something in sport or farming. I don't really know why I got involved in what I am doing, but it's the way things happen, isn't it? I keep threatening that if I was made redundant I would sell up and move to the coast and something completely different. I sometimes wonder if it's all worth it. Why not just be a postman? I'm getting very deep now. But the mortgage hanging round my neck, I do regret not doing other things, finding out whether I would enjoy them...

Why was it such a *deep* thought, to be questioning one's work? Perhaps men do spend most of their time on the surface, for fear of what lies underneath. One man, Bob, suggested to me that men do not resent the burden of their role because they have been sentenced to life, and resign themselves to that fact fairly early on. Women, on the other hand, live with the hypothetical existential choice, whether or not they realise it, between making work the be all and end all of existence, or spending a few years of life doing other things. In the context of this image of men, I came across a poem, written by a real-life prisoner, entitled 'Lifer'[5]:

> For him no world exists beyond
> The boundary of his eyes
> Within the wall, within himself
> The absolute disguise...
> There are no trees in the exercise yard
> For security spirits such chances away
> And after a while the thought of a tree
> Fades slowly out of the mind.

Lifers have to adjust to prison life, as the only life they know. For those who are not imprisoned for life, who cherish the possibility of seeing a tree, the memory haunts, and is not so easily banished. However much women today recognise the increasingly inescapable reality of spending most of their adult lives going out to work, they are also aware of an alternative way of life to that of plodding up a ladder for forty hours a week for forty years. They know that a life devoted to work misses out on much of the quality of existence, the reward of spontaneity and close, intimate relationships with other human beings, devoid of any functional vested interest.

Whether or not women's own careers end up following the male pattern, women are aware of the existential alternative, created by the female role, because other women do take a few years out, or risk starting again at forty. And for vast numbers of women who have children the decision to resume fulltime work becomes a positive choice rather than an unquestioned continuous necessity. Is it simply because women are more aware of the real personal sacrifices made in centring life around work that these men's *wives* happened to be the ones who complained and questioned the amount of time and effort they put into their jobs?

But what about the rest of the quoted part of this poem? Is

work, for men, an 'absolute disguise', and if so, what part of themselves are they covering up? You have to look behind the façade of normality in order to understand men; you have to question the way they are brought up and live their lives. You have to decide you want answers to questions like: Why do men prefer to drive round in circles trying to read a map balanced on the steering wheel rather than ask the way? Can their aggressiveness simply be hormonal? What are their attitudes towards women and the women's movement, and why do some of them seem so resistant to a freedom which would also free them? But most of all you have to ask whether there is something deep down in their childhood, in the way they are brought up, which causes them to need the defence of their role, the 'ultimate disguise' of work, something that has been taken for granted and overlooked, simply because male development has been seen as the norm.

In choosing to interview the other half of my generation, I happened to choose the age group least likely to suffer the effects of unemployment, but I also chose the generation of men which did begin to reject the work ethic back in the late 1960s, and whose lives pinpoint some of the changes beginning to happen to men, very slowly and almost imperceptibly, held back by the fact that for each they involve an individual odyssey, because for men the problem not only has no name but is not recognised as a problem. This must change, for it is important for both sexes to understand that men are fallible, equal human beings too.

## NOTES

1  Tracy Kidder, *The Soul of a New Machine* (Little, Brown & Co, Boston, Mass, 1981; Allen Lane, 1982)
2  Henry B. Biller, *Paternal Deprivation* (Lexington Books, Mass, 1974)
3  Betty Friedan, *The Second Stage* (Simon & Schuster (Summit Books), New York, 1981; Michael Joseph, 1982)
4  Mary Ingham, *Now We Are Thirty* (Eyre Methuen, 1981)
5  Gyles Brandreth, *Created in Captivity* (Hodder & Stoughton, 1972)

# Chapter One

# A MAN'S WORLD

*A great deal of their experience—especially emotional
and introspective experience—has to remain unnamed
for them. Their chief means of self-expression is
consequently through action: this is one of the reasons
why the English have so many 'do-it-yourself' hobbies.
The garden or the workbench becomes the nearest they
have to a means of satisfactory introspection.*

*The easiest—and sometimes the only possible—form
of conversation is that which concerns or describes
action: that is to say action considered as technique or as
procedure. It is then not the experience of the speakers
which is discussed but the nature of an entirely exterior
mechanism or event—a motor-car engine, a football
match, a draining system or the workings of some
committee. Such subjects, which preclude anything
directly personal, supply the content of most of the
conversations being carried on by men ... in England
today ...*

*Yet there is warmth in such conversation and
friendships can be made and sustained by it ... It is as
though the speakers bend over the subject to examine it
in precise detail, until, bending over it, their heads
touch. Their shared expertise becomes a symbol of
shared experience. When friends recall another friend
who is dead or absent, they recall how he always
maintained that a front-wheel drive was safer: and in
their memory this now acquires the value of an
intimacy.*

(John Berger[1])

To LOOK at them, you wouldn't think they were suffering
from anything, you wouldn't think they were suffering at
all. Each has a good job, a car, a house, a wife and a family.

They all exude a calm confidence, a capacity to cope, which underlies the lives they have carved out for themselves, a basic, practical, matter of fact, competent approach. They talk in pragmatic matter of fact terms, too, about their individual areas of expertise, the work they do. And the surest way to start them talking is to ask about work.

Among them are accountants, telephone engineers, travelling salesmen, office managers, window cleaners, company directors, teachers, surveyors, electricians, policemen, polytechnic lecturers, bank and building society executives, social workers, civil servants, farmers, firemen, local government officials, photographers, advertising executives, journalists, market analysts, environmental health officers ... And what they do defines them, guarantees their worth, as well as their privilege. For, as Freud claimed, work is the individual's strongest tie to reality. It plumbs you in, fixes you on a grid of functional interconnection with others, offers identity and self-expression as well as the means of survival. Work creates status and for many people a sense of belonging which they do not derive from the community in which they live, a place, an involvement with the affairs of the world.

Nearly all these men have now reached positions of prestige and responsibility, supporting several other people, singlehanded. They are almost casual in the way they shoulder the burden of their responsibilities. At the height of their powers, they have every reason to exude a self-satisfied aura. Many of them would be happy to carry on talking about work all evening. After all, you did ask ...

The glint of their self-determination is almost blinding. You could drown, and nearly do, in the swamp of detail which marks each one's daily life out as different from all the others. Yet with talk, and more talk, around the subject of work, certain patterns and with them certain puzzlements begin to appear. Frank, a plastics salesman and one of the few men who professed to hate his job, nevertheless says that he enjoys working and won't be taking his annual holiday this year. Dennis, a bank executive who has already been penpushing in the same place for twenty years, and faces at least another twenty, seems only capable of expressing the mildest resentment at the narrowness of the major part of his short span on earth:

> I've probably got Williams & Glyn's Bank printed on my chest underneath my shirt. I do feel like that. Once you've taken their cheap mortgage they've got you by the throat... But they've never done me any harm. We seem to have got on pretty well over the years, so I don't really feel trapped. But I sometimes do feel, oh gosh, it's Williams & Glyn's Bank again.

Gary, another bank official, who claims he used to be overworked but isn't any more, doesn't have time to wash the car.

Over two-thirds of all the men I interviewed worked more than 40 hours a week on a regular basis, either because they needed the overtime pay, because the responsibilities of the job necessitated it, or because they were self-employed. Many of them worked more than 50 hours and one or two of the self-employed claimed a working week of over 70 hours. These included an electrical contractor who claimed a 95 hour week. Pete explained that he preferred to stay late on a job and finish it, that he could not afford to turn work down as he never knew when he might have a slack week and only work two days, but that equally he could not afford an assistant. (He stressed the 'freedom' of being his own boss as the compensation for the long hours he worked.) Yet few of these men were prepared to claim that they felt the stresses and pressures of their role.

According to Britain's last General Household Survey[2] (1980), 34 per cent of male fulltime employees worked over 45 hours a week and 16 per cent worked over 50 hours. Of those working over 45 hours 31 per cent claimed they were very satisfied with the hours they worked; 25 per cent of those who worked over 50 hours said they were dissatisfied, and only 10 per cent said they were very dissatisfied. It seemed that pay levels and the work itself were more important factors in job satisfaction than hours of work. And among fulltime male employees in Britain in 1980, 38 per cent regularly worked paid overtime and two-thirds of those who did relied on this to make their pay up to a reasonable amount.

If so many men are so tied to their breadwinner role, why

don't more of them complain? Ironically, in my sample, the only men who said they felt the burden of their financial responsibilities as breadwinners were the ones whose wives worked full time. Otherwise, they seemed cheerfully prepared to tie themselves to earning money. When I asked them which they would choose, if they had the option, extra spare time or extra pay, over 85 per cent chose the money, saying they could always find a use for spare money, whereas they didn't know what they would do with spare time. 'You can have too much leisure time' was one comment.

Similarly, although to me the prospect of *having* to do the same line of work year in year out without a break is appalling, they really didn't seem to feel they were missing out. They had realistically adjusted to the fact that you have to earn your own crust anyway. So when I offered them the hypothetical opportunity of a few months' paid, leave, a number of men freely admitted they wouldn't know what to do with it, after they had gone on holiday and done what needed doing to the house. Some of them were so plumbed in to their working reality that they said they couldn't possibly leave their job for that long—and wouldn't want to, in case somebody came along and pinched it.

It is well known that male trade unionists agitate for more pay rather than any other work benefits. A 1980 MORI survey revealed that although men are on average paid 36 per cent more than women in Britain, only 72 per cent of the men (compared with 82 per cent of the women) considered themselves fairly paid. The most obvious explanation for this would be the male role, as provider. But as one man whose wife worked full time and who didn't have any children said to me:

> I'd love a three-day weekend. We've got quite a bit of money coming in, but I think I ought to be better paid than I am. I deserve more, because other parts of the industry are getting more.

A mid '60s study of perceptions of work in a British factory[3] showed how male workers differed from females in their priorities at work. The women stressed good conditions and friendly relationships, while for the men good pay and job security were the primary considerations, followed by working conditions and promotion opportun-ities. Worthwhile interesting work came last (this was, after all, a study of a factory) but friendly relationships mattered very little either.

Nor does friendship seem to matter very much outside work. A recent nationwide survey revealed the fact that 50 per cent of men in this country have no friends, apart from work colleagues. In my sample of men nearer 80 per cent admitted they had no close friends. The friendships they did have tended to centre around work, and it was a general rule not to see too much of these people outside work and never to confide in them. Friendships had often gone the same way as spare-time interests:

> I used to go fishing with my mate, but he doesn't bother ringing me up anymore, because I'm always working.

And it wasn't really missed, or so they said.

Although the demands of their work obviously detracted from their home life, hardly any men reckoned that they didn't have enough time for their personal relationships. It was their wives who complained—'my wife thinks all I do is work' became a familiar refrain. And Chris, a financial director of a small company, added:

> I love my wife and my two children and enjoy their company, which is the bit she doesn't always understand, that I do like to come home. And I would, if I could get things sorted out.

But the men themselves seemed to feel no kind of conflict. Work simply came first. 'Targets are targets' as one man put it. Only Jim, a computer project leader, seemed ever to have actually put in a complaint higher up about the demands of his job:

> I always feel I've got too much to do. I keep saying it but nobody listens. Somebody makes a decision that we're going to do ten things and we've just got to do them.

Dick, a chief quantity surveyor, expressed similar resentment, muted by resignation:

> They've got you if you're conscientious. I can't walk away from it. I get home between 7 and 8pm. My wife complains I never leave the office. They expect you to do a lot of things you can't do in five days a week.

Gail Sheehy[4] quotes from a survey[5] of 780 chief executives drawn from 1300 of the largest American corporations, according to which 80 per cent of these men acknowledged that their family lives suffered because of their careers, but six out of ten believed a business executive must make 'personal sacrifices' to succeed.

It seems that work demands are irresistible, partly because of the competitive nature of work. No one wants to lose status, so they all pedal as fast as they can. And they all suffer.

The trouble with work, according to Alasdair Clayre,[6] is that it creates either a compensation or a 'spillover' effect into one's leisure, so that you either act differently at home to make up for what you can't express at work, or else you become the same person at home, due to the spillover effect, that you are at work. Work, therefore, has the larger say in the kind of person you become. A mid '60s study[7] suggests that in middle management men are much more likely to suffer the 'spillover' effect, because they pursue a process of self-rationalisation at work. In striving for promotion, they internalise company goals. So by learning the best way of functioning to succeed, the executive becomes the very person he has been presenting. This book estimates that 80 per cent of men would carry on working even if there were no financial necessity and proposes that a man:

> ... enters the organisation predisposed to accept its influence, to be pervaded by its values, to intertwine his fate with it, to make its concerns his own, to identify himself with it and it with himself.

Although a number of men described a necessary unwinding period at the end of the week or at the beginning of a holiday (sometimes up to three days), only one or two described themselves as playing a different role at work from the one they played at home, feeling a different person at work. One man described feeling different when he got into his car to go to work, wearing a suit. But hardly any of the others seemed to know what I was talking about. And yet the skills of office politics are very different from those, hopefully, you use in your personal relationships. The Americans have apparently studied the art of office politics, calling it 'Organisation Development' (OD) and describe the requirements.

> The illusion of being honest, compassionate and generous is crucial, but so, too, is the necessity in practice of breaking one's word, being cruel and being mean

was how Machiavelli put it, and Jane McLoughlin,[8] after conferring with Dr Virginia Schein, a consultant in OD, summed it up as 'an exercise in self-aggrandisement'.

How easy is it, then, to come home, kiss the wife, play with the kids and generally be loving and caring? It is probably easier to fall asleep in front of the television rather than face a struggle that you don't recognise and you might lose, like the man Gail Sheehy[4] describes meeting, who said:

> 'Being "nice" to people is not what you're paid for . . . So I became basically antisocial. I don't have any true friends.' His pale blue eyes filmed over with that gelid impersonality with which people learn to defend the decisions that have diminished them.

I didn't notice my men's eyes glazing over when they admitted they had no close friends; but neither did they appear unduly concerned about it. It was as if whole sides of themselves were shut down, shut off, because all their energy was concentrated elsewhere, and I remembered one man saying 'You have to be selective with your energy, pick your sphere for the attack.' In the same book, Sheehy quotes a *woman* as saying:

> 'The really tough thing I had to learn after I started back in the rat race was the conserving of emotional energy. Anger is a very tiring experience'.

It seems to me that although work identifies you it also labels you, traps you within that identity and all the assumptions that go with it as soon as you have told someone what you do. But most of the men I talked to just didn't seem to feel that either, except those like the village policeman, who was acutely aware of his vocational role. They seemed totally identified with their work, even though surprisingly few had actually chosen their career, let alone were living out a burning ambition. Most had drifted out of school with very little careers advice and, despite the role models women lack, little idea of what they wanted to do. A few followed in father's footsteps or went along to the interview he fixed up. Most had simply randomly applied to advertisements for jobs they knew little about.

So why do they let their work rule their life? A Marxist might simply call it a case of alienation, victims of the capitalist consumer society. I think they are men who are so dependent upon their traditional role that they are in danger of becoming addicted; in fact some are addicted. They are workaholics. The symptoms are all there, the most classic being denial of the problem. It's something temporary, it's under control. Take Chris, the financial director, who is just waiting to get things sorted out:

> I've been known to still be at my desk at 3am. I can work at that time in the morning, get things done. All last week, we had an industrial tribunal and I was getting home about ten to one. My wife has rung me up about six times in the last eight or nine months and said Chris, it's absolutely stupid, it's 10.30 at night. Why don't you come home? But I'm that sort of person. Once I start something I have to finish it, wipe the slate clean, I can't wait till tomorrow... I mean, I've been in a succession of jobs where I've had to start from scratch, so it's always meant late working.

The last time Chris got home from work on time was around the time their daughter Debbie was born. Not only was that ten years ago, but he left that job, because it didn't stretch him, it wasn't a challenge any more...

'I keep thinking I'm going to turn a corner,' says a publishing editor who not only does a fifty-hour week but keeps his briefcase beside his chair in the evenings, to flip through the odd journal he doesn't have time to catch up with at work. Some men fail to notice the extra time they spend at work:

> I don't feel I've got too much to do. I usually get into the office about 8.15 and leave about 6.15, whereas the working day is officially 8.45 to 5.15, so that's 1½ hours extra a day. But a lot of it is simply that you don't even look at the clock and it's not until everybody's packed up and gone and the place has gone quiet that you think oh, they've all gone. And you just have one or two things to finish, just finishing off the day . . .

Some men seem to think that problems can't be problems if you know you've got them:

> I try to do too much, that's my trouble. It takes me three days to unwind on holiday, but I don't think I'm heading for a problem, because I'm aware of it.

And some men, like the man who didn't have time to wash his car, put their problems firmly, and safely, into the past. If it is in the past, it's possible to admit it was an obsession:

> I just lived and breathed that job, and it made me ill eventually. My wife would be very angry if I ever came into work at a weekend.

Why is it never the men themselves who are angry at having to work weekends?

In her book *Pathfinders*,[4] Gail Sheehy explains how men commonly turn to work to protect themselves from change, uncertainty or distress, just like turning to drink, or drugs: 'When the heat is on, they work harder and deny the pain.' Sheehy cites a thirty-six year old single man who insisted he wasn't workaholic, yet could only fit in time to see her at 7am. Another man would arrive at the office at 4am. I didn't meet anyone quite that bad (at least anyone who was prepared to admit to being that bad), but I met plenty of men who allowed their work to dominate their lives, without seeming to feel they were missing out on anything. In this way, men can rapidly become workaholic, every other relationship collapsing except that with the drug. Addiction grows out of the need for a hidden crutch, for fear of admitting one's weaknesses or depending on others. So one leans more and more on the crutch until one cannot move without it, and then when one cannot move at all, except to cling to it, the crutch becomes crippling in itself. Addiction is very hard to cure because addicts spend a lot of time convincing themselves that they aren't dependent, hiding their dependence from others, because to reveal it would be to lose control, to show weakness, to slip, to fall.

Men are much more prone to workaholism than women because of the irresistible pull of their role, because of their competitive need for status, their fear of showing weakness. For without the basic inner insecurity that afflicts most men, they wouldn't need the armour plating of control.

Just before I began interviewing men, I read an article by Jill Tweedie[9] on money and the freedom to love, in which she claimed that earning a living freed her to 'get on with the real business of living. Love.' It seems to me, at the opposite end of my research, that in this respect the sexes are diametrically opposed. My research among men led me to conclude, endorsed by male friends, that, to misquote a certain Romantic poet

> ...*work* is of *woman*'s life a thing apart,
> 'Tis *man*'s whole existence

The trouble is that whereas Byron's original quotation about love carries the sting of contempt of romantic emptyheaded foolhardiness, work, like that other socially acceptable drug alcohol, carries public support. Work is realistic, practical, responsible, and the worker is to be rewarded. The capacity for hard work is a talent to be recommended, applauded, because work is the bedrock of all survival, all innovation, all achievement, and nearly all status and success. People are valued, assessed, identified and classed according to their work. Such respectability is bound to mask the unhealthy dependence many men have on their work.

Of course there are certain things work cannot give us. It

cannot give the freedom to be ourselves effortlessly and spontaneously and to follow life where it takes us. It rarely allows for changes in self-development which cut across its path. The long quote at the beginning of this chapter is from John Berger's sensitive portrait of a doctor[1] with a strong sense of vocation but nevertheless a man who, married, with children, reached a point in his mid-thirties when he began to question and rethink the kind of doctor he had become. He became very withdrawn during this period, still functioning, to all appearances, but withholding much of his former energy and enthusiasm while reforming and reshaping his ideas. He emerged from this crisis a very different and in his eyes more effective doctor, as well as a more developed human being.

He was a fortunate man indeed, who had been able to weather this crisis because his working position gave him a great deal of freedom, because he worked on his own. But what if he had emerged from the crisis with the realisation that he no longer wanted to be a doctor? And what about men whose jobs would never allow them time to withdraw and reassess themselves and the meaning of what they are doing, the direction of their lives?

The mid-thirties does seem to be a time for reassessment and growth. Dante was thirty-five when he found himself 'midway in the journey through life... lost in a dark wood strayed from the true path'; Jung placed the most important changes in the human psyche between the ages of thirty-five and forty, which Gail Sheehy, in her book *Passages*[10] also cited as the beginning of the 'Deadline Decade', a period of uncertainty and prevarication, during which the individual is brought to a halt by feelings of restriction by personal and career choices made during the twenties. She stresses that people need, at such times, to shed a protective layer in order to grow:

> ...people who allow themselves to be stopped, seized by real issues, shaken into re-examination, are people who find their validity and survive.

Yet the traditional career pattern is hardly suited to

accommodate doubts about one's direction in life, especially at thirty-five. By this age, men are expected to be half-way up the ladder juggling a mortgage, a car and two children, not a very good position from which to start shedding protective layers, become more vulnerable, less effective at the job. What would become of management objectives? The new five-year plan? The forward planning schedule? Targets are targets. Women may suffer many handicaps, but their lives are often much freer in midlife to take a break from an established pattern. They simply don't have so much to lose.

Work rarely allows us to express our real selves, meaning the weaker, vulnerable sides of us that only our close friends see. It cannot be any kind of substitute, therefore, for honest, open, intimate relationships, although many women, usually in subordinate positions, do achieve intimate friendships at work. Men don't. It's against all the rules of office politics. In a book published in America, *The Private Me*,[11] Bill and June Noble counsel women against self-confession sessions:

> Men have traditionally competed with each other, so talking about themselves could mean losing what they had. Women, until recently at least, simply haven't lived in an atmosphere of rivalry. For them, therefore, confession isn't as threatening.

We have to maintain our credibility at work, and this self-protection and occupational therapy during a crisis can be helpful, but not a solution to problems, which rarely go away on their own. The big problem, of course, that you can't work off, is unemployment.

And this is why, however hard unemployment hits women, its effect upon men is devastating. Feminism has portrayed men as the self-confident sex, who put failure down to bad luck and readily ascribe success to their own skill and achievement. But remove them from the main-stream, cut off the channel through which they pour all that positive energy, and they wilt like cut flowers.

Unemployment carried much greater hardships, material-ly, during the 1930s depression than it does in the recession today, but comparative studies have shown that the psychological effects are very much the same, that the unemployed go through various stages of reaction to redundancy, ranging from initial shock and disbelief to ultimate fatalism and depression. At first they may lie in bed in the morning as if they are simply on holiday, catching up with jobs around the house, even going on holiday. But then, after a few weeks (probably when they realise no more pay slips are going to appear) the reality of their situation sinks in and they begin a confident and energetic search for a new job. When it does not come along, the mounting pile of rejections begins to have an effect. They become depressed, stay in bed later and later, and the search for another job slows up, until they reach the stage where they no longer believe they will ever get one, and become resigned to unemployment.

Men who have reached this stage often behave with mute incomprehension when asked to describe the effects of unemployment. They cannot articulate their feelings because they no longer have any frame of reference for them; almost as if, once the work itself has gone, their memory systems go with it, it wipes them out. Just as they completely absorbed and identified with the work role, felt they were what they did, so now, with unemployment, they become 'un' anything.

It is the recently unemployed, and the recently returned to work, who are very articulate on the subject. These men describe their state much more passionately than women. Women recount the boredom and feeling of uselessness, but women do not suffer the same kind of loss of face when seen out on the street during working hours, nor quite the same uselessness at home—'I just stagnate.' The loss bites much deeper into a man's sense of identity. Adrian Sinfield[12] quotes one man's reaction:

> My wife is right when she said it affects me *as a man*: it isn't the money so much as the feeling men have.

Whereas men at work rationalise money as their main reason for working, giving friendship little importance, the unemployed man realises this isn't so, as an article[13] in the *Guardian* makes clear:

It may have been hell, but there was companionship, and that's what Fred misses most about his work... 'I miss the lads at work. I've no male company during the day any longer. I still see my mates from work... but it's not the same.'

'It's like somebody cutting your throat,' was the response of one man, in a Tavistock Institute study of unemployment in the late 1970s.

'The longer you are out of work the more paranoid you become'.

'The longer it goes on the more you get careless with your self and about yourself. I sometimes wish I was dead and gone'.

As John Hill described,[14] writing on the findings of this study:

...when the father of a family ceases to be in fulltime work, the balance of the family shifts. He feels he loses not only his occupational but also his sexual identity and comes under pressure to take on a more 'feminine' role: doing the housework, taking the children to school.

To which one man reacted, 'I can't stand it—you go mad.' A teenage boy (quoted by Jane McLoughlin[15]) who had never had a job summed it up by saying 'Life is what happens to other people.' For men, a job is the ticket for membership of life, work is all they have, to prove they exist. The fact that men cling to work and work-derived status in such a potentially self-destructive way is all too easily rationalised simply as a fact of life. It slithers into social acceptability, slips back under the guise of normality, away from any allegation of abnormality, dependence, addiction.

Yet worklessness is what we face in the future. Unemployment in the Western world has apparently tripled in the past decade, with one person in eight out of work, and nearly 40 per cent of the unemployed out of a job for six months or more. In Britain, the long-term unemployed increased from 1 in 250 twelve years ago, to 1 in 25 today. In 1982 it was estimated that 1 in 4 workers in Britain (about 6 million people) had been unemployed over the previous twelve-

month period.[16] And in November 1982 official unemployment figures in America reached 11.6 million (10.4 per cent
of the work-force). Unlike the depression in the 1930s, there
is no anticipation of total recovery, no end of the road in
sight. Trade unionists Clive Jenkins and Barrie Sherman[17]
claim that the productivity gains made possible by new
technology suggest that even if substantial economic growth
in Britain does resume, it will have to be much greater than
most economists expect, to have any effect on the
unemployment figures.

And Leisure Consultants Ltd[18] maintain that output will
need to grow at a rate at least 1 per cent greater than the rate
of increase of productivity if the unemployment rate is to
be reduced to 3 per cent of the UK labour force by 1991.
Meanwhile, a recent report[19] anticipates that unemployment
in the north of England may reach 20 per cent in five years
and some schoolleavers in the region will never work.

There are various proposed solutions to this problem,
which boil down to job creation and work-sharing schemes,
achieved by implementing a shorter working week, more
part-time work, longer holidays or earlier retirement, or all
of these. As the vice-president of the Organisation and
Manpower Planning Institute of Personnel Management
put it:[20]

> We already have a very expensive work-sharing scheme: it is
> called unemployment. Three million have no jobs, whilst the
> rest of us have all the work there is. We need a much better
> scheme.

However, part-time work, as women well know, is still very
difficult to come by, and work-sharing schemes remain a
novelty, the isolated case reported in the newspaper.
Meanwhile men run faster in a game of musical chairs, cling
more desperately to the treadmill of fulltime work. A large
proportion of male employees work regular overtime. And
as I discovered, most men are extremely resistant to the idea
of any decrease in the working week, despite the fact they
work so hard. Comments included:

A shorter working week doesn't appeal to me at all. I don't believe in these 35/40 hours, never mind what ridiculous hours it's projected at. I see recently someone's predicted the working week will drop to 28 hours, well that's farcical, farcical.

Although trade union action and legislation cut working hours during the nineteenth century, they have hardly shifted since the 1930s. This is largely because falls in the official working week have been taken up as overtime. The 1981 *Yearbook of Labour Statistics*[21] shows that during the 1970s the actual working week remained relatively stable: just under 40 hours in the USA and around 43 hours in the UK. Most European countries have seen a slight reduction, with some fluctuations over the decade, from around 44 hours to just over 40. Australia, like the US, seems to have remained pretty constant, at around 40.

As Beatrix Campbell has pointed out:[22]

Even when a formal commitment is expressed it is often only that. Shorter working time has been on the trade unions' stocks for years now. But there's a lethargy and boredom about the way men talk about it, and often enough it is seen simply as a route not to time off, but to increasing earnings by gaining more overtime.

A woman negotiator last month discussed a claim for a 35 hour week with a male colleague. 'What do we want that for, it would only mean more time at home, and who wants that?' he said.

True, the Ford unions' annual claims to management included demands for a shorter working week, year and working life, but the TUC's recent call for a ban on overtime, moonlighting and a policy proposal for a 35 hour week has met with little grass roots support.

Why are men so resistant to the prospect of more free time? It cannot wholly be rationalised as their concern as breadwinners, if the threatened alternative may be no work at all. The worker, or so it seems, would rather run this risk, deny the danger, rather like the soldier who is willing to go into battle because it's always going to be the man next to you who gets hit.

One of the solitary six of the men I interviewed who opted for more time rather than more money gave a partial clue. (All except one of these men were conscious of the ever pressing need for more money—they simply valued their free time more.) Barry, who found his job boring and worked a 48 hour week of shifts, said he would prefer the time to the money 'although I could always do with more of that'. He pointed out that, as with the free afternoons his shift now gives him:

> I'd probably not know what to do with it at first. I'd waste it, because it takes you a while to ease into a new space in your life and work out what you want to do with it. But I'd prefer it to the money

he added firmly. All the other men who opted for more free time enjoyed their jobs; they simply, and refreshingly, recognised their need for the other aspects of life:

> I'd visit people, give more time to friends, children, animals, do lots of nice things with the children. Saturdays and Sundays have become a bit of a ritual, it would be nice to have an extra day to do all the things you want. I can't think what they are, now, but I never have the time for them.

It seems to me that men become so distanced from and fearful of any real freedom and space in their lives, that they cling to work and status as a surrogate for self-development. The only men who mentioned development of themselves (as opposed to furthering their careers) were four of the men who opted for more free time. Otherwise, men don't discover their work-dependence until, like my father, they retire. And then it is simply too often too late.

According to Dr Joyce Brothers,[23] American analysts have discovered a correlation, for men, between death and retirement. There is apparently a peak in the male death rate in America about two years after retirement. One of my interviewees said he had discovered that his company only paid out its pension for, on average, 18 months. Which perhaps accounts for the fact that another oddball believed retirement should be taken in one's twenties, when one had the health and vitality to make the most of it. When the fun was over, you simply worked till you dropped. Perhaps he had noticed that for a lot of men that happened anyway and they missed out on retirement altogether.

Some men witness what's happening to their own fathers, but it's a problem they are simply putting off:

> I never think about what I'll do after I retire. I absolutely dread old age. A few years ago, I lost my father. I still say that father would have been alive today, had he made forward plans for his retirement. He just vegetated. He was a very active man at sixty-one, then at sixty-three, nothing, and in the end he died of a heart attack. I regret not really giving him that wee bit more time... I intend to give my retirement a bit of thought a wee bit nearer the time, in the last two or three years, but I do dread old age.

Up to now, I've been arguing that work is an ego-boosting but somehow psychologically restricting and emotionally depleting thing. But what if work actually gives men an emotional and psychological freedom they cannot feel outside it? I'd like to refer back to the quote from John Berger which I used at the beginning of this chapter. What struck me about this passage was how true it rang, except that Berger was mistaken in ascribing this idiosyncracy to the English. As his examples betray, he was in fact talking about English men, who in these respects have more in common with men of other nationalities than with their own countrywomen. English women would certainly have been the guardians of much greater intimacies than those cited here, their heads would not need the excuse of a common task to bend together.

So, do men need a functional excuse to express intimacy, in an oblique way, because they lack the skill to do it directly? It seems somewhat limiting to know little more about a person than that he considered front-wheel drive to be safer. But what if men *feel* safer with the controlled, superficial, positive, restricted emotional exchange that work permits? So much so that they actually prefer the air-conditioned controlled temperature of the workplace to the emotional hothouse at home?

In a study of Parisian white collar workers undertaken in the late 1950s,[24] Michel Crozier described the office environment as:

> ... a relatively cheap and efficient way of providing us with the limits we need in order to play the games we like: games of conflict and co-operation, in which we do not have to risk too much for ourselves or for our partners.

He maintained that:

> Work constitutes the primary and most obvious dimension of the social life of the members of a company. It is the most neutral and most impersonal ... and the [element] upon which they first project their problems.

Although workers criticised their colleagues for their coldness, egoism and distant character:

> ... nevertheless, we can generally say that relations between colleagues lack warmth. Our interviewees are quite reserved in the matter of camaraderie; they expect cordial relations with their colleagues but prefer that a certain distance be maintained; 85 per cent ... never get together with their colleagues outside work and the 15 per cent who do seem to apologise for it. The general order of the day seems to be 'every man for himself', 'we see each other enough during the week'.

He concluded that distance and coldness were ways of maintaining possible conflicts in relationships within acceptable limits, ie safe. Office relationships have probably become more relaxed since the late 1950s, but not that much. Yet psychologist Michael Argyle[25] unquestioningly accepts that men 'get more satisfaction from working relationships than women, who get more satisfaction from friends and kin'.

Other writers, however, are beginning to question men's predilection for work, as in this extract from an article by Mike Hales:[26]

> Closing the garden gate ... I would feel an immediate and disturbing sense of relief ... Within the first few weeks it had

become a daily phenomenon: closing the door on people I love, setting out for a place I hate, consciously, and feeling relieved.

It dawned on me eventually that the hatred was the source of the release. To spend all day in an alienated environment which fed me defined, technical challenges and offered material comforts (phone, restaurant, central heating, secretarial labour on tap) was the easy option.

Pauline, at home, was confronted continually by things that must be done, and done right, because we have to live with the outcome . . . human demands . . . which must be acknowledged . . . There was no way she could let up *being* . . . [while] I decline to acknowledge the people I live with in a hundred small and intimate ways . . . The great thing about work is that I'm released, by the dispensation of The Company, from the necessity of trying to live like a whole human being.

It seems that work only plumbs you into *one* sort of reality, enabling you to escape from another. Psychologist Donald Hebb apparently concluded[27] that 'the psychological function of the social environment was to protect man through institutional arrangements against being swamped by extreme emotionality.' What is a whole human being? How much emotionality is extreme? And why is *man* in danger of being swamped by it?

The gauge of a healthy human being has up to now been based on the normal adult male. This has also, up to now, coloured the research into differences between men and women, concentrating upon the ways in which women differ from men, rather than vice versa. For example, research showing women to be less competitive and aggressive than men has stimulated explanations that women repress their normal quota of aggression, rather than triggering any questioning of the higher levels of aggression among men, even though high ambition among men has been positively linked with a rejecting and punitive father.

On the basis of cumulative studies of men, David McClelland[28] divided achievement motivation into two apparently logical components: the motive towards success ('hope success') and the motive against failure ('fear failure'). Earlier, however, Matina Horner[29] had identified a third category of achievement motivation among women, *against* success ('fear success'). This was assumed to be abnormal and a symptom of the sex role pressures and conditioning to which women are subject. Horner had tested a mixed group of students by asking them to complete a story about someone of their own sex coming top of their class. Assuming violence (ie an unpleasant outcome) to be a response to the perception of danger, 65 per cent of the female students (compared with only 10 per cent of the male) felt threatened by success.

However, later research[30] suggested that women's fears simply reflected a heightened perception of the emotional cost of competition, to which men were for some reason less sensitive. And two American researchers have subsequently been carrying out research into areas which threaten men, rather than women. Susan Pollack and Carol Gilligan[31] invited a mixed group of students to write stories based on various pictures, which included a couple sitting together on a park bench next to a low bridge, one trapeze artist about to catch another in mid air, and a man seated alone at a desk. Whereas Horner had noticed what she described as 'bizarre or violent' imagery in women's stories about success, Pollack was struck by what appeared to her as bizarre *and* violent imagery in the men's stories based on what seemed such a tranquil scene, the couple sitting on a bench. Over one fifth of the men had concocted stories of homicide, suicide, kidnapping, rape or stabbing based on this picture, whereas none of the women had projected violence into this scene. Analysing differences in the distribution and substance of violent fantasies, Gilligan and Pollack discovered that men projected much more violence into the pictures showing personal affiliation or co-operation than those showing work and achievement. Gilligan saw this as symptomatic of a dichotomy between the sexes, whereby women fear 'danger-ous separation', but men have a greater fear of something she called 'explosive connection'.

It is around an exploration of this fear in men, and how it originates, that this book is centred. For I believe that it carries the key to men's dependence upon work and the suffering they experience deprived of work, because work for men is a necessary defence against depth and closeness in relationships. Men need work because they cannot comfortably relate without it or some other functional organised activity, hence their need to play games, *do* things together. Work gives men a connectedness with others in a way that direct relationships would do, if they did not fear them. Men need relationships as much as women do, but they also need some object, goal or purpose between them and other people —hence the games men play, the most useful of which is work and the most lethal is war.

Many men therefore actually prefer the controlled working environment, and this creates ambivalence in their behaviour, which women, who often feel more comfortable and safe at home than at work, find hard to understand. And because men feel safer at work, their role becomes a mask, a defence against that which they fear, the struggle for emotional growth, depth and honesty which is so central to the lives of women. Carol Gilligan[32] says:

> We might . . . begin to ask, not why women have conflicts about competitive success, but why men show such readiness to adopt and celebrate a rather narrow vision of success.

It is time for women to acknowledge that in some respects they are stronger, more skilled, better off than men, to question and encourage men to question the myth of male dominance and privilege. I was moved to write this book because I feel men are struggling for wholeness just as much as women are, only theirs is an inner battle. The questioning of sex roles and their limitations strikes very deeply in all of us, for these roles are rooted in the powerful early emotional influences which mould our identity and personality. Dredging this pool churns up so much mud, obscuring everything. What is male, what is female, masculine, feminine, nature or nurture, and will we ever know?

Psychoanalytic theorists (particularly Freud) have been criticised in this area for appearing to rationalise the status quo. But it seems to me that Jungian theory relates quite appropriately to the changing situation between the sexes. Jung argued that in each of us there is a developing process of 'individuation', stimulating us to strive for wholeness of self. The human psyche, according to Jung, embraces both masculine and feminine attributes. Their respective physiologies and roles encourage men to develop 'masculinity' and women 'femininity', while opposite-sex attributes exist within us all, in varying stages of development, but often primitive and undeveloped, rudimentary through lack of use.

Characteristics which remain undeveloped, however, are either expressed very crudely or projected on to others. Jung called the latent male in woman her 'animus' and the latent female in man his 'anima'. Traditional sex role relationships encourage these to be simply projected on to the opposite sex. Women have recently taken the initiative, in developing their animus. Part of that process has involved the struggle to reclaim as an integrated part of themselves what was formerly projected on to men, a struggle not yet complete. Perhaps this process of realising the 'animus' accounts for their present interest in exploring the reality of those characteristics, what it is really like to be a man.

Women have perhaps shied away from this genuine understanding, for fear of the martyred tolerance or self-denial that went with 'understanding men' before. It is not easy for women to appreciate the confidence and skills they have which men lack, that what they take for granted may be difficult and threatening for men. Whereas men have tended to read women's lack of skill as inability and ineptitude, women are prone to interpret male reluctance to enter into domestic responsibilities (on every level, from emotional honesty to picking up dirty socks or working out the shopping list) as a conscious, exploitative ploy. If women really want to encourage men to change, they will have to climb down from the pedestal of moral impunity, and acknowledge some of the power they wield over men.

## NOTES

1  John Berger, *A Fortunate Man: The Story of a Country Doctor* (Allen Lane, 1967)

2 Office of Population Censuses and Surveys, *General House-hold Survey 1980* (HMSO, 1982)
3 H. Beynon & R. M. Blackburn, *Perceptions of Work: Variations within a Factory* (Cambridge University Press, 1972)
4 Gail Sheehy, *Pathfinders: How to achieve happiness by conquering life's crises* (Morrow, New York, 1981; Sidgwick & Jackson, 1982)
5 A joint *Wall Street Journal*/Gallup Organisation survey, reported by Frank Allen, 'Chief executives say job requires many family and personal sacrifices' (*Wall Street Journal*, New York, 20 August 1980)
6 Alasdair Clayre, *Work and Play: Ideas and Experience of Work and Leisure* (Weidenfeld & Nicolson, 1974)
7 Cyril Sofer, *Men in Mid Career: A Study of British Managers and Technical Specialists* (Cambridge University Press, 1970)
8 Jane McLoughlin, 'Why we're all off to see the wizards of OD' (*Guardian* 'Workface', 10 May 1983)
9 Jill Tweedie, 'Sex and money: freedom to love' (*Cosmopolitan*, January 1982)
10 Gail Sheehy, *Passages: Predictable Crises of Adult Life* (E. P. Dutton, New York, 1976; Bantam, 1977)
11 June and Bill Noble, *The Private Me* (Delacourt, New York, 1980)
12 Adrian Sinfield, *What Unemployment Means* (Martin Robertson, Oxford, 1981)
13 Geoffrey Beattie, 'A hell of a career' (*Guardian*, 18 June 1983)
14 John Hill, 'The psychological impact of unemployment' (*New Society*, 19 January 1978)
15 Jane McLoughlin, 'Muffled ignorance does not help the young jobless mountain' (*Guardian* 'Workface', 2 November 1982)
16 Joint *Observer*/NOP poll, reported in 'Quarter of work force lost jobs' (*Observer*, 5 September 1982)
17 Clive Jenkins & Barrie Sherman, *The Leisure Shock* (Eyre Methuen, 1982)
18 W. H. Martin & S. Mason, *Leisure and Work* (Leisure Consultants Ltd, Sudbury, Suffolk, 1982)
19 Commissioned by BBC TV from the Centre for Urban and Regional Development Studies, University of Newcastle upon Tyne
20 D.J. Bell (letter to *Sunday Times*, 23 May 1982)
21 *Yearbook of Labour Statistics, 1981* (International Labour Office, Geneva)

22 'Brothers in male chauvinism' (*Guardian*, 'Guardian Women', 9 August 1982)
23 Dr Joyce Brothers, *What Every Woman Should Know about Men* (Ballantine Books, New York, 1981; Granada, 1982)
24 Michael Crozier (trs David Landau), *The World of the Office Worker* (University of Chicago Press, Illinois, 1971)
25 Michael Argyle, 'Pleasures and pains of working together' (*New Society*, 9 June 1983)
26 Mike Hales, 'Disappearing into The Company' (*Guardian*, 'Guardian Women', 2 December 1980)
27 Marie Jahoda, 'The psychological meanings of unemployment' (*New Society*, 6 September 1979)
28 David McClelland, *Power: The Inner Experience* (Irvington Publishers, New York, 1975)
29 Matina S. Horner, in J. M. Bardwick, E. Douvan, M. S. Horner & D. Gutman, *Feminine Personality and Conflict* (Brooks-Cole, New York, 1970)
30 Georgia Sassen, 'Success anxiety in women: a constructionist interpretation of its sources and its significance' (*Harvard Educational Review*, 50, (1980), pp 13-25)
31 Susan Pollack and Carol Gilligan, 'Images of violence in T.A.T. stories' (*Journal of Personality and Social Psychology*, 42, no 1, (1982), pp 159-167)
32 Carol Gilligan, *In a Different Voice: Psychological Theory and Women's Development* (Harvard University Press, Mass and London, 1982)

# Chapter Two

# MEN ABOUT THE HOUSE

*So until the male section of the population wants
equality on the domestic front (they'll hardly have to
fight for it!), recognising the career sacrifices it would
mean, perhaps it would be kinder to forget all this talk
of equality and train our daughters to be happy,
contented wives and mothers. That would help the
unemployment figures and deal with frustrated feminists who have no answers (only questions)—at a stroke.*
(Letter to *Guardian* Women, Open Space[1])

CARTOONIST JAMES Thurber vividly illustrated the relationship of men to their homes in a drawing he called 'House and
Woman'. A tiny bowler-hatted figure cowers on the step, as
an enormous apparition—a glowering woman—looms
round from the back of the house. Yet how can this be, when
women seem to be fighting a losing battle in the home?

It's extremely hard to ask men what household chores, if
any, they regularly or occasionally do around the house,
without it sounding like a loaded question. That's because it
*is* a loaded question. Every time it came up, I could feel,
hanging in the air between us, the weight of feminist
pressure on men to do more, or was it male guilt about not
doing enough? They may do more than their fathers did, but
they still don't do enough, as the damning statistics tell us.
According to a recent French report,[2] domestic duties take up
4 hours in a working woman's day, and 1 hour and 40
minutes in a working man's day. Women with children who
work outside the home have 1 hour and 10 minutes less
leisure time than their husbands, and very often what is
called rest for a woman is in fact housework or child-

minding. Danish working wives are even worse off (3 hours versus 15 minutes) and while superwoman in America spends 26 hours a week on housework, her husband only spends 36 minutes.[3]

On this issue, more than any other, I could not sink into a shared pool of empathy, the comfortable feeling of having been, or being, on the same side. More than anything else, talking about housework laid out the demarcation lines, with me on one side and the men on the other. For it is on this messy ground that the battle between the sexes is really being fought. And I felt a bit like Chamberlain visiting Hitler and wanting to come back with the peaceful solution.

Many women are familiar with male reluctance, ineptness and apparent blindness when it comes to household jobs. It seems to me that the feminist answer is far too glib, and the statistics actually tell us nothing about why men don't do more around the house.

Before interviewing, I had already discovered that housework was not an issue about which, intentionally or not, men are entirely honest with interviewers. An EEC survey[4] has actually measured what it describes as the 'margin of male exaggeration', meaning the difference between what men claimed to do and what their wives vouched for (based on the assumption that wives did not exaggerate husbands' lack of help). Italian men were the worst culprits, with a 21 per cent discrepancy between word and deed, and Danish men came off as the most honest, although even they exaggerated by 5 per cent. British men were about average, with a 10 per cent margin between their claimed and acknowledged contribution. (See note.[5])

I planted a question, which I hoped sounded fairly innocuous, in the preliminary questionnaire sent out before each interview, to use as a yardstick against what men actually said. They were asked to list any electrical gadgets they had used during the previous week, either inside or outside the house, and given a few examples which included domestic items. So I had a rough idea, depending on whether they had put 'TV, stereo, electric kettle', or 'cooker, iron, washing machine, blender, power drill, etc', of the response I should expect.

In some instances I also had the benefit of a lie detector sitting in on this part of the interview. A glance at his wife's facial expression when he said 'I do my share', or her vocalised 'huh!' when he laid claim to half the washing up, was a fair substitute for electrodes on the palms of the hands. But of course wives were much more than that, because the ensuing discussion revealed a lot more on the state of play between the two parties over this issue. Some couples had obviously never discussed it, either openly or rationally, before, judging by their comments. 'This is very interesting...' one wife was prompted to remark, in the middle of her husband's explanation, which began with the flip comment 'It's keeping in your good books, isn't it?' and ended up explaining the difference between himself and his father—'I never saw him pick up the Hoover or wash up'—because 'You're more compassionate towards your wife now, because of the women's movement, you respect women as equals, don't I darling?'

For others, it was something they had sorted out and talked about, although never entirely resolved, and for a few it was part of a long-running, sometimes acrimonious battle. One man's immediate response to the question was 'I'm glad she's upstairs!' Divorces do notoriously happen over 'the little things', innocuous domestic details. When a male friend of mine joked that his wife divorced him 'because I left the top off the toothpaste' it was possibly not far from the truth. Such irritants often engender an atmosphere of resentment, under which other storms tend to brew. The couple in the flat downstairs have innumerable battles in which she complains that he has left dirty washing lying about, not taken the rubbish out, never cleans anything off his own bat, she always comes home to a tip...

Although one or two men baldly stated they did no housework at all:

I've tried, and I don't get anything from it and if I don't get anything out of something, I don't want to do it anymore.

and one man's contribution, apart from shopping expeditions, consisted of 'eating the dinners', generally men are doing more than their fathers ever did. And although men who do little often claimed:

> Basically it's what you've seen and what you've been used to. My father would never dream of wiping a cup, like flying to the moon. And that's got to have come out in me.

most men heartily disowned this image:

> My father did next to nothing. I wouldn't like anyone to say I was like him. It was quite an occasion if he actually helped with the washing up, got out of his chair.

One man summed it up as being the '1980s equivalent' of their fathers' generation, that men help more because of the changes in attitudes generally, the increasing equality between husbands and wives, and the decline of the dominant/servile marital relationship, along with the increase in companionship. This seems upheld by their greater willingness to do more than just deputise in emergencies, like their dads did, their lesser insistence upon deference as the breadwinners, and less sensitive role demarcations about 'woman's work'.

However in the majority of cases, what men do still only really amounts to a token gesture, relieving women of the continuous burden rather than sharing the demands of domesticity equally. The EEC study mentioned earlier[4] gives figures for the amount of help given by married men according to age, level of education and nationality. Overall, 85 per cent of men in the 25 to 39 age range claimed 'I help my wife often or sometimes' and this percentage increased with educational standard. In the Community as a whole, 33 per cent often helped, 49 per cent sometimes, and 16 per cent never. The job most often quoted as reasonable for a man to take over from his wife was shopping (73 per cent), then washing up (53 per cent), organising a meal (43 per cent), cleaning the house (40 per cent), and, bottom of the list, ironing (14 per cent). Italian men showed the least inclination to wash up (21 per cent) but British men were more likely to wash up (85 per cent) than do the shopping.

But are they washing up in order to wash their hands of any further responsibility, much as our fathers' generation began to do? (My father ceremoniously played the helping husband on Sundays, shortsightedly washing up after lunch.) My interviewees would willingly and fairly frequently wash up, superficially tidy up and hoover round. But (with some impressive exceptions, of course) their wives were more likely to cook, clean, wash and iron. And they tended not to notice things that needed doing of their own accord. They would wait to be asked, and were generally reluctant to take domestic responsibility—they might go shopping but needed their wives to make the list out. It is this inability to notice what needs doing, or do things off their own bat, which most infuriates women about men around the house, that men don't seem to appreciate the 'bind' of continual responsibility for seemingly 'light' housework. A lot of men discounted the time taken to load and unload machines like dishwashers (in which one man invested in order to get out of doing washing up) and washing machines, although men do load these more since automatics have replaced the twin-tub. However, they aren't aware of the supervisory effort of keeping up a constant flow of clean clothes.

There were one or two consciousness-raising sessions in the course of conversations with couples, in which the wife took the opportunity of my assumed support to remind her husband that socks don't dematerialise from the bedroom floor to re-appear in neat pairs in the drawer without some thoughtful human intervention, just as the drying up and putting away of cutlery and crockery is not a twice daily miracle performed by God.

Various men were aware of, yet resisted, their wives' need for a break:

She resents the fact that I don't help her

My wife thinks I should cook, and I don't ever think I should need to

My wife frequently says you don't do anything in the house, you expect me to do it all

and some men admitted that, on top of working all day, they

didn't want any more responsibilities:

> I don't mind doing something if I feel like it, but I shouldn't like to feel I *had* to do it.

Of course, in one fifth of British households, and the majority of those I had chosen, the traditional roles of breadwinner and housewife/childminder are being played out. While they are at home looking after the children wives are seen to be in a better position than their husbands to tackle the bulk of housework. Most of my interviewees were prepared to relieve their wives of twenty-four hour duty and didn't expect to be waited on with slippers warming when they came home tired at night. But they also felt, because the responsibility of supporting the family was theirs, that help should be offered, not expected. This all seems very understandable, in view of the hours these men work, except that it doesn't work out as a neat equation, with the proportion men do in the home depending on the proportion of time their wives spend going out to work.

Nearly a third of the men I interviewed had wives who worked full time, and about half that number had wives working part time. But many of the men whose wives worked part time did less than many whose wives were fulltime housewives, and although, generally speaking, men with fulltime working wives did more around the house than the others, and saw the work as a shared chore rather than 'hers' to be helped with, only a handful came anywhere near shouldering half the burden of housework and cooking. In fact some of the men whose wives didn't go out to work at all did more around the house than some whose wives worked full time. There seemed to be two reasons for this. The men whose wives worked full time invariably worked much longer hours (they were often self-employed) than their wives, who got on with household jobs before their husbands arrived home. Or else they were busy renovating the house or doing some other DIY or repair job. Both halves of the working couples were often quite happy with this arrangement, because one wasn't sitting down while the other was working, and the wife felt he was doing things she didn't particularly fancy doing anyway. One man reckoned he did 70 per cent of 'handyman' jobs while she did 70 per cent of the housework. Some couples seemed a bit embarrassed (the wife, rather than the husband) to be so traditional in practice when they 'believed' in sharing, and quite a few wives complained of having to nag their husbands into their part of the bargain.

Although men always used to be responsible for handyman work around the house, there was never the do-it-yourself boom, the big business operation which exists today. You had furniture rather than fitted wardrobes, you didn't plumb in washing machines, insulate lofts, install central heating and double glazing, tear down partition walls, convert attics and basements and build extensions like people do today. And you simply couldn't afford constant redecoration. If it looked presentable, it stayed where it was.

However, a lot of men react to household repairs and maintenance in the same way they react to housework, and many men confessed they were constantly being reminded that the shower was still only half built and the kitchen hadn't been started. Nevertheless, they unanimously see it as their responsibility, even though some feel more distaste for it than housework; with the exception of one man, Frank, a former travelling salesman who seemed to have abdicated all responsibility for his home other than as somewhere to eat and sleep:

> Helen does all the decorating, wall-plugging, drilling. It's not that I can't do it, but I make out that I can't.

Some men are frightened of electricity and scared of water because any mistake makes such a mess, although one man said 'Half of it is steeling yourself to do it'. Tony, the editor, wouldn't agree:

> I tried putting a sink in. The frustration of night after night under this sink in old clothes, getting wet, with the ridge of the cupboard in my back, trying to mend where the U bend went. I bandaged it and smeared it with red gooey stuff Pat's father lent me. But the water went blupp, blupp, blupp at the top of that. So I put some more on and in the end there was this huge

festering blob. It was a nightmare. Or you'd buy a tool and it was
the wrong tool and you'd bang your knuckles in the middle of
winter because that's when the car always breaks down, on
Sunday afternoon when you need it to travel 35 miles the next
day. And you'd be there with a spanner and again, crunch, you'd
come in and Pat would say 'Mended?' and your hand would be
bleeding with grease in it, you'd taken all the skin off and the car
still wouldn't work. I think if somebody took the company car
away, I'd need Valium very badly.

Another man complained wearily:

> Yes, she has to nag me to do things that, yes, I should do, even
> though I feel too tired or put it off. I can get flipping frustrated
> and annoyed even putting up shelves. I can't think three moves
> ahead in woodwork. She's more practically minded than I am. I
> do it with her help, but it takes four hours for something her
> father could have done in thirty minutes.

Why is it that couples stick to traditional roles, even with
such evident distaste? Why do some men readily tackle jobs
seemingly beyond the capacity of most men? And why was
there, in my sample, a strange discrepancy between the
appreciation men showed for their wives, and the amount of
help they offered? Men who described their wives as
housewives, mothers etc were far less likely to help out than
men who ostensibly did not recognise (by leaving a blank or
N/A) the work of their wives. It is easy within the context of
feminist logic to explain away male lack of domestic *savoir
faire* as a conscious, insensitive and exploitative ploy, for
which men's mothers are partly responsible. But that offers
no real explanation, nor, in the light of the quote at the
beginning of this chapter, any real answers.

Various studies claim that the lower down the social scale,
the more rigid are men's attitudes towards domestic roles[6].
However, among the men I interviewed, the reverse appeared
to be true. The French report mentioned earlier[2] gives blue
collar workers as marginally better than their executive
counterparts. And in Hannah Gavron's mid '60s study,[7]
working class husbands seemed much more home centred,
31 per cent sharing housework and childcare completely.

More recently, Dr John de Frain[8] confirms this among American blue collar workers; even though they don't pay as much lip service to women's rights as professional men, they do 15 per cent more around the house. He reckons that blue collar men 'let the barriers down at home' because housework compares quite favourably with what they have to do at work.

What came across in my sample was that these men often came from families where mothers had worked full time, their fathers had helped and they had been expected as children to help, and they often now had working wives themselves. In these, and in other households where wives worked full time, practicality dictated who did what. Shift-workers who got home before their wives would put the dinner on, men who worked nearer the shops did the shopping, like Ken, a central heating engineer:

> I do the shopping. I don't mind, I don't like it, but I do it. With Cathy working up in the city, there's nowhere for her to do any shopping. I do a lot of it when I'm working.

Nigel, a self-employed insurance broker, even found it a welcome break:

> I don't mind shopping, it gets me out, half an hour to escape. But that wouldn't change if I had an office in town, because I'd just walk out of the door and do it and then put the bags in a corner till I got home. My wife's work is very inflexible in that way, whereas I'm in the sort of job where I can put the pen down for half an hour. My way of relaxing for half an hour can be doing the ironing in front of an old film on the TV.

Men whose wives were hospitalised for some reason cooked, shopped, washed, ironed and cleaned, but it was very conspicuous that the ones who carried on doing these things had had some kind of experience in childhood, or when they were single, of fending for themselves, or else they had watched their fathers deputising around the house. Nigel's father had always stayed in the pub at night, until his mother had a nervous breakdown, when he was eleven:

So my dad stopped going to the pub as much and took over a lot of the cooking and housework. He was quite good at it, used to cook things that I'd never dreamed of having, like scallops.

Barry, a shift-worker, who claims he does 'the lot, even the occasional cake' had a mother who was:

The world's worst cook. My father cooked at weekends. During the week we had spam and salad all summer and sausage and chips all winter. My mum couldn't make cakes or anything. So my dad would show us, or we'd help.

Men who had fended for themselves before getting married were also much more capable and aware of what needed doing, having learnt the hard way, like Adrian, sharing a flat with six other men:

At first I lived out of tins and dinners for one. Then I thought this is revolting, there can't be much to this cooking business. I made a few mistakes, like mixing peas with scrambled egg—the most revolting colour, and it didn't taste too good either. And I used to save the blood to make gravy. I thought it was having the heat wrong that always made it curdle. I had to learn to cook. We took turns to make a roast at weekends. If you didn't do it properly, you were told in no uncertain terms.

Adrian still does his own mending, because it's something his wife goes out of her way to avoid: 'If it was stuck on your nose, you'd have a habit of forgetting it was there!' Jim's mother wouldn't let his sisters into the kitchen, but got him to help with the gravy: 'That's how I discovered that you can't go wrong with a roast.' And Alan started getting the dinner ready because his shift ended before his wife got home from work. It was lucky he was a fireman, because he set fire to the kitchen twice, but in the process discovered he really enjoys it, especially exotic things.

Dick, on the other hand, whose mother was a housewife, has to go without the exotic food he enjoys:

It's difficult if a woman isn't really a good—I musn't say that—isn't really into cooking. I've said I'll buy her some really nice cookbooks, but why should she be a good cook any more than I'm good at looking after the car? I *can* look after myself, it's not... It's just, because you don't do it very often, the silly things put you off, like how much salt to add.

An otherwise helpful and understanding husband, he felt inhibited by his own lack of expertise, but also rigidly aware of conventional roles, of usurping his wife's status. Most men claim they don't feel 'effeminate' doing 'women's work', yet both sides *are* affected by subtle social pressure to toe the stereotype line. Several couples mentioned face-saving operations to cover up what may be seen as a slur on the man:

> Although we have this sharing attitude, if there was a job that so obviously was a bloke's, she would never take it off me. She's very sensitive in that way. We did some concreting which she got very involved in, but if anybody came round she would give the impression that I was doing it, as the chap, although she would be doing as much as I was.

Many women are familiar with passing money under the restaurant table, and of course these strategies become self-perpetuating, with public behaviour masking less rigidly role-defined practices in private. Few men said they would be embarrassed being seen doing housework, although Tony admitted:

> I used to feel embarrassed, if people were coming round to dinner and they arrived while I was hoovering the hall. Ding, dong—and then, Ooo, look at Tony! It doesn't bother me now, though. I think I really have grown through that.

Many men won't hang washing out, however, although they'll fetch it in. Ken, whose wife spent a long time in hospital, discovered why:

> The neighbours used to take the rise out of him when he put the washing out, but he put them in their place. You should have given it to me, she said, I'd have put it out for you. So he said I'm quite capable of hanging a piece of washing on the line. Then the man said something about I see you've got your apron on. So Ken said, at least I do help my wife, which didn't go down too well.

Another man came under pressure from his father, for ironing his own shirts: 'He told me I was a fool.' And Jill, Adrian's wife, feels that it reflects on her, not Adrian, when her mother is tracing the dust on the rubber plant. He says:

> I don't know that I really consider that certain things are a man's job, except that perhaps there's an image I think one ought to present to people who don't know you very well. I don't carve the meat when there's just two of us, but if there were people here I might get a bit disgruntled if I was shown not carving.

As one man said, 'How much you care about what people think depends on how confident and carefree you happen to be feeling.' Those who are susceptible to social pressure are those who suffer an inner sense of insecurity. Jill pointed out that they use humour to bridge the gap:

> If I get a screwdriver out, to take off the bathroom cabinet, I say in mock indignation, I shouldn't be doing this, this is a man's job. And the same when Adrian's ironing, he grimaces and says I hope nobody turns up and sees me! We joke about this role business, don't we?

There is a tendency, even among couples like Jill and Adrian, who share a great deal, for a kind of see-saw effect of sliding back into traditional roles, whereby Adrian's cooking has gradually diminished to breakfasts at weekends:

> And when you start to do less, it becomes harder and harder to do more again, you just fall into roles.

He turned to his wife and added:

> You automatically expect now that you'll be cooking the main meal. And I assume you're going to do it.

This of course also means that Adrian can no longer compile the shopping list: 'I never know why it's there. You also hide things in obscure places.' Besides, it's more practical for Jill to do the shopping, because she can finish early one afternoon, near a big hypermarket. But Jill also admits that the things she does, she does out of preference:

I do most of the housework and Adrian does most of the gardening. From that point of view we've fallen into those silly traditional role stereotypes. But I do the housework better than Adrian does and I moan about it but I don't really mind doing it. We each choose what we like to do best, then share out what's left, like ironing. He does all his own shirts. But with the car, when I was single I used to check the oil and pressure, but now I just sort of expect Adrian to do it. And if he is out there working hard, I think, well I don't want to be doing that, so I get on with the cooking. It's easier to let one person get on with something and not interfere.

Division of labour does neatly avoid some of the 'let's do it my way' squabbles of sharing. In the garden, men do the heavy spade-work and grow the vegetables, while women potter about among the flower-beds: 'I say we can't eat flowers, she says we can.' The problems of sharing come to a head over decorating, which only a few men considered their wives not competent enough to tackle ('I won't let my wife decorate, because she tends to fall over.'). It's usually over the wallpapering. Some couples admitted shouting at one another, while another couple decided on a truce:

We don't speak. We used to argue for hours over it, so I'll mark the top and she'll mark the bottom and she'll cut across—she's better at straight lines than I am—then I paste and stick it on, and so on...

This kind of conflict offers a clue to an understanding of the real reasons why men tend not to pull their weight in the home, the deep, inner reasons which men themselves can't admit and often aren't consciously aware of.

The traditional role relationship may mean that men are the ones who pay for their homes, but women are the ones who take possession of them. And when it comes to whom the house really seems to belong to, possession is, as James Thurber realised, nine-tenths of the law. How can it be his home, when it bears such a heavy stamp of her presence on it?

The women's movement expects men to understand women and their position from a woman's point of view. Although women do try to understand men, I would suggest that they find it hard, domestically, to put themselves into the opposite position, to understand how it feels to come home to a house where things have been given a place by someone else, things you may have been using have been tidied away, where the furnishings and décor reflect another person's taste, even down to the colour of the toilet roll. Yet this is the experience of many men, especially men whose wives are in the housewife role. It may appear trivial, but it is crucial. Most of us can remember how important it was, during adolescence, to have our own piece of territory, where a diplomatic treaty had restrained our mother's colonising influence. Home is part of individual self-expression, just as much as the clothes we wear, the cars we drive and the furry dice we may or may not have suspended from the rearview mirror.

Yet many women fail to appreciate their territorial advantage, that not only do they feel more at home at home, in the way that men feel more at home at work, but they are at home when the man arrives, having appropriated the place before him. Not only do women plan meals, choose décor and establish a place for everything, but every time they clean its contents they are fostering an intimacy, a connectedness their husbands lack: they are reaffirming, reappropriating, repossessing it. Women may resent this greater involvement as a burden, but it does give them a special territorial advantage. (Women who commit murder apparently do it in the kitchen, the focal point of their power, whereas men murder in the bedroom, where they can exert their physical dominance.)

The power and control women wield in the home is of course often hardly matched by status or influence outside it. If women are honest with themselves, most of them feel highly ambivalent about men helping, especially in the kitchen. They yearn to lose the nagging burden and the skivvy role, but cling to the power and control. One wife who had to leave her job to follow her husband's promotion, began to ask him to do less around the house, because she was starting to feel a sense of redundancy in every aspect of her life. Although women complain about men not helping, there is a fine line between helping and a clumsy interfering takeover bid. As our mothers said 'I don't want a man getting

under my feet when I'm cooking', so women find it hard to
disengage from involvement with domesticity, sit back and
let him do it his way. As one wife admitted:

> In a way, I must admit, I want it both ways. I resent David when
> he does do things, because he does them wrong, not the way I
> would do it and I feel anxious, or I keep checking up on him.
> Even if I leave him to get on with it, I'm inspecting what he's
> done afterwards. I don't give him any room to feel it's *his*, in the
> way that I *care* about doing it, because it's mine. I'm better with
> our little daughter helping, than when my husband does
> something. What often happens is that I'll rush to do
> something, and then resent it afterwards, that he hasn't done it.

In the past, men counterbalanced female power in the home
by insisting on ritual acknowledgement of their position as
head of the household. Some men still insist on being served
first, carving the meat and sitting at the head of the table,
even if the distinction is purely metaphorical:

> I like to think I sit at the head, although the table is actually
> round.

The men who insist on this kind of deference tend to be men
who acknowledge their wife's role as the homemaker and
avoid doing much around the house, since acting as kitchen
assistant is not really commensurate with a position of
assumed authority. In this way men of my father's
generation masked their domestic helplessness by treating
the house like a hotel, waited on by their wives because they
were footing the bill. A hotel is not a home.

Nowadays most men don't insist on this kind of deference
because couples want more equal, companionable, shared
marriages, even though they don't necessarily share roles.
This creates a difficulty for men because it exposes the
imbalance of power in the home. They may of course defend
their disadvantage in other ways, by keeping a piece of
inviolable territory, like a certain armchair in the best
position or a den that mustn't be invaded or disturbed, but
this seems a little old fashioned too. Men don't necessarily,
however, despite the spirit of equality, feel any less

threatened in the home, so they defend themselves in other ways.

The technique in which they are particularly adept, is that of distancing, cutting off. This can be done literally, as many working class men used to do, by staying in the pub or the club all evening, which some of these men's fathers used to do, and one or two of my interviewees still do. One man described the breakdown of his first marriage as stemming from the excluded feeling he felt when he walked into his home. He regularly stayed at work until 7 or 8 at night, because he was more at home there than in the house he called his home, and ultimately the couple, divided by their separate roles, split up.

So overwork may be a symptom of cutting off from home, just as bringing home a bulging briefcase (only to return with it next morning, unopened) may reflect the need to reinforce a threatened sense of identity rather than conscientiously catching up with work. Of course the two may dovetail into the perfect collusion, the demands at work and the cutting off from home, which may be why so many men find work irresistible, rather than a frustrating conflict of divided loyalties.

Men who do come home at the right time may distance themselves psychologically, so that they simply don't notice their surroundings, and therefore numb themselves to the threat of their wife's control. One man had decorated the whole house according to his wife's taste, but couldn't remember the colours in the upstairs rooms. He never looked: 'If she said paint the walls red, I'd paint the walls red.' The trouble is that this attitude of uncaring, and lack of awareness of their surroundings carries over into an inability to notice cups left lying about, dirty socks on the bedroom floor, dust or dirt or things that need doing. Some men manage to make some sort of territorial statement in the living room, while backing off from everywhere else:

Ninety per cent of the time Ann chooses the décor, for peace and quiet, really. I chose this room, because I like to look at wallpaper that appeals to me, but the rest of the rooms are entirely Ann's choice, especially the kitchen. I don't mind.

This cutting-off capacity is what gives men the ability to tolerate levels of untidiness which might otherwise be infuriating:

> I come in sometimes and the place is a complete mess and I just sit amongst it. Other times, I blow my top and get the children to clear everything, everywhere.

Another man said:

> It doesn't bother me whether the house is clean and tidy. Sometimes, though, I get annoyed if it's a mass of Lego and Action Men just where I want to sit down.

Children have their own way of making a claim on family territory, by strewing their toys around. It isn't only children who make a territorial statement in this way. Women usually interpret the toothpaste left out with the top off, shoes and socks in the bathroom, wet towels on the bed and a dirty comb sitting on top of the refrigerator as thoughtless laziness. But in some ways it's more aggressively (if subconsciously) deliberate than that.

Marking is something animals do to indicate the boundaries of their territory to other animals. Fortunately men don't go round spraying all the rooms in the house, but just as there is an assertively proprietorial element to cleaning something, there is an assertively proprietorial element involved in making it dirty, messing it up, sabotaging it, leaving a symbol of one's presence.

The things that men choose to do around the house also reveal a defensive element. The most popular domestic chores men volunteer for are washing up and hoovering. Both activities combine a minimum of acquired skill with a sensation of directing and controlling, doing something decisive, rather than acting as a menial or revealing lack of skill and expertise. Clearing up after a meal involves three tasks: clearing the table, washing up, and drying and putting away. Of these, washing up is the central pivotal task, which men prefer even though the others involve less effort. Greater prestige and control, therefore, attaches to washing up. Similarly, vacuum cleaning is a decisive, directional act, like

mowing a lawn, or driving a machine. One man declined to
do the hoovering because it wasn't an upright model that
you push backwards and forwards in a forceful manner;
dragging a cylinder about, poking a nozzle into corners,
simply wasn't the same.

And many men who insisted on their ritual position of
dominance in the home showed a distinct defensiveness
about tasks involving any kind of exposure of their lack of
skill. They seemed to prefer to hide behind the idea that it
would be boring, rather than betray their own inexpertise in
an area in which their wives happened to excel:

> I've never cooked a thing in my life and it's a bone of contention
> between my wife and myself. If she was ill, I'd get by. She often
> says to me, one of the joys of life would be if you were to cook a
> Sunday meal for me. I'll never do it. It's the time, I haven't got
> the time. I consider I do sufficient things to please her, like
> taking the kiddies out at weekends, without cooking.

The same man, a bank employee, did take time on one
occasion to have a go at the washing while his wife was out,
but in relating his failure hid behind nonchalance, even
selfishness, stressing the insignificance of the task, rather
than admit he couldn't actually do it when he tried:

> I know it's a rotten thing to say, but it amused me one evening to
> have a go at the washing. I got the spin-dryer making the most
> awful noise because I'd got the weight distributed wrongly, but
> you see I get very frustrated doing a job which takes a long while
> and I feel I'm getting nothing out of it. There's no job
> satisfaction. It's selfishness, I know.

Interestingly, quite a few other men mentioned spontaneously doing something when their wives were out, when
for once they had the house to themselves:

> Sometimes if I get up in the morning and she's gone out, I'll do
> something that takes my fancy—go and polish the dining
> room table.

Several other men mentioned having a go at the washing,
almost as if they wanted to see whether they could do it,

while their wives weren't there:

> She rushed out one day and I thought she'd probably want to get this washing done, so I sorted it out into what I thought were the right lots, for woollens, delicates etc, and put it in. It was my stuff that came out worst... That was me trying to be helpful.

This of course smacks of a conscious helplessness, although the same man said his wife 'says I do a far better job of ironing sheets, so I finish up doing them'.

It was noticeable that men, like Nigel, who spent part of the day at home, alone, and probably did the most (with one or two exceptions) towards taking over responsibility for housework, shopping and cooking, tackling skills like ironing, were also the men who cared least about playing the ritual head of the household, as if they felt secure in their own territorial claim.

Otherwise, I listened to the enumeration of cooking, polishing, bedmaking, window-cleaning, dusting, cleaning baths and even toilets, but washing, no, not unless she's sorted it all out beforehand, and ironing—*never*. To women, washing and ironing appear perfectly straightforward tasks, easily mastered with an intelligent assessment of the colour and fabric and in many cases simply requiring the ability to read a manufacturer's washing label. Yet men with highly responsible jobs, like Dennis, who runs a department in a major bank, admitted:

> She has to tell me what number on the dial you use, because I turned everything pink once, making it too hot or too cold.

And Ken, a central heating engineer, in every other respect more than competent around the house because his wife works full time and has a physical disability, confessed that he can't iron, or rather:

> I can do it, but I don't like it. I do muck a few things up, my wife's blouses and things like that. I used to stick a hot iron on them and that's goodbye to them.

This apparently entrenched incompetence appears to

women as a convenient avoidance technique, but it isn't necessarily so. It reflects the lack of an acquired skill which many women probably take for granted.

Women are more sensitive to touch than men and they are also better at distinguishing and naming shades of colours. (See note.[9]) (Paint manufacturers have finally cottoned on to the fact that women tend to choose the decor in the home—90 per cent of the wives in my sample did—and now aim their colour ranges at women's taste.) Most men acknowledged that their wives had a better colour sense than they had. A great deal of attention has been given to the spatial-mechanical skills which girls fail to develop during childhood, because they are not encouraged to construct things and run round testing their reflexes and co-ordination, but not much notice is taken of what girls are actually doing while boys are out grazing their knees.

While girls are dressing dolls and playing house, they are not wasting their time, but developing their acute sense of touch, which is actually twice as sensitive as that of a man, discerning the differences in texture and tones of colours of materials. This skill is carried forward into dress sense and interest in clothes. For women, the intimate handling, the touch and feel of materials becomes so much like second nature that they assume it's a natural facility, that everyone has it. The positive effects of female sex role conditioning, against the negative effects of male sex role conditioning, tend to get overlooked. It is not easy for men and women to share domestic roles, because both sides have got to go so far against the grain. And the barriers involve not just compensatory control, competence and conditioning, but a powerful emotional pull as well.

The interest and attachment which female children develop towards dolls and doll's-houses creates what I would call an emotional focus. Children are at their happiest when they are playing, most spontaneously and unselfconsciously. For a child, a favourite game is a kind of meditation, a kind of magic ritual against upsetting experience. When I was a child, woken in the night by a bad dream, I would hold the horrible images at bay by mentally redecorating my doll's-house. This, the emotional aspect of conditioning, is what becomes most engrained in us, as Colette Dowling found, in *The Cinderella Complex*.[10] Women home in on home because they are emotionally drawn towards replaying childhood games. Men invariably seem to describe housework as 'boring', saying that they can only tackle it when the mood takes them, and couldn't bear the responsibility of *having* to do it. While women also feel trapped by housework (and are in reality much more trapped than men) they derive more satisfaction from it, according to the EEC survey.[4] (See note.[11]) Men often spoke to me of the only satisfaction being that of seeing the difference between dirty and clean.

This, and the difficulties inherent in sharing as opposed to division of labour, is what makes it so difficult not to fall into traditional roles. Women simply care more about the house and doing it yourself is often less effort than reminding, or nagging someone else who never remembers to do it. So much does seem to depend on how much the woman *resists* doing it herself, even though she invariably does it better. Tony admitted:

> If I do clean, I tend to skip over things, whereas Pat will actually rip things apart, get underneath beds. Neither of us likes doing it, we've always shared. I think if Pat had spoiled me, given me one inch I would have been in there like a shot but she actually made it clear—I just cooked this meal, if you don't wash up, Tony, it can sit there for a week till it gets fungus on it. Just to get through your life you have to do certain things and they're chores, so we share it, which is very different to my background.

Tony's wife Pat never *played* at housework as a child. She was forced to do it for real, from the age of eight. As an adult, therefore, she readily rebelled against it, allowing the cleaning threshold to drop to the point at which Tony began to notice:

> This is the type of house that when I was a boy, my mother would whisper, afterwards, it wasn't very clean, was it? And although that doesn't bother me, when the hand-basin starts to get scummed I think well, that's not on, Tony. It's nice to be a little bit in control of the entropy in this house.

Nevertheless, Pat and Tony still slip into traditional roles. Tony sees it as Pat gravitating to the tasks she can handle, leaving him floundering, a dinner party joke, in his traditional role:

> These stories become folklore, and that one about the letter rack will be used for forever and a day, as an exmple of my apathy. 'I asked Tony five times a week on average for a year and he never did it . . .' and 'then we had this light that we never used. There's been a piece of sticky paper over the switch for the past year'. Pat doesn't actually do anything about it because she likes to have things she can get me for! She does a lot of things, which happen to be the things she likes and can cope with, and leaves me to do the other things . . .

But what about men who aren't in a couple role relationship? Single men seem to fall into two distinct domestic groups: those who become houseproud and derive satisfaction from looking after themselves (down to admiring fourteen shirts hanging from the picture rail, ironed in one evening), and those who neglect their home, eating out, spending the evening in the pub, anything to leave until the last moment facing an unmade bed in a room full of clothes strewn where they happened to be taken off. Some of these men live with the fantasy that this is only a temporary arrangement, while they're working so hard, or because the flat isn't worth it. What they seem to be saying is that they are waiting, holding some part of themselves in suspension, and in so doing making a statement of need: need for someone to come along and take care of them. In the meantime they are content to put up with squalor and hardship because they consciously cut off from that need and can find no resources within themselves to provide for it.

As single women have been discovering through economic necessity, it is a hard slog to face all of life's responsibilities on your own. In this respect the male/female division of labour performs a valuable function of protection from simultaneous exposure to *all* of life's demands. It allows for the need to regress, recharge batteries for a while. We all have residual needs for parenting, however old and independent we are. The emotional regression couples indulge in is not confined to babytalk. It is commonly expressed by women 'mothering' men, and men 'fathering' women, like Adrian taking over the care of Jill's car. To take Jill and Adrian as an example, they are aware, as they say, that they came together as independent people who cared about one another, not because he needed a housekeeper and she needed a meal ticket. And to a great extent they have maintained that independence of spirit, but the ghost of the dependence is there, still, as they came round to admitting. It seems, though, to be more on his side than hers:

> I think Adrian still feels he ought to support me. I'm sure you don't like the fact that I couldn't give up work tomorrow.

> Maybe so. But it's not that I consider it an affront to my manhood that I can't support you. It's purely selfish, it's very nice to come home and have everything there...

We are not just playing out our parents' roles because of our conditioning, but as part of the close comfort of a couple relationship. This is emphasised in the polarised situation where couples are really playing mothers and fathers, each partner taking the full brunt of their separate responsibilities. Yet men seem to express a greater need to regress than women. A survey carried out in the late 1950s, for a Chicago housing company, apparently revealed that a house has a different emotional meaning for men than it has for women. To a woman, it means an extension of her personality and creative possibilities. To a man its meaning is conveyed in one word—Mother. Perhaps men need to regress into the symbolic hold of a mother figure because that regression, for various reasons, is denied them through life. Not only, therefore, do men struggle against women for domestic equality as husbands and fathers; they struggle against themselves.

## NOTES

1 Lizanne Winter (letter to *Guardian* 'Guardian Women', 10 May 1983)

2 Official report from *La Documentation Française* (Paris, 1982)
3 Danish and American statistics quoted by Dr Joyce Brothers, *What Every Woman Should Know about Men* (Ballantine Books, New York, 1981; Granada, 1982)
4 *European Men and Women in 1978: A comparison of their attitudes to some of the problems facing society* (Commission of the European Communities, Brussels, 1979). Based on interviews with nearly 9000 respondents.
5 Ibid. British men topped the list of those claiming to help often (48 per cent), against 15 per cent in Italy, which allowing for Italian exaggeration amounted to a minus quantity of men. However, 54 per cent of Italians claimed to help their wives 'sometimes', against 39 per cent in the UK, which came bottom in this category. Italian men were also the most to admit to 'never helping' (30 per cent), with 12 per cent of UK men, and only 11 per cent among the paragons of honesty in Denmark.
6 Elizabeth Whitelegg et al, *The Changing Experience of Women* (Martin Robertson, Oxford 1982)
7 Hannah Gavron, *The Captive Wife* (Routledge & Kegan Paul, 1966)
8 Dr Joyce Brothers, op cit
9 Otto Jesperson, *Language: Its Nature, Development and Origin* (Allen & Unwin, 1922). He noticed women's language involved more colour distinctions, with precise discriminations in naming of colours (eg 'fuchsia' as opposed to 'red') which men were more likely to consider trivial or irrelevant.
10 Colette Dowling, *The Cinderella Complex* (Summit Books, New York, 1981; Michael Joseph, 1982)
11 This survey found that 59 per cent of women felt that housework could actually be enjoyable (against 43 per cent of men), and that 31 per cent of men felt it was purely a necessary burden (against 23 per cent of women).

## Chapter Three

# SONS AND FATHERS

*How sad that men would base an entire civilisation on
the principle of paternity, upon male legal ownership
of and presumed responsibility for children, and then
never really get to know their sons or their daughters
very well; never really participate, for whatever reason,
in parenting, in daily, intimate fathering . . .*
(Phyllis Chesler[1])

MY FATHER once explained to me that in the 1930s, when he
first had children, it would have been 'beneath a man's
dignity' to be seen pushing a pram. When I asked him what
that meant, he simply repeated 'undignified'. When I
pressed the point, he explained that, just as having a
working wife would have implied that he could not afford to
keep her, pushing a pram would have signified that she was
failing in her job, her side of affairs, looking after the
children. I had always assumed men were too embarrassed to
be seen doing anything so essentially feminine and caring,
but he denied that embarrassment came into it, and repeated
the word again, 'undignified'. I never thought at the time to
ask whether he'd pushed me in a pram, after the war, and
now it's too late to ask. Somehow I doubt that he did. Some
fathers did, but most men were the product of two periods of
military service, that short-back-and-sides mentality which
helped segregate the sexes roles even more.

One of the first films I ever saw, in the 1950s, was *Doctor in
the House* from Richard Gordon's novel, with Dirk Bogarde
playing Simon Sparrow the young medical student who
finds himself having to deliver a baby. I can remember
watching mystified as he kept running downstairs asking for

kettles of hot water. But however it happened it was obviously a mothers' affair and fathers had nothing to do with it. Films of that period would show fathers pacing up and down a shabby hospital waiting room, chain-smoking, until a distant cry halted them in their tracks. An American doctor apparently capitalised on this by holding a microphone to the newborn baby's mouth, calling the appropriate father over the waiting room intercom and then smacking the baby's bottom so that he would hear the first cry.

Novelist Deborah Moggach[2] recently vindicated (in an article in the *Sunday Times*) my suspicions that 'few men of middle age have seen this overwhelming event', by referring to her own father who confirmed that:

> Chaps simply weren't around. No question about it—far too indelicate. If it was a home birth one was despatched elsewhere... the whole process was nothing to do with the male sex.

It was a female mystery and part of the shyness between couples which prevented some of them from ever seeing one another naked.

This article was smartly followed up by a letter[3] from two famous childcare experts of the 1950s and 1960s, John and Elizabeth Newson, dismissing Deborah Moggach's father as an 'unreliable informant', since their own study[4] at the end of the '50s showed that 13 per cent of home births were attended by the husband (no lay person being allowed in for any hospital delivery). However 87 per cent of the fathers were presumably *not* present, but it does prove how much the climate of popular opinion has swung towards assuming the father ought to be there. The Newsons, who had three children between 1955 and 1961, add that 'There was never so much as a raised eyebrow from any of our midwives about our sharing these births, nor even about filming the last one', but then most fathers of the period were not professionally involved in the study of *Patterns of Infant Care*.

Whatever the experts practised themselves, they were prone to agree that the mother was the all-important figure as far as a child's physical and emotional development were concerned. The great guru of childcare and the attachment theory, John Bowlby,[5] writing in the 1950s, hardly gave fathers a passing mention. Studies of that period tend to refer to fathers as 'husbands', endorsing Bowlby's belief that the father was basically there to provide for the child and support the mother. Mothers were warned of the dangers of leaving the child, while the father's presence (or absence) was hardly mentioned. Bowlby's actual immortal words were:

> ... Little will be said of the father–child relationship: his value as the economic and emotional support of the mother will be assumed.

I have to strain to remember my father when I was small. When I say remember him, I mean remember being with him, what he meant to me, our relationship. Perhaps it was because I was a girl. When I asked my elder brother, though, if he could remember Dad taking him out, there was a long pause. 'I don't remember going anywhere,' he said finally. I had to remind him about the cricket matches, where I tagged along, cross and bored, made to trot back with the empties of fizzy drinks for the money back on the bottles.

> Yes, he took me to two test matches, at Lord's. But really we were never very close. I suppose I didn't miss any relationship that wasn't there, because I'd plenty of friends, I didn't need too much parental attention. I remember his absence, during the war, when I was about five. And drawing pictures for him. And I remember him coming home on leave and that was quite a happy occasion. But I don't really remember him spending much time with me.

Distant, a stranger in a dark suit, the ultimate deterrent if we were naughty—'wait till I tell your father'. But it was rare for him not to miss when he swiped out half-heartedly with a slipper. If I felt apprehensive of him, I think it was largely because his own shyness of us, as children, transmitted itself. He was gruff but inarticulate when he had to tackle us about anything we'd done wrong, although he could be quite stern, right up to the last day of his life, when he sharply forbade me to fetch the nurse because he wanted to get out of bed by himself—and I disobeyed him.

He once cryptically remarked about his own father that Grandpa Ingham was fond of volunteering. He had run away from teacher training college when the Boer War broke out to enlist, without telling his parents, in the Imperial Yeomanry, and then on 4 August 1914 volunteered again. Apparently he didn't come back until 1919. He had been fighting in Salonica, in Greece, caught malaria and travelled through Italy and France in an open cattle truck for four days before reaching England, whereupon he was sent out to Archangel to fight the Bolsheviks. My father, meanwhile, continued his schooling. Between the ages of seven and fourteen he hardly saw his father at all.

Yet although he was there, with us, living in the house when we grew up, I don't believe he really knew us, not like our mother did, and we certainly didn't know him. I can't remember how I felt about him at all as a father, although one vivid memory returned to me when I was in my mid-twenties. Lying in bed one night, on the brink of sleep, I suddenly saw myself, felt myself, with my father when I was very small. It could have been a dream, but it wasn't. It was like a flash of emotional lightning illuminating a forgotten recess of my mind and in the few seconds that it lasted I could feel and see everything as if I was really there. I was sitting on my father's knee, crying, and he was bouncing me up and down pulling faces to try to make me smile. And with this memory image came an amazing rush of longing, of feeling, of love for him, and of safety because he cared enough about me to try to stop me feeling sad. That is the only recollection that I have, submerged, disassociated, disconnected from any time or place, of any tender spontaneous affection from him.

Many men I've spoken to since have similar snapshot memories of important, fleeting instances when their fathers were really real to them:

> I have one vivid memory, I can see it now. I don't know how old I was, but less than ten and more than two, on the back of his moped, going off to feed a horse with some bread one Sunday morning. I can smell the petrol in the moped. It was such a rare occurrence, as he was always working. He never looked after us on his own, my mother never went out.

And yet paternal deprivation wasn't supposed to exist.
Mother was the significant parent when it came to the
emotional development of the child. True, over 90 per cent of
all the men I asked claimed to have felt closer to their
mothers than their fathers when they were children, even
though fathers were more likely to share their interests. A
small number of men do remember their fathers as warm and
caring, encouraging and supportive, but for most the
relationship was either problematic, or non-existent, or
both:

> I have very negative memories of my father. Mum was
> smashing... but my image of my dad is the one that was never
> there. It was the neighbour across the road who took me to
> football matches, not my father. With him, you couldn't even
> play football in the garden, in case you knocked a plant over.
> The only time I ever remember him taking me out was going for
> a cycle ride into some woods one Sunday. I can remember sitting
> on the lines at the gateway. But that's the only time. He didn't
> like holidays, anything to disrupt his routine.

Graham, who followed in his father's footsteps to become a
policeman, before switching careers to social work, conjures
up a picture of his father as a man who didn't like being with
children, or didn't know how to be with them, who perhaps
resented his wife's capacity to abandon herself to them in a
way his job prevented him from doing. For many other men,
Dad was simply that, the absent provider:

> I didn't see much of my father, he worked long hours, which was
> why I was a mother's boy I suppose. She was around more. He
> only had Saturday afternoons off. Who is this man? That might
> have a lot to do with it. He never took me to matches, I often tell
> him off about that. But he worked a 6½ day week, and that was
> that.

At a time when labour-saving devices in the home were
perhaps giving mothers more time to devote to their
children, fathers were working just as long hours as before.
Any drop in the basic working week was swallowed up by
overtime, since the consumer society meant greater earning
power as well as greater spending power. At a time when

only working class or professional wives went out to work as a rule, the full burden fell on men, especially fathers of young children:

> He just used to come home and fall asleep.

> He never took me out much, we never had a great rapport. He used to work long hours, he was always tired when I knew him.

There was also an element of neglect, of fathers who pursued their own interests, regardless of the family:

> I looked forward to him coming home, but it was always fairly late, around seven o'clock, and he was very involved in local politics, so I didn't see much of him even then.

And the physical distance, the stranger relationship, was compounded by the psychological distance which seemed to go with it:

> The closest I ever got to him was on some occasions, when I was seven or eight. We used to go into the wood collecting sticks and leaf mould, and sometimes I could get away with holding his hand. I remember the nice feel of this big rough hand. It wasn't that he didn't like me. Of his two sons I was apparently the favourite, but he wasn't able to express it in any way. I wanted to be close to him, I was very impressed with him. He was always right about everything. He wasn't authoritarian in a punishing way, but the whole household lived in fear of him...

The traditional father role didn't leave a great deal of scope for playing a part other than the serious and responsible authority figure, as Tony remembers his father:

> I felt closer to my mother because she was there most of the time. My dad was more of a stranger. When you banged your knee, it was mother you went to. He was more distant, he did this job and you didn't know where he went out during the day. Mum was homely, familiar; he was more severe. She could be cross with you, but the threat was 'wait till your father...' and that *was* a threat, because he was more of a stranger, simple as that. He would come home and if mum said 'Tony's been very bad today,

you must speak to him,' you quaked in your shoes a bit, because
you weren't sure how he was going to react. You didn't feel you
knew every facet of this man. He never took me out on his own,
except when I was about nine or ten. He introduced me to
football and cricket—wonderful father/son thing, you know—
but those were special occasions. My strongest image of him is of
him locking up, shutting up the house having ushered us all
out, locking and checking, very slow and very sure.

Nick, now an office manager with a Lloyd's insurance
broker, feared his father because of what he represented,
rather than what he was:

> I was afraid of my father, irrationally, really, because I only
> remember a couple of times when he spanked me ... but I saw
> very little of him and mother was always saying wait till your
> father gets home. She didn't invent the phrase, but by God she
> used it.

For some men, like Frank, who actively disliked his father,
that fear was very real, and paramount:

> I lived in fear of my father ... He was not averse to hitting me,
> from a relatively young age. And quite badly, in fact very badly,
> ie the police etc. Because he drank tremendously, frighteningly.
> I have a terrible memory for childhood, mainly I think because
> I've got a mental block and don't wish to remember. But I can
> remember between the ages of seven and ten, which was the
> worst of all. He got drunk every night of the week ... Mother
> lived in fear of him coming home. You could hear him park his
> bike in the back of the house and then all the banging and
> crashing as he was trying to find his way into the house, and then
> all hell let loose.

Just as a few men's fathers resembled Mr Morel in
Lawrence's *Sons and Lovers*, causing them to hate their
fathers and idealise their mothers, there were a few men who
idealised their fathers for being less accessible, powerful,
someone to look up to, and easier to get on with because they
weren't always there. Potentially, and sometimes actually,
dad could be much more fun than mum, because he played
your games with as much (sometimes more) enthusiasm as

you did, to make up for the times when he wasn't there. And in the holidays, or after school, he would sometimes show you the important grown-up world he lived in:

> The train would come in at 5, and shunt for an hour in the yard. If you went up he'd put you on the train with him and you'd shunt up and down the sidings, sit and wave to all your mates on the platform.

Some men remember getting up at 5 or 6 am, just to have breakfast with him, or help him get ready for work 'and in the holidays I would cycle down to him, see what I could scrounge out of his lunchbox, but no more than any other kid'. There was no such note of defensiveness in the way Andrew talked about his father, a tiling contractor:

> I felt closer to my mother because she provided the greater security, the environment I needed, but all my spare time was involved with him. I went everywhere to work with my father, visiting sites and clients. I was his sidekick from a very early age, six or seven. Everywhere he went, his shadow went with him, until I was twelve or thirteen when I had my own job, as a tea boy and helping the blokes—getting in the way, I suppose. The strongest impression I have of my father was him at work.

Some boys felt closer to a father they idealised, because he was interesting, because he was something glamorous, like a train driver or a footballer:

> I don't think I could ever reach my view of my father, he's the best man who ever lived. He was quite a good footballer, played in the county league at thirty-six, without any training—which just shows how football's changed. I used to go with him when I was five or six, as a mascot I suppose.

Barry sees his dad as the ideal father:

> I suppose my mother was interested in us in her way, but he always had time to tell you things, show you things and do things with you, he fostered our interests. I bought a stuffed goose with its wings outstretched, hissing, and two or three weeks later he brought home these two squirrels, motheaten things. There was more fur in the bottom of the glass case than there was on the squirrels. 'There y'are, little lad, Harry Fant's

given you these, look.' And he'd hunt round for bits and bobs for us, stuff that people threw away in the bottom of the shed he'd bring us. If you went to the seaside, you wouldn't just have a toffee apple and come away, you'd be walking down the bleedin' beach looking at pebbles and shells and things and sometimes I'd think oh, shut up, will you, go away; but when you look back he was doing the ideal thing.

Feelings for dad were sometimes far less straightforward, full of conflict between what you wanted him to be, and needed him to be, and what he was, or appeared to be, so that in a way you felt you were playing his part for him:

My mother was a dominant woman, whereas with my father, it was anything for a quiet life. I felt closer to him, I suppose, because I sided with him. I used to say for God's sake, dad, stand up to her, tell her you're a man, but of course it's the British character to stick up for the weaker one. I felt sorry for my dad, but now when I think about it, I'm not sure I really do. He rarely took me out, never to sports, never really bothered with me, never looked after us on his own, because my mother never went out.

Increasingly, however, dads had to deputise in emergencies, because the battery of female kin was no longer close at hand. For Mike, whose mother had a nervous breakdown, this marked a turning point in his relationship with his father who had previously spent all his spare time down at the pub.

Dads may not have been much good at cuddling and caring, but they did things with you rather than for you, joined in your games. That was why you treasured the memories like precious stones.

Most of the men I was talking to are now fathers themselves. Many of them, now the roles are reversed, are trying to re-experience their own childhood in a more positive way, often expressing a desire to make up for what they felt they lacked:

I do a lot for the children, because I missed out a lot with my father. He didn't have the time. I'd like more time. Coming back to your question about a shorter working week, what I'd like to do with the time off is play more, and it would give me more time to mend their toys!

This man, however, was one of the few who expressed the desire for more time with their children. Most men, despite their better intentions, seem more or less locked into the pattern they grew up with, not realising how much more of themselves they could perhaps give to their children, not experiencing the conflict between work and home as a conflict. They still come home tired, around the children's bedtime and Rick, quoted above, was one of the half dozen men who opted for more spare time rather than more money, and one of the even smaller number who opted for more time to spend with their children. He was also one of the few men who, when contemplating paid leave and how they would spend it, mentioned the constraint of school holidays or family commitments, or the possibility of family coming too.

Yet it must not be underestimated to what degree today's fathers *are* more involved, less strange to their children than their own fathers were, partly by their own initiative, and partly out of a new expectation to be more active, positive fathers, endorsed by pillars of the establishment like Prince Charles. It all seems to have started in the delivery room about ten years ago, when wives began asking their husbands to be there, and gradually hospitals came round to the idea, so that now, as one father put it:

> I didn't have much choice in the matter. The nurse said here you are, Mr So-and-so, put this on, gave me a gown and mask and there I was, helping with the gas.

Being in at the birth is now generally much more popular than being absent, although the suggestion often seems to come from the wife, reflecting the closer companionship needs in the marriage rather than the father's interest specifically in the child. Ann Oakley[6] recorded 43 per cent of fathers in the mid 1970s wanting to be present at the birth. A slightly later study[7] chalked up 52 per cent, and only 1 of 13 fathers interviewed in a study by Lorna McKee[8], in the north of England in 1976–7, did not want to be present, because he was 'squeamish'. For most men in this last study, attending the birth was part of a desire to share the experience, express their commitment and a joint responsibility towards the child, help their wives through it and satisfy their curiosity as to 'what happens'. However, none of these fathers mentioned having wanted to be there to consolidate their relationship with their child, although some made this connection afterwards.

Generally, the fathers I interviewed were glad to have seen their children born, (they were more likely to have seen the younger ones born), but did not consider the experience brought them any closer to those particular children, and they were often very inarticulate when it came to describing such an 'amazing experience'. Lorna McKee,[8] however, describes how although men would attempt to hide their own nervousness because they felt they should be the reassuring male presence ('the sturdy oak ideal'), their role as perceived by the medical staff was far less clear. Five of the thirteen fathers described waiting up to two hours while their wives were prepared for delivery, without any explanation of what was being done or how long it would take. They consequently experienced a mixture of 'loneliness, confusion, anxiety, boredom and annoyance', felt neglected, abused and in the way:

> I noticed it very soon after arriving... my role had been shed at the door. And we'd been working through pregnancy together and relying on each other so much and I was just left really like a spare part without any clear instructions as to how I could help. I was really regarded as a burden and I'm fairly sure that some of the midwives regarded me as the villain of the piece that had caused all this. There was that sort of air about... People spoke to me as if I wasn't there, spoke about me to Sally or asked Sally to answer questions on my behalf even though I was standing there. And I felt very much as if I was in the way.

McKee's fathers described 'balancing their attention between their wives and their infants' and, like my own interviewees, found it hard to find the words to sum up the experience, resorting to abstract expressions of 'joy, strangeness, wonderment and elation', at seeing their children born. All the birth attenders felt they had experienced something 'very unique, emotional and lasting', which in some cases reduced them to tears, and yet McKee was forced to sum up by criticising the neglect by the medical profession of the father's involvement in the process, or feelings for the child:

> The injustice and contradictions of a system which on the one hand encourages participation and responsible parenthood and on the other denies a feeling of involvement and individual choice... it is a pity that the father's place cannot be made more coherent, explicit and accepted.

And Sheila Kitzinger warns,[9] 'Once the triumphant phoning is over the new father comes face to face with his isolation and expendability.' From the evidence of thousands of births between 1979 and 1982 she concludes that hospitals which allow fathers to be present at the birth exclude them from their wives and children soon after the event. A report from the Thomas Coram Research Unit stressed that few fathers had the opportunity to develop confidence in handling, feeding or changing their babies while they were in hospital, as medical staff often felt fathers might transmit germs.

These findings are part of a recent long-term study entitled 'Transition to Parenthood', undertaken by the Thomas Coram Research Unit (affiliated to London University) which chose a random sample of first-time parents, all between twenty and thirty-four. (See note.[10]) Out of eighty-five couples, three quarters of the husbands had attended the delivery (although only one father had had time off as part of a paternity leave scheme) and these men apparently expressed 'love' for their children sooner. In fact, fathers were more likely than mothers to report positive feelings at first sight of the child (78 per cent to 45 per cent) and less likely (8 per cent to 20 per cent) to report no feelings.

However, only three fed their babies in hospital, none bathed them and after seven weeks one fifth of fathers had still never bathed the baby—'If I said bath it, I think he'd faint'—or changed a nappy. The researchers concluded that although fathers now attend the birth and take a few days off work afterwards, and although they are usually first on call to help out with childcare (grannie no longer being round the corner), only a very small number actually share half and half when they are at home. Apart from a handful of men who admitted to doing nothing at all, most fathers made token gestures and most couples apparently expected it to be this way, with the mother doing the lion's share because the father is busy being the breadwinner. Because of this, though, many mothers complained that fathers didn't realise how demanding the baby was:

> I didn't think he could ever really understand unless I left her with him for a couple of weeks.

A street survey of 50 men carried out in London by Haringey Childcare Campaign found that although between them they had 100 children under the age of 11 almost half had never taken their children to the doctor or to school, two-thirds had never washed their clothes or arranged a babysitter, and 4 out of 5 had never mended their clothes, although, according to Peter Moss at the Coram Unit, mothers do three-quarters of childcare tasks when fathers are not at work.

Among my interviewees there was a fairly similar response, that they did not *mind* doing things which their fathers might have been embarrassed to be seen doing. They had all pushed a pram (possibly because pushchairs are more common now than old-fashioned sprung baby carriages), and claimed that they didn't feel embarrassed because they were 'too proud', or, conversely, talking about a different kind of pride, masculine pride as opposed to paternal pride, they were 'not too proud' to be seen doing it. However, those with their wives present, and, oddly, those who tended to be more involved with their children, remembered, or were reminded, that they did 'feel a bit stupid' when they first had a go. Some admit they still won't do it unless their wives are beside them. The majority had taken part in the everyday intimacies of bathing and feeding, but were more likely to admit:

> I always seem to be out of the room when nappies need changing, but if one of them has been sick, it's whoever gets there first starts cleaning it up.

And I suspected from the monosyllabic replies to these

questions that most of the men didn't do this kind of thing with any responsible regularity. The way one man summed up the extent of his 'share' of these tasks—'Because I'm not here most of the time you can take it that probably for every ten times she does something I do it once' seemed probably fairly near the mark for most. Even men who were more involved than most were less likely to do as much as their wives because they were away at work, and considered their breadwinner role as their principal responsibility and contribution to childcare. Those whose wives worked full time were more likely to look after the children on their own.

The breadwinner responsibility is of course a very real one. (See note.[11]) Men, especially white collar workers, are wrapped up in their work and find it hard to switch off and change key into the very different role of a parent. (This is often why working class men get more involved with their children. I found the working class fathers much more likely to say that the family was more important than work, or 'the kids are our life'—because they are more likely to work for the sake of the family rather than for themselves and the advancement of their own ego.) Yet few men actually experienced conflict between their work role and their expressed desire to be close to their children in the way their fathers hadn't been with them. This seemed partly because they accepted without question the role of the father as guide, mentor etc, a role which fits in more easily with the kind of roles men play at work (expert, specialist, 'doer'), and one man, a middle class parent, actually said he saw no difference between his job as an office manager and his role as a father, since they both involved advice and guidance!

If men now do things their fathers ne'er dreamed of, they still seem to cling, waving rather than drowning, to the traditional notion of the father figure role, disciplinarian, moral guide, tutor. One or two felt there was no difference between mother and father roles, but most men saw their parental role in terms of commanding a child's respect, and therefore necessitating a certain distance between themselves and the child:

I called him the 'old man', because he was my stepfather and I didn't like him so I didn't want to be seen as his son. I missed not having a father but I think you should be slightly afraid of him, his word goes, although it's important to share as much as you can with kids. I wanted to start a family, because you only really become a man with a son, don't you?

Only a very few men mentioned 'loving and caring' when asked to express a father's role and what being a father meant to them. One man declared he would be happy if his son loved him as much as he had loved his own father—in his case, a great deal. Another man qualified his opinion that he was more loving and caring than his father had been by adding 'perhaps he was, but didn't show it... I know that like him, I can have my nose in a paper too often...'

Men's limited notion of the father's role may be something which, despite the increased emphasis upon fathering, is subtly reinforced and fed back to them in various ways. Expectant fathers are inevitably physiologically more distanced from their new status than their wives. Those who suffer sympathetic pains or put on weight tend to become the butt of derision rather than taken seriously as they are in some 'less civilised' societies. Only half the fathers in the Coram sample had been to an antenatal class and mostly it was only one class. Yet as the Coram report pointed out, men seem in more need of parentcraft classes, since most have no relevant educational or work experience, and little previous experience of close contact with young children.

The wife becomes, inevitably, the more practised and confident caretaker and may unwittingly collude in this by not encouraging or expecting her husband to take more responsibility with the child. Meanwhile, he feels the financial pressures of parenthood, to get on and get promotion, more money. So it becomes hardly surprising that, as a self-help group for distressed parents of crying babies (Cry-sis) recently discovered, male partners walk away from the crying baby with much more ease because 'they don't experience the demands in the same unremitting way'.

A recent study[12] of the part played by fathers in their babies' health care showed that although most fathers were knowledgeable and concerned about their babies' health, they tended to defer to their wives as the 'experts', and were expected by the health care staff to play the secondary role and treated as relatively incompetent. It was hardly surprising, then, that the Coram researchers found that fathers readily assumed women were more capable parents than men and showed more opposition to the idea of changing roles because it would therefore be bad for the child. (See note.[13])

Peter Moss[14] from the Thomas Coram Research Unit, points out that it is very difficult to combine paid work with family life:

> The qualities which are good at work—like speed and aggression—are no good with kids. If you go home and act like that you'll get nowhere. And you can't have managers getting so caring that they can't fire their workers. What we have to face is a society divided into people who want and have children, and people who don't want children but want to hold, and do hold, positions of power.

This seems to me rather a dangerous division. However, most of the men I spoke to seemed content to be part-time, peripheral parents, often too preoccupied, although they do lovingly rough and tumble with the kids, at this point in their careers to devote any more time. Nor do they feel the need to devote more time to their children. Should it, could it ever, be any different?

In the same way that women started requesting their husbands' presence when they were giving birth, women are largely behind the impetus for men to be more active parents. Since the mid '60s (when, in 1966, Betty Friedan cofounded the National Organisation for Women with 'shared equal parenthood' as its expressed aim), there has been growing pressure from the women's movement for men to give more of themselves as fathers. Although the emphasis during the early 1970s was upon equality in the workplace, it has gradually been realised, during a decade in which more and more women have been going out to work, that the greatest practical obstacle barring the way for many women has been the large lump that child rearing slices out of their lives while men carry on carving careers for themselves. Men have been criticised for concentrating on glossy picture-book parenting, being there at bedtime but avoiding the messy nitty gritty of the fulltime burden which leads to baby battering; funking the frustrations for the fun bits.

Some unions are now beginning to press for paternity leave as well as maternity leave agreements, but the male-dominated unions do still seem slow to respond to this idea. Meanwhile the attitude of many employers is that fathers are an unnecessary luxury accessory to the birth of their children. Most men are expected to take time out of their annual leave to be there, as the men I interviewed did, and a considerable number missed the event because it happened during working hours and they couldn't take time off.

Most of my interviewees also took time off from their annual leave around the time of the baby's birth, in order to help their wives. The husbands in the Thomas Coram study took on average a week off work, but hardly any of them got paternity leave. The Alfred Marks Survey on Fringe Benefits for Office Staff in 1981 found that only just over 1 employer in every 10 had any sort of paternity leave policy, and in the majority of cases this was a discretionary type of compassionate leave. (See note.[15]) The main organisations responding to paternity leave are those which employ considerable numbers of women, like publishing companies, communications and public service industries. Britain, in this respect, compares very unfavourably with other European countries.

A recent survey of 230 fathers by the Equal Opportunities Commission showed that although 217 took time off work for the birth of their child, over half had to take this on annual, sick or unpaid leave. France and Sweden, however, have statutory provisions. (See note.[16]) In Sweden, parents have the right to nine months' paid leave and there is government pressure to make fathers take at least three months of this allowance. In 1979, a new Swedish law came into force giving parents with children under eight the right to a six hour working day, while those with children under eighteen months can take fulltime leave of absence, so one parent can be at home receiving the benefits, while the other could be working a shorter day. The Swedish programme seems to be the most progressive, offering real opportunities for men to participate more fully as parents. Previously, the take-up rate had only been small and slow growing, rising from 2 per cent in 1974 to 10 per cent by 1977.

Last year, the EEC Commission officially launched a proposal that would 'promote a more equitable sharing of family responsibilities between working parents'. The idea is for parents to have the right to three months' leave to be taken before their child is two, although this would not necessarily be paid.

The rationale for men as active parents, aside from the women's movement, remains relatively hazy. The main reasons put forward by British unions promoting paternity leave are roughly as follows: the mother may wish her husband to be present at the birth; the husband may help around the house while the mother is indisposed; men can care for their other children; paternity leave enables fathers to play a more positive role in childcare. It is only this last rather vague reason which implies that the father himself (rather than any caretaker substitute) has any real and valuable part to play in his own right. Otherwise paternity leave is sold to employers as allowing planned rather than unplanned absence, creating improved industrial relations, and encouraging white collar workers to make up work after their period of leave!

The fact remains that very few couples in this country are in a position where it would make economic sense, apart from any personal preferences, for them to swap roles or share parenthood jointly. I only came across a handful of men who were interested in the idea, regardless of practicability. For the majority of men being at home all day with the children appeared laughable, unthinkable, an anathema, seeming sadly to express the distance between men and women in that the life of one half of a couple could seem so alien to the other.

I was compelled, in fact, to step outside my chosen sample in search of men who have become real active fathers, rather than evening and weekend fathers. I had come across one or two who were contemplating giving up the rat race for home-based employment to allow greater personal flexibility in their lives and more involvement with their children, but I specifically contacted and interviewed three fathers outside my sample, two sharing the upbringing of their children by working part time and one self-employed father who has taken over the major caretaking role from his wife. All are also in their mid-thirties, and all three live in London which may, or may not, merely reflect the means by which I was able to contact them.

John is a part-time civil servant who shares a house co-operatively with his wife and another couple with a child, so child-minding is a shared arrangement between all four parents. Paul, a part-time physics teacher, job-shares as well as sharing the care of their child with Anna. Roy, whose wife works full time, takes care of their son while operating as a therapist from home.

For Roy the decision to be the one to stay at home and look after their son was a logical as well as personal choice. His work was more flexible and home based, while his wife's regular salary was necessary for them to obtain a mortgage. Paul and Anna found themselves not automatically considering the usual childcare arrangements because Anna earned more than Paul. Although the job they share is on a lower grade than previously, they are slightly better off with two individual tax allowances than if one of them had given up work completely. And anyway, they decided it would be nicer to share childcare than do the conventional thing. John and his wife, who have always shared everything, having a 'strong commitment to doing things equally', realised when they were approaching thirty that this was the crunch point, if they wanted a child. They knew they didn't want to farm the child out to other people if they were going to bother having children at all:

> I decided to wait until I had the letter saying I was promoted to principal, and then wrote back saying that I wanted to work part time. It was a difficult point, for them and for me, because no man had ever done that before. But my thinking was that we have decided to have a child therefore I must arrange my life to do my share of looking after it. I was doing quite well with my job, but I was prepared to take risks with it. Most people told me I was a lunatic. I was taken aside and told, this isn't going to do you any good, old boy.

According to John, his employers were quite floored, and intimated they would have difficulty finding him a job, putting him off for a month while they investigated official policy 'during which time my file had grown considerably'. But because of the Sex Discrimination Act they couldn't treat John differently from a female employee, although surprisingly they didn't require him to return full time after six months.

> I don't think the recession had anything to do with it. My working part time is actually a bit more reliable than many of the women working part time, because they are fully responsible for their children while they are at work, whereas I am not. I believe my employers get a better deal from part-time workers. You're more awake. I think you can't work effectively more than twenty-five hours a week, so they are buying my best time. [See note.[17]]

Paul and Anna chose an opportune time to put forward their job-sharing proposal, because the schools they each worked in were amalgamating and jobs were being reorganised anyway. The head wasn't happy about the prospect of the alternative, losing a physics teacher, and the shortage of physics teachers definitely influenced the school's acceptance of the arrangement. Paul also feels that their employers don't realise the bargain they are getting, that two half teachers give more than one, not counting the unofficial time they spend communicating with one another, and the children benefit from different teaching skills as well as the different perspectives of a male and a female teacher.

John feels that they've perhaps treated him better than many of the women civil servants who transfer to part time:

> They moved me out of a job that was relatively prestigious to one that hardly existed at all, but which has since become a good job.

There's a fair amount of short-term flexibility about his work anyway, and the people working under him quite like the arrangement, although he thinks his superiors are less likely to:

There was a lot of interest, and a certain amount of hostility—
'Nice to see you in today', meaning that I've got a cushy number.
But *they* don't want to do it. It's the usual story. I can't because
my wife can't earn enough; I don't want to spend that much time
with my children. And of course they'd be worried about the
career aspect of it. I'm ambitious, but not that concerned about
it. Most people are going to lose because only one winner gets to
the top, so it doesn't really matter what level you end up at.
Whatever else happens, I can say, well, I've done this thing. A lot
of older men say to me that they don't know what they'd do
without their work. I feel as involved as anyone else is in the
actual job, yet I hardly think about my work outside it, whereas
when I was working full time I thought about it much more.

John believes he is emotionally different from most other
men his age.

The people I like best and talk to at work tend to be women. Men
don't soul-bare. They don't talk about fears or feelings, because
you have to believe that the system is all for the best.
   I'm like my father in a lot of ways, but he wouldn't have done
what I'm doing. I don't remember him spending much time
with me, although he did things around the house. Women like
my mother, housewives, tend to resent me. I used to take the
children to the one o'clock club, but I wasn't made welcome
there at all, I was encroaching on female preserves. And my
mother-in-law didn't believe I was really competent to look after
my daughter, couldn't believe I was really doing it. When I go
out, older women will intervene, much more than with my wife.
   But I've become much more confident in talking about
domestic things.

Paul also feels that although he was used to being with
children through his job, looking after their son on his own
has given him a tremendous amount of confidence he lacked
when Anna was the chief caretaker. He describes it in terms
of being able to 'innovate, suggest things, whereas Anna very
much ran things before, and I simply took over; but now I
know him well enough to be able to introduce things
myself.' Paul too has noticed the kind of isolation that
pioneer fathers are likely to experience, because social
networks are built up around women, who are unused to
sharing the intimacies of childcare with men, or whose

husbands object, because of the sexual innuendo of having a man round while they are at work. The solution chosen by another father, a single parent, has been to socialise with other single parents.

Roy also mentioned the coolness, the distance from the mothers at the playground, and was told over the phone by one husband that he didn't want his wife making friends with a strange man. Otherwise, things are working out very well, with a very different father/son relationship developing than Roy had with his own father, although when his son hurts himself badly, he will still go to his mother. Roy talks in terms of the different physical contact there is between males, the rough and tumble, rather than cuddling or hugging or holding hands, and enjoying together the very male toys that are around. Paul mentioned feeling less concerned about discipline, probably because a real relationship exists.

John talks about the process of looking after his daughter as a

> ... very emotional experience, which most men don't have. Very important and fundamental. I enjoy the things we do, pottering about, going for walks, visiting the zoo. Being eccentric at work has made me a lot more eccentric in other ways, like running to work. It's good to have more space, it's increased my self-confidence at appearing different. There are ways in which it makes you harder, you have to be very confrontational, have fights, more active emotionally than I think men are used to being, because there are more arguments—and more cuddling.

These men may be unconventional, but they are giving the lie to the idea of women as the best caretakers for young children; they are showing that men don't have to act the breadwinner/disciplinarian role; and they are enriching their own lives by reaping the benefit of close, caring relationships with their children, something most men missed with their own fathers. They are untypical, but they reflect a shifting of the balance towards real fathering.

Most men only seem to realise the importance of their relationship with their children in a crisis, usually when, following divorce, they lost their children at the same time as they lose their wives. In the past, the bitterness of divorced men seemed wholly on the level of the material loss, moving into a rented bedsitter while their ex-wife hogged the family home, although somewhere under the skin of emotional silence, the loss of their children, however shallow the relationship, must have diminished them. But it is real relatedness that creates real caring; their position as bread-winner was simply etched more starkly than before. Perhaps, also, there was little to tell between the occasional parent and the weekend parent they had been before.

Today, the situation is superficially slightly different. In two months of 1982, out of nearly 14 000 custody orders in Britain, over 11 000 went to the wife, only 1 707 to the husband, and a mere 638 to 'joint custody', reflecting society's judgement of the mother, psychologically and morally the more deserving parent. The document[18] from which these figures are taken advises that a 'clean break' should be avoided when parents separate, and that access visits should start right away, and advocates that the term 'one parent family' should be discarded, since children have, and need, both parents.

The reality, according to a book called *Surviving Divorce*[19], is that between 40 and 50 per cent of children whose parents divorce lose all contact with their non-custodial parent, which usually means their father, and 50 per cent of fathers contacted by the authors of this study of the impact of divorce upon men had lost contact with their children because it was too painful and difficult to stay in touch.

Last year there were an estimated 700,000 'non-fathers' in this country, and according to a survey[20] carried out by Gingerbread and Families Need Fathers formal access orders don't work. Between 60 000 and 70 000 children a year are losing a parent, usually their father. Almost a third of divorcing families dispute or have difficulty in maintaining access by the absent parent.

Families Need Fathers is a registered charity, set up to promote equal parental rights, believing that children need a continuing relationship with both parents, but while the majority of fathers leave the real-life responsibilities of changing nappies, drying tears and wiping noses and bottoms to their wives, it is fighting a losing battle. All the tears shed by suffering non-fathers and their personal anguish will only really be recognised as legitimate, and wrong, when ordinary everyday fathering is invested with more tangible feeling and effort, and when women, forced to sacrifice so much for their children, feel less tempted to abuse what must seem their only privilege and power.

Meanwhile, as the small daughter of one of my interviewees remarked in passing, 'I don't think any of my friends will remember their dads on Father's Day.'

*The Good Father*[21] is a novel by Peter Prince which explores the dilemma of a father whose divorce has separated him from his son, although he has always been sympathetic to the women's movement. In Hooper's confusion and rage he urges another deprived father to fight for *his* son through the courts. The victory turns out a hollow one. Hooper then spends a weekend with his own son, staying with friends in a cottage in the country. Sleeping in a double bed together, he dreams vividly that he is strangling his little boy and stays awake all night for fear that if he sleeps he might really kill him. He convinces himself that it was the pain of the loss of his son he was trying to destroy, not the child himself. But later, talking with a friend, he comes to a more terrible realisation:

> 'He broke us up,' he told her. 'Emmy and me—we could have made it if we hadn't had him. We'd have got past the bad times. We'd have looked after each other always . . . He finished us. He grabbed all the kindness and we had nothing left . . . I didn't leave home because of Emmy,' he said, feeling as he spoke the words as if a fissure was opening in his heart. 'I left because of Christopher.'

Tragically, the exclusion of fathers from an active role with their children can distort and warp their feelings of care to those of jealous resentment of a closeness between women and children which cuts them out. But more than that, it can painfully reactivate early conflicts of their own, which they are then helpless to work through, but which hold the key to the male dilemma. The conventional father-child relationship points to their real problem, cuts very close to the bone. Yet all the movements to redefine fathering as something more than the simple blood tie, an act of procreation, are floundering, not so much because of the practical obstacles which perpetuate separate roles, but because they are not fixed to a firm theoretical base, to a theory which really shows the importance of the father's role, what it really means.

That theory—and the evidence to support it—already exists and has done for most of the lifetime of my generation of men. But when it first emerged it was overshadowed by something more socially acceptable. It has since been restated, but somehow absorbed and lost within the rhetoric of the women's movement. Meanwhile, in the absence of a real appreciation of the part fathers play in the emotional and psychological development of every child, fathering has remained condemned at best to a holiday relief activity with no strings, at worst to a duty men must share, a burden they must assume so that women may be equally free. But it is not enough to argue the father's need of his children, his right to have a relationship with them, or the need of children for two parents, like some interchangeable circus double act or elegant variation in a child's life. The indispensability of the father in the full and healthy development of the child, and the tragic consequences of his frequent absence, have got to be fully recognised. Until they are, the real cost cannot be counted. Fathers are not simply stand-ins for mothers.

## NOTES

1 Phyllis Chesler, *About Men* (Simon & Schuster, New York, 1978; The Women's Press, 1978)
2 Deborah Moggach, 'When did you first see your baby?' (*Sunday Times*, 27 June 1982)
3 John & Elizabeth Newson, 'Middle aged fathers missed nothing' (letter to *Sunday Times*, 11 July 1982)
4 John & Elizabeth Newson, *Infant Care in an Urban Community* (Allen & Unwin, 1963); *Patterns of Infant Care* (Penguin, 1965)

5 John Bowlby, *Child Care and the Growth of Love* (Penguin (Pelican) Books, 1953)
6 Ann Oakley, *Becoming a Mother* (Martin Robertson, Oxford, 1979)
7 H. Graham, L. McKee, *The First Months of Motherhood.* Summary report of women's experiences of pregnancy, childbirth and the first six months after birth (Health Education Council Monograph Series, No 3, 1980)
8 Lorna McKee, 'Fathers and Childbirth: "Just hold my hand" (*Health Visitor, 53* September 1980)
9 Sheila Kitzinger, *The New Good Birth Guide: How to research and plan the kind of birth to suit you and your partner* (Penguin, 1983)
10 The research, carried out between 1978 and 1981, included five in-depth interviews with the parents, at different stages both before and after the birth, to assess the impact of parenthood on both sexes. Copies of the report may be purchased from the Thomas Coram Research Unit, 41 Brunswick Square, London WC1
11 Peter Moss, in 'The choice will be children or power' (*Guardian,* 9 December 1982) made the point that twelve months after the birth of their child, the first-time fathers in this study worked an average forty-seven hour week, excluding lunch and travelling to and from work.
12 M. Kerr & L. McKee, 'The father's role in child health care' (*Health Visitor, 54,* February 1981)
13 Husbands were twice as likely as wives to say that men would make worse caretakers than women and 53 per cent of men as opposed to 29 per cent of women were against changing roles for this reason and also because they felt it would be bad for them. Nineteen per cent of fathers said this, and both sexes generally felt that men get a better deal in life than women. Only a third of both sexes actually felt the traditional roles (man sole breadwinner, woman sole childcarer) to be preferable to women working part time or full time outside the home and men helping out with childcare. However, only 22 per cent of fathers felt they had been missing out, and said they felt left out since the birth. The vast majority were satisfied with the limited contact they had with their children.
14 op cit
15 Incomes Data Services in their comprehensive 1981 *Guide to Maternity Arrangements,* found 13 firms offering one day; 11 firms offering two days; 15 firms offering three days and 15 firms offering five days. The Civil Service and British Telecom

gave special leave 'to nurse a sick relative'; the BBC allowed male employees up to two weeks compassionate leave if necessary. The TUC's model agreement states that 'All male employees are entitled to ten working days paid paternity leave around the time of the birth of a child'. Unions which are also pressing in Britain for joint responsibility include ACTT, APEX, ASTMS, NALGO and the NUJ, whose claims vary between ten days and eighteen weeks.

16 French men can take three days' paid leave following the birth of their child, and a law in 1978 extended parental leave for the upbringing of children to fathers for one year if the mother is not taking it. In Finland, from 1978, a father staying at home to take care of the child became entitled to the allowance of just over six months around the birth.

17 During the three day week, ten years ago, output only fell by 10 per cent, as opposed to the 40 per cent expected.

18 A discussion document, *Children and Family Breakdown— Custody and Access: Guidelines for a New Approach* (Available from Dept CP, Elfrida Hall, Campshill Road, London SE13) 1983

19 Peter Ambrose, Richard Pemberton & John Harper, *Surviving Divorce: Men beyond Marriage* (Wheatsheaf Books, 1983)

20 Gingerbread & Families Need Fathers, *Divided Children: A Survey of Children After Divorce* (1982) Available from Gingerbread, 35 Wellington Street, London WC2 and from FNF, 37 Carden Road, London SE15

21 Peter Prince, *The Good Father* (Jonathan Cape, 1983)

*Chapter Four*

# THE MALE DILEMMA

*I knew children who had no fathers, on account of the
war or of some disastrous accident, but I could scarcely
imagine having no mother. David had no mother.
When I got to know this, it fully explained why he
called for our pity. There would have been nobody to
bandage him when he cut himself, or make him a hot
drink when he'd been out in the rain, or cuddle him if
he woke up with a bad dream, because fathers didn't do
that kind of thing. I loved my Dad, but it was clear to
me—as it was then clear to all children in rural Wales
anyway—that fathers stood for authority and mothers
for reassurance. I began to understand the sources of
David's silence.*

(Mervyn Jones[1])

THE DISRUPTIONS of World War II brought to the attention of
many health workers the importance of a stable environment
in the growing-up process. Around the time that my
interviewees and the other men of my generation were being
born and starting to grow up—to be exact, in April 1948—
the Social Commission of the United Nations decided to
make a study of the needs of children who were homeless,
orphaned or separated from their families as a result of the
war. The World Health Organisation appointed, in January
1950, a certain Dr John Bowlby to study the mental health
problems and he began visiting France, the Netherlands,
Sweden, Switzerland, the UK and the USA, publishing his
results in 1951 under the title *Maternal Care and Mental
Health*. But Bowlby's more influential and widely publicised account came out in 1953, entitled *Child Care and the
Growth of Love*.[2]

It was at this point that the role of the father was officially rubber-stamped as of no consequence to the development of the child. Ironically, the same year saw the publication of the obscure American psychoanalytic work which revealed the real and vital significance of fathering, but it was a case of being in the wrong place at the wrong time. It was too wide of the mark of accepted ideas about sex roles, whereas Bowlby's theory simply slotted into the all pervasive notion of a woman's place being in the home. (It would take another twenty-five years, and the kiss of the women's movement's questioning of the female role, to revive it.) According to Bowlby it was essential for a child's normal mental development to have a warm, intimate, continuous relationship with its mother. Any disturbance of this relationship could impair the child's capacity for affectional bonds later in life. Such was the reaction to this pronouncement that Bowlby felt obliged to qualify, in his second edition in 1965, that the mother's continuous presence did not mean being tied to the offspring for five years constantly. Deprivation meant more than occasional short absences, although 'leaving any child of under three years of age is a major operation only to be undertaken for good and sufficient reasons and... planned with great care.'

Mother and child need to feel closely 'identified' with one other, but in his three-volume work, *Attachment and Loss*,[3] Bowlby did acknowledge that in some cases the father plays the mothering role, since it is with the person with whom the child socially interacts, rather than the person who feeds the child, that the primary attachment bond is made. Some mothers are socially unresponsive, so the child turns to its father. Bowlby also allowed that fathers signified as 'subsidiary attachment figures', becoming more involved as the child grows older, and on hand to stand in at times when the mother is not available. He was not, however, successful in living down his more famous earlier remark that dismissed fathers as financial and emotional support systems for mothers, echoing Margaret Mead's rather acid observation that fathers were 'a biological necessity but a social accident'.

Bowlby argued against Freud's 'cupboard love' drive theory (that 'love has its origin in the attachment to the satisfied need for nourishment', which proposes that attachment behaviour arises out of the infant's desire to preserve the presence of the source which satisfies its needs) by quoting Harlow and Zimmerman's famous '50s experiments with cloth and wire-covered surrogate mother monkeys. The baby monkeys fed from a bottle in the wire monkey yet clung to the more 'comforting' presence of the cloth monkey. But Bowlby was somewhat hard put to it to find any satisfactory theory to account for the function, as opposed to the proven significance, of attachment relationship. He described attachment behaviour as seeking and maintaining proximity to another individual, and pointedly differentiated it from mere dependence, which he saw as a rather disparaging term, especially when carried into adult life. To be attached to someone, on the other hand, implied something positive and admirable. Bowlby plumped for the notion of safety in numbers, that attachment gives the individual social protection, and decided that 'attachment behaviour is regarded as what occurs when certain behavioural systems are activated'. However, most psychoanalytic theory and most generally accepted child development theories now see personality development as something more than a set of 'behaviour systems' to be activated in the context of the security of a cosy protective presence. The significance of the primary caretaker now tends to be seen in terms of the infant's gradual dawning consciousness of itself as a separate and autonomous being, the process of individuation, which is seen as a development from identification to differentiation. Babies themselves have yet to pipe up and confirm or deny this theory of personality development, but most theorists agree that the newborn baby does not readily distinguish between itself and its environment. This is often termed the 'autistic phase' and is seen as lasting up to the second month. The child then passes into a 'symbiotic phase', between the second and fifth month, during which the boundaries between itself and its 'mother' still seem to merge, but it is gradually becoming aware of being cared for, of the processes of caretaking, although it still cannot separate itself from the adult who is looking after it. This symbiotic relationship is seen to involve a regression on the part of the mother to identify with the infant state, while the infant, to refer to Freud's theory, becomes dimly aware of its separateness through some frustration of its immediate needs, at the same time internalising an image of its mother, in an attempt to preserve her presence, thereby remaining fused with her, but in a more conscious sense.

Gradually, as the child's motor development increases, as it crawls away, its awareness of its physical separation from its mother grows; but so does its anxiety, its fear of being without its mother, causing it to come back for emotional support. At about eighteen months, the child appears to discover, along with its capacity to walk unaided, that it is a separate and very vulnerable being. Hence, along with the urge to explore comes possibly greater concern than previously about the whereabouts of its mother. New phases of development towards autonomy are therefore marked by regression into earlier, more fused states of identification with the primary caretaker, which are an essential part of normal development since they allow the child to proceed without too much anxiety at its own pace—*reculer pour mieux sauter.*

Fathers are seen to enter the child's world as it becomes more active and independent, representing to the child the world outside the confines of domesticity, and facilitating the child's first tentative entry into that world. Fathers are also said to play an important part in the establishment and reinforcement of gender identity. Most personality theorists stress the importance of the first five years of life, during which time the mother is accepted as the primary caretaker, but agree that a secure sense of gender identity is vital, and possibly central, to stable personality development, and that this self-perception of its gender is usually established in a child by the age of three.

The process by which the child recognises and identifies with its sexual identity is the subject of several different theories, the most influential of which has been Freud's, which defined this stage of development as the Oedipal stage, after the Greek myth of the prince of Thebes who unwittingly murdered his father, Laius, and married his mother Jocasta.

Freud argued that biological differences between the sexes predispose different behaviour patterns, endorsed by the successful resolution of the Oedipal conflict, which as far as the boy is concerned seems mainly dependent upon hostile perception of the father. As the male infant becomes aware of sexuality, his love for his mother becomes erotically and sexually imbued. Threatened by the powerful hostility he then imagines he has stimulated in his father, the rival with whom he cannot hope to compete, he resolves the anxiety this arouses by repressing his feelings for his mother and according to Freud breaks through the Oedipal conflict by focusing on his father, who then becomes the model of his masculine development, on the principle of 'If you can't beat 'em, join 'em.' The girl, whose pre-Oedipal phase lasts longer, finds the transition more problematic. She turns to her father as a love object by rejecting her mother for not having, and therefore not having given her, a penis, but often cannot completely break away from her continuing dependence upon her mother. (See note.[4])

However, just as World War II had sparked off Bowlby's investigations into the importance of the mother figure, it had also stimulated studies, particularly in America, of the effect of father absence upon personality development, due to the number of children who had lost their fathers, either temporarily as POWs, or permanently as casualties of war, in Germany, Japan and later Korea, and the noticeable increase in 'problem children' and delinquency.

Early absence of a father figure was associated either with subsequent tendencies towards crime and violence, or the propensity for sons to play with dolls and express aggression verbally, in a more feminine way. The researchers concluded that male children growing up without early contact with their fathers seemed unable to acquire appropriate (ie male and mature) ways of handling and expressing their aggression. Similar studies showed that weak and ineffectual fathers tended to have hyper-aggressive sons whereas the sons of dictatorial and uncaring fathers suffered from shyness and inferiority complexes. Men with accepting, caring and supportive fathers were lacking in ambition compared to men with disregarding, cold or critical fathers, indicating that the way a boy develops very much depends on his father's personality and attitude towards him, but by implication upholding the idea that a father should be a cold authority figure, rather than someone caring.

These findings were supported by more extensive research in the 1970s. Studies of American GIs' children, whose fathers were away for up to eight years in some cases, as POWs in Vietnam, showed that they suffered more than the normal amount of behavioural problems and nervous habits, were lacking in independence and confidence, and tended to be withdrawn and antisocial. Father's return did not readily undo the impact of his prolonged absence, possibly partly because of his own difficulties in adjusting to hostile, fearing or simply strange children, usurping his relationship with an equally estranged wife. It was often concluded that the difficulties of boys with over-punitive or ineffectual fathers, who compensated by becoming over-aggressive or too passive, were not so much a result of the father's failure to serve as a good model for moral authority and control, but because the male child was threatened by his mother's overwhelming presence which he either succumbed to or rejected, for example by joining a delinquent gang.

Between the mid 1940s and the mid 1970s a mass of piecemeal research on the significance of the father figure accumulated, mostly confined to obscure journals of orthopsychiatry and the like, unpublished papers and doctoral theses, attempting to measure the effects of paternal neglect. Much of this material might have sunk without trace but for the dedication of Henry B. Biller, professor of psychology at the University of Rhode Island, as the extensive bibliography in *Paternal Deprivation*,[5] published in 1974, bears witness. Biller constructed a picture of the father as a vital influence not only in his daughter's capacity for relationships with the opposite sex but in his son's early sex role identification and development:

> A warm relationship with a father who is himself secure in his masculinity is a crucial factor in the boy's masculine development. Boys who have punitive, rejecting fathers or passive, ineffectual fathers generally have less adequate sex role functioning than do boys who have interested, nurturant fathers...

Research findings indicated 'the need to modify traditional views that the infant's attachment is usually exclusively and primarily with the mother and that the father does not become an important figure for the child until post infancy.' Specifically quoting research which suggested that the father-infant relationship is important even during the first year of life, Biller argued that the influence of the father on the male child's sex role development was demonstrably crucial, since secure gender identity is central to security of self. Therefore the father is all important to the male child's overall personality development, not just his handling of aggressive impulses. (See note.[6]) Yet when the child is under three, the father is hardly ever available, because of increased pressure to provide for a growing family at the ever rising standard of living. But the *degree* of father availability had never been measured.

Similarly, much research while purporting to examine gender identity had actually only observed one particular facet of it, often in the context of masculine traits which have since come under question. The so-called 'ineffectual' father of the '50s might come across as the caring father of the '80s, whose sons, in the post-hippie, anti-career counter-culture age feel less confused about the male role than those forced to grow up in the macho fag-fearful America of the 1950s.

In discussing paternal deprivation (and the inadequacy of conventional theories of gender identity formation) Biller touched on the ideal of the warm supportive father, against the stereotype of the strong, silent ambitious male; he pointed out the discrepancy between early gender identity formation and lack of early father involvement, and he raised the issue of the hazy meaning often ascribed to the word 'identification', but he failed to grasp the full importance of questioning this key concept. He simply concluded that the paternally deprived tend to adhere more rigidly to stereo-typed sex-role behaviour, missing the implication that this could be universally applied to the vast majority of men.

Though sympathetic to feminism, Biller's work sat uneasily upon the stage reached by sexual politics in the mid '70s. In the '50s, some since much quoted research by Evelyn

Goodenough (a child specialist and later director of the Gesell Institute of Child Development) revealed that fathers, rather than mothers, reinforce sex role stereotyping in their children. (See note.[6]) Fathers are therefore left caught redhanded, with feminists likely to conclude that if that's what father involvement means, children are better off without him.

Biller's work was ignored by mainstream personality theorists, who were more concerned about assimilating non-sexism into their language. One of the most comprehensive and authoritative works on the subject of personality development, *The Person*, by Theodore Lidz,[8] was first published in 1968. By 1976, when the second edition came out, its flavour, and the subtitle, had changed to acknowledge a person as male or female. Like Biller, Lidz accords the secure sense of gender identity a central importance in the development of personality:

> Security of gender identity is a cardinal factor in the achievement of a stable ego identity and a child's sex is among the most important determinants of personality traits ... A child does not attain sex-linked attributes simply by being born a boy or a girl, but through gender allocation that starts at birth and then develops through role assumptions and identifications as the child grows older.

Lidz describes the process of individuation and bond formation as taking place during the second year of life at the same time as the formation of gender identity, which is well established by the age of two to two and a half. From this age the child is internalising parental sanctions, and around three must complete the task of differentiation from its mother to become autonomous. (Separation, Lidz points out, creates anxiety, which is a fundamental stimulus for the individuation process, but can also create repressive ego defences which impair full and healthy personality development.)

Lidz[9] endorses in part Erik Erikson's theories of gender identity which are based on the psychological experience of physiological differences:

... a boy, in response to the presence of his penis and the feelings it engenders, tends to become intrusively active, whereas a girl, responding to her external and internal sexual organs, feels receptive and even ensnaring... the girl develops feelings and ideas of an inner space, a creative space that profoundly influences her way of relating and her feelings about herself.

Gender identity, however, also depends upon ways in which parents relate to the child, interact with one another and regard themselves; therefore all sorts of variations in gender identity security may develop. Lidz also stresses that no child grows up purely masculine or purely feminine, because people are not embodiments of sexual stereotypes; no parents are fully consistent models as males or females.

He acknowledges that little boys must shift from their initial symbiotic relationship with their mothers to identify with their fathers. But he does not explore the difficulties that overcoming their initial identification with a woman may create for a boy, although he presents the girl's later adolescent problems, having failed to resolve her continuous identification with her mother, as a real crisis. The fact that 'many boys of three or four will openly express their belief or wish that they will grow up to be a mommy' passes without comment because of Lidz's unquestioning acceptance of male development as the norm.

By the mid '70s, the women's movement had gone through various stages of questioning the female role. Although Betty Friedan[10] had called for 'equal, responsible, shared parenthood', she had endorsed and accepted that the mother should be the primary caretaker, advocating that women plan their lives to include time out for childcare in the early years. Fathers were simply expected to be more active support figures, rather than given any definite role of their own. Hannah Gavron's study The Captive Wife[11] referred to fathers as 'husbands' in the same way that the medical profession, in the late 1960s and the 1970s, began to encourage fathers to see their role as supporting their wives, rather than having relationships with their children in their own right. Though they were described as 'helpful' or 'interested', the prevailing current of opinion on the importance of the father was summed up by one case study, a mother whose husband was a child psychiatrist: 'He hasn't got time. He works so hard he literally never sees them.'

In the early 1970s the young radical element of the feminist movement turned its back on motherhood, endorsing what de Beauvoir had so eloquently stated in *The Second Sex*[12] that, with women lumbered down by the fruit of their bodies, left holding the baby, motherhood was the means by which men exerted their existential advantage, because the male sexual role concurred with self-expression instead of conflicting with it. In the absence of active partners, let alone active fathers, young women bought their personal freedom with abortion and the pill. During this time it was considered vital to play down the role of the mother as the crucial indispensable caretaker by denigrating Spock and Bowlby and rejecting the notion of the nuclear family altogether. People should live co-operatively, ensuring the presence of several caretakers so that children would not grow up neurotic and mother-dependent and anyone, irrespective of sex, could undertake the job of childrearing. The early 1970s was a defensive time of playing down sex differences, since for women they were tied to prejudice and inferior status; playing down differences simultaneously muted discrimination and subordination of women.

Earlier in the decade, in the spirit of *vive nulle différence*, Michael Rutter published *Maternal Deprivation Reassessed*,[13] which gave a logical and empirical critique of Bowlby's original work and assertions. Rutter assessed experiments over the years to test out Bowlby's thesis and attacked Bowlby's concentration upon the mother (despite the latter's recent mitigation of this). (See note.[14]) However, although he also claimed that bonding, caretaking and play are three separate functions which may or may not be performed by the same person, this was not to say that it makes no difference in terms of individual psychology who that caretaker is:

> A child, for example, who fails to develop a bond with his father or any other male figure in early childhood may not be able to make a really close relationship with him later.

He then raised the point that:

It may well be that youngsters who have developed bonds with adults of only one sex are at a disadvantage later with respect to heterosexual relationships and to the development of sex-appropriate attitudes and behaviour. It is probable that... bonds need to be formed with people of *both* sexes and... that early attachments will influence the kind of close relationships which are possible later.

Having questioned the general drift of child development theories up to that point, and tentatively begun to suggest that young males might have problems through being raised by women, Rutter was opening up the field not only to acknowledgement that fathers could perform the primary caretaking role, but also that the sexes react differently to being brought up almost exclusively by women, *possibly to the detriment of the male.*

*Sex, Gender and Society*[15] was also published in 1972. Ann Oakley endorsed the movement against sex role conditioning of small children to confining sex role stereotypes. In playing down sex differences and stressing the effects of conditioning, Oakley presents girls as more restricted. However she does acknowledge that men are vulnerable too, more likely to die from stress diseases, and, in a world where men apparently have every outward freedom and advantage, 'The boy's development of gender identity is more problematic and causes him more anxiety than that of the girl... boys find it harder to grow into men because they are brought up by women', and yet they are encouraged to be consistently masculine in their gender roles from early childhood on, with fathers rather than mothers focusing anxiety on this matter.

The contribution this book makes towards a proper illumination of male personality development lies in its questioning of the ill effects on men of sex role conditioning as well as sex roles themselves, which exclude men from 'mothering'. In her later book, *Housewife*,[16] Oakley pointed out that fathers can become good 'mothers' and reiterated that no one had yet studied the importance of father's role.

These works which grew out of the reassessment of the female role had begun to question the negative effects of traditional sex roles upon men. Yet although each of them touched upon the crucial point, they all seemed to gloss over it. They were all perhaps too dazzled by the myth of male dominance and advantage, the assumption that the dominant cannot also be victims and are somehow freer, through their power, to be fully themselves.

Every reason having been established why men should 'mother' and no reason why they should not, it took a book which was prepared to look behind conditioning for the real reason why women mother and men don't, to expose the handicap in development which men suffer, because they lack a primary caretaker of their own sex. And even though Nancy Chodorow does spell out what other writers merely imply, or ignore the clues to, she does it in a series of footnotes to her main argument in *The Reproduction of Mothering*.[17]

Chodorow's thesis is perfectly simple. Why is it, she asks, that it is invariably women who are attracted to mothering, who turn to mothering, and who show the greater facility for mothering? She rejects all the straightforward simple solutions such as biology or sex role conditioning as insufficient explanations. Being a woman and being encouraged to play with dolls is not enough. She argues instead that the *capacity* as well as the desire to be a mother grow out of the early and continuous mother-daughter relationship itself, reinforced by the fact that this same relationship produces sons whose nurturant capacities and needs have been repressed and denied. This is what predisposes men to function in the impersonal public world and women in the close domestic affectional world of relationships, of childcare, and caring about people. This is why women mother, want to mother, and get satisfaction from it; why men don't seem very eager to swop places or to father actively enough to imbue the word with any more meaning than that of fertilising an egg.

Her thesis that mothering involves something more than the sum of biology and sex role conditioning is based on the implications of the fact that infants don't just need physical caretaking but also 'affective bonds and a diffuse, multi-faceted, ongoing personal relationship to caretakers for physical and psychological growth' without which they do not flourish, and in some cases die. Although those concerned with the overthrow of the Bowlby attachment theory which effectively imprisoned the mother with her child for the first five years of its life, claimed that from the child's point of view it does not matter what sex its mother is, Chodorow insisted that 'Parenting... requires certain relational capacities which are embedded in personality and a sense of self-in-relationship,' because parenting is 'participation in an interpersonal, diffuse, affective relationship'.

She then goes on to explain how conventional personality theories fail to deal with the asymmetry in the fact that men are parented by women and women by themselves. Important stages in infancy are accepted as being vital to the establishing of a secure sense of self, during which the infant gradually emerges from a fused identity lost in its mother to realise itself as separate, but linked to her, and to develop a responsive relationship with her. As it becomes more able to exercise independence, so paradoxically it becomes more aware of its actual dependence.

It has been recognised by the personality theorists whom I have already discussed that this period of development is not a straight path towards independence, but a yo-yoing process, in which the child regresses to an earlier, more fused state with its mother to re-contact the comfort of the symbiotic bond and allay the anxieties of its new-found independence.

When a little girl begins to perceive and develop a sense of her own gender identity, this same process, the sense of self-in-relationship, into which she is free to regress if she needs, continues to develop. But as soon as a small boy begins to become aware of his own gender identity, he faces a developmental conflict. In order to continue the process of individuation and differentiation, he needs to reject his identification with his mother, whom he perceives as different from himself. In order to preserve his developing identity he must relinquish the former sense of self-in-relationship, but in order to allay his anxiety about this development, he still experiences the need to regress into the self he must reject.

The problem, on the other hand, that the girl faces, which

may often not be resolved until adolescence, is how to experience herself in a differentiated relationship. However, if she has a warm, supportive active father, she can turn to him to discover her sense of herself as close but separate, safe but different, and accepted for what she is, while still retaining that deep sense of relatedness, of self-in-relationship, with her mother. But a boy, even one with a warm supportive father who encourages a close relationship, will nevertheless be developing a sense of self that is disconnected, because however close his relationship with his father becomes, it cannot reach that part of himself shut off from his mother, the part of himself which identified with her.

This is because, having experienced the symbiotic identification solely with his mother, it becomes associated with identifying with a female and therefore for a boy implies loss of self. It is also likely that this kind of regression feels dangerous, because these residual identifications meet with disapproval from his father, the figure with whom he is becoming more and more aware he *should* identify. For most men, however, the relationship with their father is more distanced anyway, so their identity is bound to develop with a sense of self apart. The little boy cannot reach out to that which is a part of himself in his father, and in which his own sense of himself is deeply and positively evoked. Instead, he must be content with a negative, with repression of his sense and capacity to identify because it is bound up with being feminine, and become separate, distant, in order to be a man.

This means that in order to develop their sense of maleness, boys turn away from the part of themselves which was fused with their mothers. But if their relationship with their father is inadequate for replacing this sense of self-in-relationship (which it normally is) then they begin to define themselves as *not* female, as separate, as distant, because in that sense they can at least feel self-contained. They will be unable to tune into an essential part of themselves which is fused with a symbiotic sense of maleness, because they do not develop their sense of self-in-relationship hence the tendency of many men to be unable to generalise about male experience, to refuse to believe that it is possible to talk about men 'in general', because in that collective sense, they do not mutually feel they exist.

Lidz and Biller noticed that in the absence of a close relationship with their fathers small boys need to reject that which is feminine in order to reinforce the fact of being not female, because they are unsure of what it is to be male. But what Lidz did not appreciate is that the little boy is not simply turning away from little girls, but turning away from the core of himself, the centre of his own being, which was fused with a female.

Also, the boy's sense of being male will not be modelled upon a person who embodies male characteristics, as Lidz claims, including some contrasexual (ie feminine) elements, but upon what the child sees around him as indications of what it is to be masculine; his role image will be the flat two-dimensional cultural stereotype, reinforced by the person he cannot quite reach. Ironically, therefore, but obviously, in the light of more recent history, it is girls who are freer from sex role conditioning, because girls have the inner freedom of having based their sense of self upon a person who happens also to be female, rather than a cutout male type.

This goes a long way towards explaining girls' readiness to wear men's clothing and embrace the male role without feeling a threat to their gender identity, while men find it hard to return the compliment and are often reluctant to tolerate anything which they feel to be non-masculine, especially, as has been noticed, in their sons. They are shoring up their identity by so doing, because they feel threatened by that which remains at the core of their being. During my research it was very noticeable that men whose own relationship with their father had been problematic, and who seemed insecure in themselves, were most vehemently intolerant of the idea of their sons playing with traditionally feminine toys.

And if little boys who are placed in a conflict situation when developing their gender identity react by what Freud described as 'breaking through', perhaps that violent reaction is not so much a resolution of the Oedipal gender conflict as a repression of it. Because the avenue of retreat, of safe regression to allay anxiety becomes cut off, they activate the other, more damaging ego defence mechanisms in its place: denial, sublimation, displacement, etc., which then follow them into adult life, blocking off their inner selves and their capacity for emotional growth.

Because Chodorow's book was angled towards women, her point about men has simply been assimilated into the feminist debate, mentioned in passing in various subsequent works. What to me lifts Chodorow's theory down from the shelf of what has been called 'interesting and plausible' is the way in which it is possible to weave around it so many other strands: the variety of research already done on fathers, what is observable about men and their relationships with one another, with women and with children; and lastly, but for me not least, the way in which it illuminates what I have been able to learn about men myself.

As mentioned at the beginning of this chapter, it was an American psychologist, more than thirty years ago, who first proposed the theory expounded by Chodorow. O. H. Mowrer[18] simply pointed out that Freud's analysis of the Oedipal triangle was wrong, because he described the relationship between the infant and the mother as a 'love object' relationship, the male infant's love for the mother becoming imbued with sexuality while the female infant turns to love her father because he has something she has not. However, as Mowrer pointed out, the infant-mother relationship is one of *identification* rather than love, and therefore 'normal' development requires a shift in the object of identification on the part of the boy rather than the girl. Other journal articles in the late '50s theorised that the girl has the initial advantage in progressing towards appropriate gender identification, and D. B. Lynn[19] added, in 1961, that if the boy does not make the shift during infancy 'it is extremely difficult, if not impossible, to make an adequate masculine identification'.

It seems to me that the difficulty in accepting this theory is twofold. Firstly, it requires an enormous shift in thinking, away from the idea of the male as the norm and towards a notion of masculine disadvantage in the normal course of development. This is a difficult step both for women who are feminist and tuned to the idea of male dominance, and for men themselves who are socialised to repress and inhibit recognition of their own fallibility or weakness. Secondly, it involves a major rethinking of the whole of accepted personality development theory, which although it contains clues to the male dilemma, is modelled on the male path as the normal route to healthy maturity. Thus although Freud's twin goals of maturity—love and work—are acknowledged, it is assumed that the route to the former is via the latter.

Most theorists simply hold that personality development is a slow process of differentiation towards total autonomy, at which point it becomes possible, because the ego is not threatened by engulfment, to make a close intimate sexual relationship; other theorists simply mention the capacity for a fully 'genital' relationship, without the idea of emotional intimacy entering into it at all. Anthony Storr, in *The Integrity of the Personality*,[20] acknowledges that the capacity for differentiation and the capacity for intimacy proceed alternately, step by step, but still concludes that the former is the prerequisite for the latter, that one must refine one's sense of separateness before one can develop one's capacity for intimacy. Storr sees the child making several important identification relationships, as the vehicle for the evocation of latent and undeveloped parts of the personality. 'Personality is like a harp with many strings. Not all the strings are plucked at once and some may lie silent throughout life.' But he firmly adds that 'Identification with another person is a bar to being able to have an adult relationship with them.'

The difficulty, in this respect, is that the concept of identification, in most personality theories, is very limited and expressed as a negative state out of which it is necessary to grow. To quote Anthony Storr once more:

> To identify with another person is to lose oneself, to submerge one's own identity in that of the other, to be overwhelmed, and hence to treat oneself ultimately as less than a whole person.

I would argue that this is the concept of identification seen from the male point of view, as a threat to the central core of being, because it is associated with the early experience of being merged with a female, rather than any later, more separate period of development.

What remains missing from the definition of identification as the term is used by most personality theorists is the understanding of it as a developmental process in itself, a capacity which is not abandoned in early development ('normal' male development almost invariably requires this) but refined to become part of a mature personality, just as much as the capacity for differentiation; and a necessary component of the capacity to form loving and caring relationships (not just the mother-infant relationship, where the mother regresses at the same time as playing the parent role, but adult relationships) in which empathy, as the mature manifestation of identification, plays an important part.

Identification involves a kind of emotional resonance, a sense of being under the same skin, yet mature identification is not the gazing absence of a sense of self experienced by the baby, but the capacity to merge ego boundaries from a firm and secure ego base, the sense of self within the context of influence and relatedness with another, a fine-tuning to the nuances of difference as well as an ability to see another's point of view.

Male theorists perhaps retain a primitive defensive idea of identification because their own experience of the identification process was blocked and cut off before it was allowed to mature. Hence identification for them signifies loss of self, and they are at a loss to describe the capacities by which mature relationship is formed other than in the rather anodyne and flat tones of Anthony Storr as 'appreciation of the other person', using the word empathy without really knowing what it means.

If we accept Chodorow and Mowrer's theory, many other things seem to fall into place: the difficulty men experience in the primary caretaker role, because it involves partial regression to the symbiotic, identified state; the difficulty male children experience in grasping a firm sense of their gender identity; why fathers and male children tend to defensively reinforce the barriers of sex role stereotypes; not to mention the seeming inability of men to experience a common sense of maleness, by which all males are linked.

Women can experience that common sense of fusion, which is the basis of mutual understanding and co-operation, because they are unafraid of being lost in it; they have Ariadne's thread.

Given that each sex retains an unexpressed, contrasexual side, the anima, or the animus, it has been assumed that women feel freer to express masculine attributes, the animus, maleness, acceptably as tomboys, because of the superior status of masculinity. But the real reason for male rigidity in this respect, for the pejorative of the term 'cissy', is that men fear—in a very deep-rooted way—any expression of femininity as a threat to their sense of identity.

Women learn within the security and continuity of the primary relationship to develop their sense of self from the inner core of their being which is part of themselves and yet at the same time accessible to others. Lidz makes the point that the disidentification process is a gradual one and any break in it is likely to be accompanied by damage to the developing ego. Storr says that, 'It is a remarkable and interesting fact that parts of the personality which have been disowned in early childhood remain infantile.'

The small boy is forced to make such a break, disown such a part of himself, in the rejection of his primary identification relationship, which leaves him no regressive temporary retreat when anxiety threatens, unless he has been able to make a sufficiently trusting primary relationship with his father. Even then, it is unlikely that he will be able to tap the same level and quality of identification in order to continue where he left off with his mother.

Instead, he becomes aware of distance, and the need to make a leap at the exteriorisation of himself as the only way to develop. He has to reach, grasp beyond himself, and, for fear of overbalancing, create an artificial support structure around himself. If the psyche were to be seen in concrete terms, the female would radiate from an energy centre where the intensity remains at the core, while the male psyche would grow brightest around the outside, disappearing into darkness at the centre, like the coolness in the middle of a flame.

Erik Erikson described the growing male and female psyches as reflecting their differing physiologies. Boys, with their external genitalia and their sexual function are concerned with the exteriorisation of their energy. Girls, whose genitals are hidden and whose sexual function is receptive and nurturing, become more concerned, inwardly, with their emotions and reflections. Whatever truth that interpretation contains, the present mother/father roles only serve to reinforce such oppositions, in that girls develop their inner feelings while boys neglect the inner self and concentrate upon that which is detached, outward and outgoing.

Women learn within a relationship to discover themselves; men are forced to relinquish their deeper needs and attempt to realise their potential in a void, grasping at the externals of masculinity, at what is around them rather than within themselves. Masculinity sits on men as a discontinuous coating, a consolidation, shored up with tremendous fortifications, but vulnerable to the slightest earth tremor, because of its shaky foundations. Unable to find their masculine identity in the relationship with their fathers, who are often relative strangers, men hunger after ideas and images of themselves. As D.B. Lynn pointed out, males tend to identify with a cultural stereotype of the masculine role, rather than aspects of their own father's role specifically (see note[21]).

Another psychoanalytic writer put his finger on the male dilemma, in a journal article on fathering. J. M. Ross[22] claimed that Freud, in his interpretation of the Oedipal myth, was blind to the possibility of the positive father because of his own lack of a father. Ironically, Oedipus' (and Freud's) preoccupation with the past concerned a search for the father he never had. The masculine dilemma is really the Laius Complex, not the Oedipus Complex, because Oedipus inadvertently kills the father he has never known and therefore cannot recognise. It was Laius who, threatened by his son's existence, rejected him, setting in motion all the tragic consequences, echoed in Peter Prince's novel, *The*

*Good Father.*[23] Do fathers reject their sons because of the real fear of annihilation that regression (as part of the parental contribution to the primary relationship) represents, thus perpetuating a fatal vicious circle of privation, whereby 'each man kills the thing he loves'?

Because of their hunger and unfulfilled need for an image of maleness, boys are much more susceptible than girls to the negative effects of sex role conditioning, despite all the emphasis to the contrary. Boys are much more likely to conform to the socially acceptable image of what it means to be a man in order to complete their own sense of gender identity. That identity therefore depends very greatly upon the time and place in which the boy is growing up.

Kohlberg[24] quotes an anecdote of a five-year-old American boy who excitedly rushed to his father, an urban academic, clamouring 'Daddy, how old will I be when I can go hunting with you?' The power of the stereotype pushed out by the mass media had utterly eclipsed the frail image of the real-life father.

The little boy who is starved of a close relationship with his father has little choice but to turn to other sources to satisfy his need for confirmation of himself as male, to realise his potential male identity. Some are fortunate in finding a real life substitute—'The man next door was more of a father to me than my dad was'—but most boys learn to imitate and internalise and model their style of behaviour on the ideas and images of masculinity they pick up from their surroundings.

In this respect they come to adopt a *stereotype* of what it means to be male, rather than learn their maleness through a relationship with a man who is primarily a person, with characteristics which may not be stereotypically male. Girls, on the other hand, realise their femaleness through someone who does not necessarily conform to the feminine stereotype. My mother, for example, used to whistle very loudly. Boys, however, are likely to grow up with the impression that to be male means to be tough, outgoing and invulnerable, all the time. This 'macho' idea of maleness is most prevalent in Latin societies:[25]

Masculinity means courage whether it is employed for moral or immoral ends . . . the concept is expressed as the physical sexual quintessence of the male (*cojones*). The contrary notion is conveyed by the adjective *manso* which means both tame and also castrated. Lacking the physiological basis, the weaker sex cannot obviously be expected to possess it, and it is excluded from the demands of female honour.

In *Interaction Ritual*,[26] Erving Goffman describes how many males deliberately seek out risk situations in which they can prove their power and bravery. (This of course stems largely from insecurity, the need to try and prove that they are male and that they are strong, because they lack the inner ego strength to feel it.) They learn to desensitise themselves to the risks they are taking, by leaning on what Goffman terms 'defensive determinism', trusting that blind luck will protect them, and fate dictate when their number will be up. This fends off remorse over failure, but it also adds another layer of insensitivity, the inability to question one's actions.

To be a man takes courage, integrity and composure—meaning self-control. This can be trained as the capacity to stand 'correct and steady' in the face of sudden pressures. Goffman admires this 'stiff upper lip' ideal as the sign of a strong character. Any inability to behave effectively and correctly under stress is a sign of weakness. However, he acknowledges some recent modifications in the male image, by which men have become able to avoid testing themselves out. Increasingly, expressions of hostility can be hedged, defused into humour, without loss of face. According to him this trend began with the replacement in 1844, of part of the English Mutiny Act which obliged officers to uphold their honour by duelling by an article forbidding it.

Nevertheless, for young boys of my generation, growing up with the novelty of television, the duel as proof of manhood was re-enacted thousands of times by Hopalong Cassidy, the Lone Ranger, Brett Maverick, Rowdy Yates; in *Well's Fargo, Wagon Train, Laramie, Gunsmoke, Bonanza, Rawhide* and every backyard and playground, the West was won, over and over again:

Clint Eastwood has always been my hero. I must have seen *A*

*Fistful of Dollars* about thirteen times. Quick on the draw, the coolhearted customer who didn't give a stuff about anybody. Dale Robertson was all right, but he was a bit like a preacher, not dirty enough.

Many men echo Alec's ideal of a ruthless hero, but the western that most seems to sum up what the cowboy image meant to every small boy growing up in the 1950s was the cinema classic taken from a novel by Jack Schaefer, starring Alan Ladd, *Shane*.

The battle between domesticity and daring, fencing and free range is enacted in the story of a community of small farmers trying to hold their staked-out territory against the wild cowhands riding roughshod over the land. In the opening scene, little Joey, through whose wide eyes the story is told, is stalking animals with an unloaded rifle. Shane appears, a jumpy and rather trigger-happy stranger, identified with the baddies and told by Joey's dad, Jo, to leave them alone. Joey is visibly impressed by the fact that the stranger makes it clear that he is leaving on his terms.

However, when the cowboys ride up and intimidate Jo and his family, Shane quietly returns and indicates his aim to defend them. Jo then offers Shane a job, helping out on the farm. Riding into town without his gun, for provisions, Shane is humiliated by the cowboys in the saloon; so he returns and with Jo's help, and Joey watching, saucer-eyed, through the double doors, they administer a sound thrashing to the men who had previously intimidated them.

Shane has already given Joey his first lesson as a gunslinger, and demonstrated his own skill with a six-shooter. Joey pesters his father with questions as to whether he could 'whip' Shane? 'Maybe.' He is beginning to believe that this enigmatic stranger is braver, stronger, more of a man than his own father. He begins to hero-worship Shane. The cowboys then set a trap, inviting Jo to come and meet them. Although he knows he will be ambushed, his honour is at stake. When his wife pleads with him that it is just stupid pride, Jo replies:

> Do you think I could go on living with you and you thinking that I'd showed yellow? And what about Joey, how do you think I'd ever explain that to him?

And he adds, showing that he also believes Shane to be more of a man: 'You'd be better taken care of, better than I could do it myself...' implying his death would allow the consummation of the already growing attraction between Shane and his wife. However, Shane rescues Jo's honour, by knocking him unconscious ('No one can blame him for not keeping that date'), and goes himself, knowing he goes to meet Wilson, a man notoriously fast on the draw. Joey runs after him, and finds out that although Wilson was fast, Shane was faster, and has realised the farmer's life is not for him:

> A man's got to be what he is, Joey, can't break the mould... You go home to your ma, and your father, and grow up to be strong and straight. And Joey, take care of both of them...

With 'Mother wants you!' echoing significantly, the man on the horse rides off into the dawn.

Shane remains an enigma, a man who is gentle and considerate, yet ruthless and strong, who seems to be fleeing from something so intangible that it appears to be a part of himself, something he is trying to disown, which may be why the name Shane comes so close to sounding like shame. Yet Shane shows Joey that he can grow up to be a man by having the courage to face his enemies and emerge successful no matter the odds against him. Wounded, riding off murmuring 'It was just a scratch', Shane repairs Joey's troubled sense of maleness which had come under threat because of his father's failed masculinity, in not fending off the cowboys.

Yet while they lapped up, wide-eyed, these mirages of masculinity, the men of my generation were growing up in the latter half of a century in which, in the Western world at least, traditional notions of masculinity, in terms of courage and patriotism, were gradually being revised. When World War I broke out, young men jumped at the chance to prove themselves and hurried to enlist. It was only when they got to the front, that many of them began to realise that 'going over the top' was not so much an act of heroism as a form of mad, pointless suicide. War had been the means of proving one's mettle because it had always been a game, the 'sport of kings', in which honour and the codes of war dictated that each side had a fair chance of winning. But the superiority of the enemy's weapons and the indiscriminate use of weapons like gas, began to render any kind of valiance superfluous; if one was simply to fall as cannon fodder, like the rest.

When Siegfried Sassoon refused to rejoin his company in 1917, he would probably have been court-martialled and shot as a coward and a traitor. But because he had volunteered on the day war broke out and won the MC (which he subsequently threw in the Mersey) he was assumed to have gone insane, and sent to hospital. Although doctors began to accept during World War I that 'shell-shock' was a legitimate organic condition, whereby the brain suffered chronic concussion as a result of proximity to explosions, most symptoms of psychological distress were treated as signs of weakness and cowardice. (See note.[27])

The fact that 8 538 315 men died during that war proving their manhood, became, for a short time after the war, part of the glorious masculine ideal of honour and courage and determination up to the end. It was only gradually, as the disillusioned, like Sassoon, began to publish their memoirs and accounts, and bitter poems, revealing the blunders, the insurmountable odds, the horrors, the brutality, that public opinion started to falter, to entertain Wilfred Owen's change of heart, that it might not be such a glorious thing, *pro patria mori.*

And the representatives of a new generation of young men, at an Oxford Union debate on an evening in 1933, carried the motion moved by philosopher C. E. M. Joad, that 'This house will under no circumstances fight for King and Country.' However, by the time World War II broke out, many who might otherwise have become conscientious objectors realised that this chap Hitler was different... Nevertheless, six men out of every 1000 registered as conscientious objectors in Britain, and rather than being imprisoned, sent to asylums or shot, they were allowed to do non-combatant work in the forces or factories or agriculture. And the introduction of conscription extinguished the glory of being a volunteer.

What had previously been an act of patriotic male pride

became merely a duty, with men resigned to doing their time, like a prison stretch, until the war was over. And of course the way the war ended, on 6 August 1945, signalled the beginning of the end of the concept of war as a testing ground for courage and manhood. The gradual sophistication of weaponry had culminated in the creation of a weapon which made a nonsense not only of the idea of winning the war-game, but also of the concept of glory, honour or courage in war. What sort of courage does it take to fire a missile, to hide in a bunker and visit death on those who are themselves powerless to strike back and only have a matter of minutes in which to realise they are supposed to be playing the game?

The conventional game carried on, however, in Korea, Vietnam, Suez, Cyprus. In most Western countries young men of eighteen had no choice but to play it, and a great many were perfectly willing. In *The Right Stuff*,[28] Tom Wolfe describes the lives of young men attracted into what Charles Moran, a doctor in the trenches in World War I (and author of *The Anatomy of Courage*[29]), called 'the quintessence of manly daring', the twentieth-century equivalent of the nineteenth-century cavalryman, the career of the fighter pilot. In 1952, at Edwards Air Force Base in America, 62 Air Force pilots died in the course of 36 weeks training, nearly 2 a week. These figures did not include the test pilots, who were dying quite regularly too. The statistics were not secret, but the pilots seemed irresistibly drawn towards the risk as a challenge, whether they had what it took to pull back from the brink of disaster and then, cool as a cucumber, go up again the next day. There was a conspiracy of silence about the risk of actually losing your life. As with Goffman's 'defensive determinism', these men assumed the ones who bought it weren't up to scratch, not made of the *right stuff*, ie indestructible.

However, in Britain, after the humiliation of Suez in 1956, and with the rising cost of conventional military weaponry, it was decided to phase out national service and rely on a small professional army backed up by the nuclear deterrent. Young men, once the last national serviceman had finished in May 1963, were no longer pushed into a two-year 'character-building' training which was supposed to make men out of them. The reality, which B. S. Johnson and others describe in *All Bull: The National Servicemen*,[30] was that:

> ... almost all benefits ... seem to have been incidental, marginal to the main experience which was tedious, belittling, coarsening, brutalising, unjust and possibly psychologically very harmful.

There was a new generation of young men some of whom were growing up and rebelling against the 'macho' militaristic images of masculinity, some of whom took actors' workshops in how to fail the medical for national service. Others, wearing duffle coats and black polo-neck sweaters, joined the march to Aldermaston over the Easter weekend 1958, singing protest songs for peace. By 1960 the march, which had become an annual event in the opposite direction, from Aldermaston to Trafalgar Square, where a rally was held, had become a four-mile movement, a peace movement with which a man could now align himself and not be generally regarded as insane, or cowardly.

But little of all this confusion about masculine ideals seemed to be consciously touching the lives of the men who were still in short trousers at that time. Their reality was the endless World War II reruns at the cinema, playing cowboys and indians in the playground, finding their identity among their friends. As various men, including my older brother, pointed out:

> I didn't really miss my dad, once I started going to school. I had my mates.

## NOTES

1 Mervyn Jones, *Two Women and Their Man* (André Deutsch, 1981)
2 John Bowlby, *Child Care and the Growth of Love* (Penguin (Pelican) Books, 1953)

3  John Bowlby, *Attachment and Loss, 1: Attachment* (Hogarth Press/Institute of Psycho-Analysis, 1969)
4  Other theories propose that children simply notice anatomical and social differences between males and females and form the appropriate identification with their same-sex parent; or claim that the child's desire for approval and internalisation of the parent when absent develops gender identity. Status, envy, learning and role theory in turn explain the male child's development of an appropriate sex role identity as a kind of Pied Piper seduction process, whereby the father is rewarding and affectionate, or rewarding and punitive.
5  Henry B. Biller, *Paternal Deprivation* (Lexington Books, Mass, 1974)
6  Traditional theories of the acquisition of sex-role identity did not acknowledge the importance of the father, nor his relative absence, because they set the development of gender identity relatively late. Biller pointed to evidence that awareness of gender begins to become apparent at one, and is established irrevocably by the age of three. (It was at this age that the writer Jan Morris remembers sitting under a piano and realising she was a girl, although she resembled, and had been brought up as, a boy.)
7  Biller does mention this critically, but fails to extrapolate that fathers may simply be transmitting their own rigid insecurities of gender identity. He also uncritically accepts studies which show sons' imitation of fathers to be higher in male-dominated households, falling for the old chauvinist chestnut that men need a dominant role model if they are to become 'assertive, active, independent and competent'.
8  Theodore Lidz (Professor of Psychology, Yale), *The Person: His Development through the Life Cycle* (Basic Books, New York, 1968); *The Person: His and Her Development through the Life Cycle* (Basic Books, New York, 1976)
9  Theodore Lidz, ibid.
10  Betty Friedan, *The Feminine Mystique* (W. W. Norton, New York, 1963; Victor Gollancz, 1963)
11  Hannah Gavron, *The Captive Wife* (Routledge & Kegan Paul, 1966)
12  Simone de Beauvoir, *The Second Sex* (trs H. M. Parshley) (Jonathan Cape, 1953)
13  Michael Rutter, *Maternal Deprivation Reassessed* (Penguin, 1972)
14  Rutter pointed to a 1964 study which showed that only half a sample of eighteen-month-old children were principally

attached to their mothers, nearly one third of them forming their main attachment to their fathers. Since Bowlby himself had stated that attachment was more to do with social and emotional bonds than physical caretaking, Rutter concluded that many of the qualities for good mothering could apply to other relationships experienced by the child, and it was perhaps therefore preferable to concentrate upon the various requirements for normal development than attempt any artificial separation of functions and, since social interaction constitutes the basis of attachment behaviour:

> ... it is difficult to see what merit there is in tying the concept of attachment to motherhood if it is not necessarily tied to a female, not a function of feeding and only indirectly related to caretaking activities.

He also claimed that privation ('lack') rather than Bowlby's word, deprivation ('loss') was the more detrimental to a child's development, suggesting that it is bond formation that matters for the development of social and emotional relationships in later childhood and adult life. Distress may arise from disruption of bonds but psychopathology will develop when firm bonds fail to form.

15  Ann Oakley, *Sex, Gender and Society* (Temple Smith, 1972)
16  Ann Oakley, *Housewife* (Allen Lane, 1974)
17  Nancy Chodorow, *The Reproduction of Mothering: Pyscho-analysis and the Sociology of Gender* (University of California Press (Berkeley and London), 1978)
18  O. H. Mowrer, *Psychotherapy: Theory and Research* (Ronald, New York, 1953)
19  D. B. Lynn, 'Sex differences in identification development' (*Sociometry*, 1961, *24*, pp 372-383)
20  Anthony Storr, *The Integrity of the Personality* (Heinemann Medical Books, 1960)
21  D. B. Lynn, 'A note on sex differences in the development of masculine and feminine identification' (*Psychological Review*, 1959, *66*, pp 126-135). In this article, Lynn proposed a refined definition of 'gender role' (and therefore the terms masculine and feminine) by proposing three interacting components: sex role orientation (the child's inner sense of its own identity); sex role preference (the value of gender-linked toys, activities, interests and media influences); and sex role adoption (the publicly visible masculinity or femininity of the individual's behaviour). Studies of gender role identity had often only observed the latter, which could in fact indicate insecurity of

gender orientation, among individuals struggling to compensate for lack of inner sense of themselves as female or male.

22  J. M. Ross, 'Fathering: a review of some psychoanalytic contributions on paternity' (*International Journal of Psycho Analysis, 60*, pp 317-327, 1979)
23  Peter Prince, *The Good Father* (Jonathan Cape, 1983)
24  L. Kohlberg, 'A cognitive developmental analysis of children's sex role concepts and attitudes', in (ed) E. E. Maccoby, *The Development of Sex Differences* (Stanford University Press, 1966; Tavistock, 1967)
25  J. Pitt-Rivers, 'Honour and Social Status', in (ed) J. Peristiany, *Honour and Shame* (Weidenfeld & Nicolson, 1966)
26  Erving Goffman, *Interaction Ritual* (Anchor Books, New York, 1967; Allen Lane, 1972)
27  The French and the Germans treated these men to electric shocks, threats of imprisonment and execution. The recovery rate was understandably high. Between 1914 and 1920, British courts martial condemned 3080 men to death for desertion, of which 346 were executed before a firing squad. Many of these men had previously had distinguished war records, but this was ignored, because the idea that a man could reach a psychological breaking point, that men were simply fallible human beings, was also ignored. See: Anthony Babington, *For the Sake of Example*, (Leo Cooper/Secker & Warburg, 1983)
28  Tom Wolfe, *The Right Stuff* (Farrar, Straus & Giroux, New York; Cape, 1979)
29  Charles Moran, *The Anatomy of Courage* (Constable, 1945)
30  B. S. Johnson, *All Bull: The National Servicemen* (Allison & Busby/Quartet Books, 1973)

## Chapter Five

# BOYS WILL BE BOYS

*Often when I hear an explanation of the way someone has behaved I know it is wrong. It is an explanation from the outside, the fixing on him of some arbitrary behavioural cliché. I find it easy to imagine myself as another person and understand what they have done from the inside.*

(Thomas Hinde[1])

IT IS strange to meet and talk to amiable grown men in their clean civilised clothes and realise that only time separates me from nasty little savages with scabby knees and short trousers, greasy hair and dirty fingernails. *We* came to school in pretty smocked dresses, gleaming white ankle socks and sandals that were only slightly scuffed at the toes. *We* never rolled in dust or dirt or threw other people's caps about or smoked moss behind the bicycle sheds. Well, hardly ever. I can remember trying the moss, which made me ill, and climbing the fruit trees getting my knickers caught on twigs, and my friends and I did play adventure games with male heroes, although the boys were never seen skipping or playing with dolls.

Most children start at a mixed school but it is generally only in the classrooms that the sexes mingle. My junior school had separate cloakrooms and entrances with 'BOYS' and 'GIRLS' carved indelibly, in stone, overhead and the playground behind the building was split into two by a chain-link fence far too high to climb over. Who in their right minds would have wanted to? The playground wasn't segregated simply so that we could use our respective outdoor lavatories, wooden sheds with garden-gate latches and bolts on the cubicle doors, small squat smelly porcelain bowls with a weather-beaten wooden seat come away from its rear attachment. It was segregated to reflect the fact that, left to our own devices, we were so different, so opposite: different bodies, different clothes, different games, different enthusiasms... Most likely, as the old nursery rhyme about frogs and snails and sugar and spice implied, we were two totally different species.

The separate societies into which we had each been born had been drummed in long before reaching school—'Good girl', 'You're a big boy now', reinforced by a colour-coded uniform and the exclamations of close relatives as they commented on how much we had grown. We each had a separate cultural heritage, an oral tradition of rituals and rites handed down from generation to generation, only marginally affected by any changes in adult civilisation, since at least Brueghel's time.

Boys of my generation were more likely to play cowboys and indians and cops and robbers than space invaders, the SAS or the IRA, but boys still play Johnny on the Pony (under a variety of different names), exchange marbles (which are now becoming magnetic ones, not glass), fly kites, build model aircraft, ride bikes, kick balls about, collect stamps, bus numbers, train numbers, and numbers of almost anything that moves, race model cars and crash them or blow them up. The blowing up, also, of carefully constructed model aircraft, is the most vital part of the process, even though they never really blow up into satisfying smithereens.

Boys are now drawn towards computers and video games, but still play in teams, wrestle, fight, cheat, tease, quarrel and boast and like to be part of a group or a gang. Girls, on the other hand, still spend more time at home, hang about talking in cloakrooms, play skipping and hopscotch on the pavement, or squat over games with jacks. They still like dancing, skating, riding, swimming and of course dolls, playing house and dressing up. They are more interested than boys in cliques and secret societies, whereas boys prefer gang warfare. Girls will talk for hours in a huddle sharing hopes, fears and dreams, poring over romantic stories while boys leaf through motorcycle magazines. (See note.[2])

Many girls, however, pass through a 'tomboy' phase, in which they want to be out climbing trees and camping, just like the boys. Few boys, though, are very keen on being joined by girls in their games. They still see them as soft and silly, cry-babies wasting time holding hands and talking, little goody-goodies who behave in class, just as girls still see them as noisy and rough, primitive little animals, always pushing and shoving and scrabbling in dirt.

Jimmy Pettifer was the archetypal horrible little boy in our class. He crushed your hand in country dancing and swung you round so hard you got dizzy or fell off your feet. Whether it was to show his disdain for country dancing on a Friday afternoon, or for soppy girls, it was hard to tell. Jimmy Pettifer had no time for school work either, but he won a prize at the annual prize giving, for best attendance. He had never been late or had a day off. Only when his name was called from the platform, no one moved. His name was called again. 'He's out playing on the rec, sir' someone finally dared to shout from the back of the hall. It was the supreme irony, winning the prize for best attendance and not being there to collect it. But Jimmy Pettifer wouldn't have risked being seen bobbing up in front of everyone to shake hands with the headmaster. Jimmy Pettifer was out on the rec, being tough. No doubt he was kicking a ball about, twisting the iron railings, or pulling the wings off flies and slicing worms in half just to watch both ends wriggle away, while we would clutch the swing mounts and scream and squirm imagining the pain. Of course, that was why he did it, partly to torment us.

I could never understand that kind of cruelty, and from what I saw of being a boy, at junior school it surrounded you—brutality, cruelty and violence. I was so relieved to be a girl, to be saved from having to pick fights, or fight people who picked on you; girls might fall out and disagree, but you were never actually attacked or threatened or forced to stand up for yourself. It was only much later, grown up, when I began to envy what that trial by fire gave you: to be able to stand your ground in a world where you were bound to meet the confrontation and conflict you'd avoided on the playground at school. I began to see how growing up as a boy could be an advantage, because of the important things you learned how to do.

It was the women's movement and the urge to be independent which showed me this was so. Since the late 1960s the growing body of feminist thought has condemned what it sees as sex role conditioning in childhood, because of the way in which this causes girls to censor and deny themselves. Conventional feminist thought interprets that which Erik Erikson[3] described as a preoccupation with 'inner space' as repression, particularly of the impulse towards aggression and exploration. Boys are seen as freer, more assertive, able to be more active, boisterous, extrovert and spontaneous because they are less inhibited, less restrained, can do what they like and by doing what they like, gain confidence. As Caroline St John-Brooks points out,[4] 'Training for power play in boys begins early.' She quotes an Oxfordshire researcher's observation of 'how small boys learn to manipulate each other, bluff, threaten violence, retreat and save face, in rituals which girls rarely share'.

Boys are encouraged to learn how to manipulate the environment to their advantage, defend themselves, be confident enough to shrug off failure. Boys are apparently more likely than girls to return to a task at which they previously failed, having ascribed their failure to 'bad luck'. Girls, on the other hand, dismiss success as 'luck', and ascribe failure to an accurate assessment of their ability, allowing themselves to become discouraged and less likely to attempt the task again. Boys also tend to assert themselves in class much more, and show less compliance.

Freud described the period of childhood from preschool to adolescence as the 'latency period', when the child is preoccupied with the need to establish and develop its identity in the context of the same-sex peer group. Erikson expressed the particular 'task' of this period as 'I am what I can . . . make work', underlining another deficiency for girls.

It is well known that boys perform better on visual-spatial tests than girls. They apparently respond faster to visual displays, perform better with visual reinforcement and are more responsive to novel visual input, especially if it is brightly coloured or three dimensional. Boys have been shown to be more sensitive to novelty and to find more imaginative ways of playing with new toys. Males also excel over females at mechanical-spatial ability and maths problems which involve restructuring or the capacity to rotate or isolate visual images towards new planes or combinations. Mechanical interest is found in males as early as four to five months, and from early teens onwards they develop keen visual acuity and fast responses, corresponding to increasing physical strength. (See note.[5])

Although boys' slower language development is also well documented, as is their lesser academic ability during the prepubertal phase, they soon overcome this and outstrip girls, catching up with their reading and writing skills, since all children are encouraged to learn the three Rs, whereas few parents insist on girls developing mechanical skills.

As if this were not enough, male advantage tends also to be upheld by conventional personality theories of development and what is deemed a healthy adult personality. Freud saw the girl's inability to fully resolve the Oedipal conflict, by detaching herself from her mother, in her propensity to live through or depend on others, allowing her personality to become submerged and her outlook over-subjective. Since most personality theories stress independence as the goal for mature development through a process of 'progressive differentiation', female development is seen as more problematic than male.

Similarly, despite the fact that girls are generally acknowledged to be physically and emotionally more 'mature' than boys, Jean Piaget, who studied the behaviour of children very carefully and formulated theories to show how their thinking processes develop, defined maturity as the capacity for logical thought. He noticed that boys become increasingly fascinated with the legal elaboration of rules and the development of fair procedures in their games, whereas girls are much more likely to tolerate breaches, argue for individual cases and make exceptions and innovations. Piaget concluded that girls' 'legal sense', essential to their moral development, lags behind that of boys, because girls remain bound up in the personal rather than the abstract mode of thinking.

Therefore, while the goal of healthy personality development appears to rest upon the realisation and achievement of differentiation from others and the capacity to act independently, manipulate the environment, assert oneself effectively and acquire a mature moral sense, girls, in the way they are encouraged to develop, appear to be at a disadvantage. Whether through upbringing or aptitude, their development is seen as more problematic, their path to a healthy adult personality more difficult. Feminist emphasis upon girls' lack of advantage versus male 'supremacy and power' has endorsed this and the positive nature of 'masculine' attributes. Much energy was expended during the early 1970s (and still is) trying to rub out sex role stereotyping, in the hope that the 'positive' masculine traits will stick to both sexes.

The attitudes of children themselves seem to concur with the idea that there is something 'wrong' with the way girls grow up, rather than boys. In one school in Somerset, 64 per cent of the boys claimed they were happy with their role, but only 4 per cent of the girls felt the same way about being female. An American survey quoted in a recent study of communication[6] revealed that four-fifths of girls wanted to be boys at some time, but less than half of all boys canvassed admitted to ever wanting to be a girl.

However, this has more recently begun to be interpreted as a 'rigidity' on the part of boys, reflecting fear of being labelled a 'cissy'. A British sociologist, Dr David Hargreaves at the University of Leicester, has been carrying out research among primary school children which seems to show that apparent differences in ability between the sexes may simply be self-chosen differences in response, based on what is seen as sex-appropriate behaviour. He mentions paternal intolerance of inappropriate toys for boys, and quotes[7] research which shows that boys are more rigid in their sex-typing. Sheila A. Ross, whom Hargreaves also quotes, found that three to four year old male 'shopkeepers' were much more anxious than their female counterparts that their boy customers should choose sex appropriate toys than the girl 'shopkeepers' were when selling to other girls.

However, Hargreaves also quotes an infant school where the children were given authority to adopt opposite sex behaviour (there weren't enough girls in the school play) for which the boys became very keen, staying in 'drag' for the rest of the day. And Hargreaves himself noticed that when he asked small boys to carry out an exercise pretending they were members of the opposite sex:

> The reaction was incredulous and uproarious. The children were very excited by the idea, and I witnessed one very convincing imitation of Danny La Rue.

Lidz[8] asserts that boys adopt a contemptuous attitude towards girls and girlishness, convincing themselves that there is nothing they want less, because of the fear of regression and engulfment femininity represents—and 'repressing such wishes into the unconscious is one *task* of the "latency" period' (my italics) in order that they may become more secure in their gender identity. It seems, however, that small boys are aware of missing out on certain ways of being and acting. But are they missing out on something more than just an enjoyable game, something vital for their full and healthy development?

Slowly, writers and researchers on qualitative sex differences (mainly post- and pro-feminist) are beginning to think that they are. There is an established controversial school of thought that creative people show more cross-sex characteristics. And Jung's idea of wholeness, that a duality of masculine and feminine traits coexists within each of us, has been developed by other writers.

In general, however, personality theorists seem more concerned with accommodating a post-feminist perspective (extolling the need for 'variety' in a heterosexual society), than really questioning accepted theories in the light of research findings on sex differences. One personality textbook[9] updated in the '70s from the dark days of 1963 when it first came out, seems to say all the right things about research generalising from the male sex about both sexes, and equating male with healthy and normal. But although the authors allow for potential conflict in males over dependency, they seem otherwise content with the inconsistencies in their own theory which implicitly equates male with normal.

Perhaps they do not wish to be disturbed by what they might find if they delved a little more deeply. It seems hardly accidental that the introductory essay[10] in Lloyd and Archer's *Exploring Sex Differences* is written by a woman. Barbara Lloyd argues that psychologists have produced a theory of child development which reflects contemporary power relationships and defends the status quo, stepping lightly from what is to what ought to be, without anyone noticing. (See note[11].) One of the following essays in the book examines qualitative sex differences from the point of view of skills which men lack. It also is written by a woman. According to Diane McGuinness,[5] research during the '60s and '70s shows that although sons demand—and receive— more physical attention, girls develop greater tactile sensitivity. And regardless of their greater contact with their mothers, boys prefer objects to people and show poorer speech development. (See note[12].)

She compares female superior verbal skill, memory and social sensitivity with male superior visual and spatial ability, citing a 1957 study which showed that girls remember socially relevant information that boys do not. Girls' interest in other people is apparent at one week and at five months. Females apparently use more complex psychological categories than men when describing others. Girls respond to faces, she proposes, because they are locating the source of sound to which they are attracted, because of their greater aural sensitivity. They have a greater memory for verbal, visual and social information. McGuinness links this with a 1972 study of newcomers to a playgroup, where even three-year-old girls responded to new children with affection, interest and solicitous behaviour. Boys, on the other hand, initially ignored and excluded the 'interlopers' from their games. The two sexes have therefore already established preferences in the way they respond, and this object/social distinction between them appears pervasive across age groups.

This would seem to support and reflect Chodorow's

argument that girls retain a sense of self-in-relationship, identifying with nurturing capacities which boys feel forced to cut off. McGuinness[5] claims:

> ... clear evidence on this distinction in an experiment in which adult subjects must choose between object and social stimuli without being aware of the reason for their reactions. Photographs of objects were paired with photographs of people and presented stereoscopically. This results in binocular rivalry in which the more meaningful stimulus predominates.

The men saw the objects and the women saw the people. She also cites some very early research (in 1891) which showed that objects interest males because of what they do, how they move, or respond, while women supply communicable descriptions of objects. She stresses the fact that different *values* are put on the differences between the sexes.

Parents insist that boys learn to read and write, overcoming their early deficiency, and much concern, post-feminism, has been expressed about the lack of insistence that girls acquire mechanical skills, but there is no equally serious concern for boys' lack of what she calls 'social intelligence', meaning sensitivity and responsiveness to people. No one really questions the problems specific to boys in the process of personality development, the journey towards real maturity. And the main thing they seem to lack on that journey is skill in making relationships. When the pressures boys come under from the earliest age are appreciated, it is not hard to understand why.

Having established an appropriate gender identity, small children show little interest (in the case of small boys, much scorn) in the opposite sex. This is because the child is preoccupied with the need to establish and develop its own sense of identity within the context of its same-sex peer group. According to most personality theory, children begin to enjoy fantasy play with others around the age of three. At first this is simply self-absorbed 'parallel play' with snatching and arguing over goes with toys, but it gradually develops into participation in one another's fantasies, with imaginative role-taking as children begin to relate to one another as equals.

Segal and Yahraes[13] describe peer-group playmates as 'key instruments in the symphony of human development', whose influence is stronger the more emotional needs are not nurtured at home. But if peers are not just playmates, nor are they merely substitutes for siblings or parents. Since the child begins to feel more threatened and insecure the more it becomes aware of and exercises its impulses towards independence, the peer group provides a context in which it can act separately from and often unseen by its parents, yet not feel entirely alone and cut off, because of its membership of the homogeneous group which reinforces the old reassuring merged sensation of identification. It is not just safety in numbers, it is security in simultaneous sameness.

This is why, within the interplay of squabbles and disputes, popularity ratings and preferences, it is so important to be seen to conform, especially to gender roles, which in the case of boys involves a fierce rejection of girls. My brother and his friend played with me in the garden at home, but if we were leaving school together, I was instructed to wait at the gate, or further up the lane. He wouldn't come looking for me among the girls.

This disdain has been interpreted as children picking up on the values of the patriarchal society, but, as Theodore Lidz[8] points out:

> The exclusion of girls from the boys' juvenile peer group serves to help the boy become more secure in his gender identity and his masculine role.

Lidz as has already been noted, regarded this as a 'task' of normal male development, but as Hargreaves[14] has pointed out it can be both restricting and anxiety-provoking for the child. The small boy has already come to the peer group feeling more anxious and insecure than the little girl because his sense of gender identity is not so firmly based, as a result of the inadequacy of his relationship with his father. He joins the peer group with a greater emotional need, hungry to fill the vacuum created by the inaccessibility of his father as a model for the masculinity he seeks.

At the same time as needing to allay feelings of anxiety through a sense of solidarity within the peer group, small boys jointly aspire to a model of maleness based on social stereotypes. They may look up to a teacher who is a good sportsman (or, in the case of my generation, proved himself during the war), or they may idealise heroes in comic strips or on the television, and what each of these figures exudes is a sense of confidence, power, invulnerability, rightness, the exact opposite of the uncomfortable feelings of inadequacy the boy himself is consciously or unconsciously experiencing.

The small boy seeks, as far as he is able, to emulate this toughness, to prove to himself his maleness by being just as strong. Very early on, therefore, in the process of getting to know one another, little boys will begin to compete with one another, mimicking the adult male conflicts they witness on the screen, in the attempt to establish their own self-confidence. This normally takes the form of fairly innocuous threatening behaviour, pushing and shoving in mock hostility, although one man I know was kicked in the balls on his first day at school.

Paradoxically, the threat of violence, of being hurt, increases the sense of vulnerability and the need for security. But small boys soon discover that they cannot cling to their fathers. The response to the complaint that 'So-and-so hit me, dad,' may well be not 'There, there, kiss it better' but 'Well, what are you waiting for? Go out there and hit him back.' One man tells the story of how he went looking for a kid who hit his younger brother, taunting him to come out of his house. Far from backing up his cowering son, the boy's father joined in the taunt, telling him to go out and take his medicine. And the boy who runs to his mother for comfort soon earns the put-down label, 'Mummy's boy'.

In developmental terms, an already anxious child has become even more anxious, because he discovers he cannot temporarily regress to lick his wounds. So the child resorts to sideways self-defence. With the avenue of healthy temporary regression cut off, the psyche seeks to alleviate anxiety by sheltering in other, more distorting kinds of defence, known as defence mechanisms, all of which can impair normal personality development.

Defence mechanisms are ways of avoiding fear and

anxiety. The most common defence mechanisms are repression, regression, projection, rationalisation, reaction formation, displacement, and intellectualisation. As we have seen, although small boys appear successful in repressing their residual identification with their mothers and being female, they are unable to resort to the most natural defence, regression, which allows the personality to step back briefly and recover. Projection involves attributing unacceptable ideas or impulses to others rather than acknowledging them in yourself, and often leads to hostility towards others, hence Wilde's maxim to choose your enemies carefully, because you will resemble them. Boys see in girls the projection of characteristics they cannot accept in themselves, and react by denigrating them and regarding them as inferior. Sublimation is the modifying of unacceptable impulses into socially acceptable activities, and may be seen in sport, especially boxing, and of course war, where the 'just cause' justifies brutality and murder. It is interesting that identification, after the primary relationship, is seen purely as an ego defence, incorporating the thoughts, feelings and actions of another to increase one's sense of worth or reduce a threat from others who are more powerful. These defences all come into play in the situations in which the small boy finds himself.

They are believed to operate primarily unconsciously, and although moderate use may protect the ego, excessive use is damaging to healthy adjustment. Because of the all-pervasive power and influence of the peer group during the greater part of childhood, boys' use of such defence mechanisms is almost bound to be excessive, depending on the particular pressures they come under and the extent of their basic sense of security; meaning, largely, the quality of their relationships with their fathers. Probably the most obvious defence boys turn to is reaction formation, the transforming of dangerous or painful urges into their opposite, although the original urges persist at an unconscious level.

Small boys learn very early on to react to fear with feigned courage, which becomes real courage, or so it seems, when they have proved themselves capable of standing their ground, and shown their mettle by fighting back, or even deliberately going out of their way to provoke a fight, usually with someone smaller than the person who picked a fight with them. This is another defence, displacement, shifting impulses and feelings about one person or object towards a safer, less dangerous person or object.

Much of what takes place is on the level of sparring, threatening behaviour which isn't carried through. It is important, however, to know that you can fight:

> I think boys do wonder about fights, what do I do, how much does it hurt, so they experiment to find out, but in a safe controlled way. I used to have fights, really nasty fights in terrible tempers, where boys would say 'I'm going to fight you, Tony Taylor, but no hitting in the face.' If they said hitting in the face, that was heavy stuff. More likely they'd be, in a really bad temper, just going umph! on your arm. You didn't lose total face because you hadn't run away snivelling and you'd actually planted a couple of punches on his arm, not to hit him hard, just to draw away his anger. If I let him give me three really good 'uns, it might be enough, and it often was.

You took shelter behind unwritten rules about how far you could go in a fight (it was generally frowned upon if your victim needed medical attention) and also behind allegiance to a group:

> In the junior school it was a gang thing. You wanted someone for your gang or they'd expelled someone from a gang so they couldn't take part. They'd make a disparaging remark about your family or your sister, even if they'd never seen them. They'd say 'Your mother stinks' and you'd say 'What?'. It was a challenge to a fight. Most of the fighting started around eight or nine and ended around thirteen or fourteen, although of course the rougher kids stayed in gangs. Certain boys become the butt of jokes and attacks, like flicking custard. Sometimes I'd be on the other side of it, even with a friend, you know, how little boys go too far . . . One flick of ink, two flicks of ink, then the bottle of ink. He would come across and thump me then, he was stronger than me. But never really badly, he always remembered I was really his mate.

Group pressure could be more powerful than individual

friendship, because the group is the source of security in the jungle of violence in which boys are forced to live. You project your aggression outside the group on to some innocent victim who is 'different', and then you feel safe. Girls rarely go round in groups of more than four, and normally within this group there are dyads, one-to-one friendships. Boys on the other hand, rarely mix in groups of less than four, and are much less likely to pair off within the group.

Boys conform to group pressure to be rough and coarse and exuberant, tough and brutal, because those are the ideals you are supposed to worship, at the shrine of the stereo-typically male. Some men look back favourably on the rough and tumble as a harmless outlet, a way of letting off steam and being 'the best of mates afterwards' rather than harbouring a grudge. But most men remember yearning to be Superman or Charles Bronson so that people would shrink at the sight of them and they wouldn't have to prove themselves: 'You'd just tap them on the shoulder, you wouldn't have to hit them.'

There are usually a handful of boys in that position, to whom the others look up, because they are tall, muscular, invariably good at sports, particularly football, and with nothing, therefore, to prove. These boys, consequently, are often gentle and kind. One man, now a sports teacher, remembers being treated as a father figure at school, actually earning the nickname 'daddy' among the boys, because they felt able to come to him for advice and support. However, another powerful-looking interviewee of six-foot-three nurtured behind his controlled façade the fear of his own violence, partly because he feared the uncontrolled violence his father exhibited:

> I was hoping you'd ask me why I never got into a fight. It was because I knew I would hurt, possibly kill someone. I was very good at boxing, but I still live in fear of losing my temper. No one ever picked a fight with me.

Beneath the ones at the top who don't have to prove themselves lies the substratum of those who are jockeying to be top dog, often picking fights, 'squaring up' to other boys to prove themselves. Among them are the hard nuts who've earned their reputation fairly with their fists and also the other type, the bullies. These are often boys who are actually very insecure, unsure of themselves and do not look very strong. Unlike the tall, athletic types, figureheads at the prow of masculinity, these boys present its unacceptable face. They are often eager to demonstrate their cruelty, like one boy who has gone down in history in other people's minds as the one who was capable of stabbing somebody's guinea pig with a pair of compasses. Often such boys have ineffectual or dominated fathers, and feel a conflict between the real-life male model and the cultural stereotype, which they resolve by disassociating themselves, cultivating an image at the opposite extreme, because the social stereotype is the stronger.

Gary was such a boy, small, thin, baby-faced, with contempt for a father who settled conflict by appeasement—'anything for a quiet life'. Gary's life, consequently, was far from quiet. Around the age of thirteen he found a hero and a role model of his own age:

> I fell under the spell of the class bully. I loved him, as one guy can love another. Yet he was a violent, destructive bully. I suddenly discovered the power of confrontation, of saying 'If I say boo, jump!' and the other guy saying 'Make me.' And whereas before, I would have been the one to jump, I became instead the most awful bully, almost expelled for fighting. I prided myself on being tough, looking hard, which was difficult with such a baby-face, so I never smiled. I would 'book' a guy, stare at him until he was the first to look away, which was the moment of submission, triumph. Strutting round with my coat collar turned up. I even squared up to a friend in the school playground. I started fights, I was the one to pick on people. I regret it terribly now, I wish I could meet them and apologise. Although, in another way, I'm almost glad it happened to me, except that I wanted to be close to the blokes I really admired, but Kevin's dominant character magnetised me.

Such boys either become the bullies or the bullied. The ones who get picked on usually have some visible handicap or deformity or otherwise stand out from the group in some way. They become scapegoats for the safe release of aggression which at the same time bolsters the other boys' feelings of belonging within the group. One man described how being sent to the secondary school for the first week in short trousers sealed his fate, and his position in the pecking order:

> I tried to become immune by the only means at my disposal, humour. But I was a bad joke-teller, and went too far cheeking the teachers and ended up as the butt of laughter. Successful comedians stayed on the right side of various fine lines, which even now I'd be hard pushed to define. I did, though, gain some respect by the amount of canings I amassed—I held the record for two years until I got smart.

The ones at the bottom of the pile either try to play up, in vain, to curry favour and earn respect, or else seek protection at the front of the class, swotting to get in with the teachers. They are, of course, especially reviled for this, and generally lead a humiliating, miserable existence, always on the sidelines. When teams are picked, the rating of popularity, they are always the last to be chosen. First come the friends of the captains, then the physically tough ones, and the ones who call loudest to be chosen. Then it comes down to having to accept the duds, the ones with braces, glasses, clothes too big for them, the ugly ones and the artistic ones; or else they are left out, if it is a game at breaktime, not a lesson.

You can earn some respect by having a particular skill, like telling jokes, bringing dirty magazines, doing other people's homework for them, or else keeping on taking a beating, branded as a 'nutter', but otherwise you can never really belong. Advertisers in boys' comics played on the fear of failure. There was one brand of chest-expander regularly advertised in the *Eagle* in a strip cartoon, rather like those for using deodorant. This one, however, showed a boy who was laughed at and made miserable because he couldn't box or he couldn't swim. Of course, he buys himself a chest-expander and within a few weeks he is beating his 'friends' in front of their girlfriends.

However it isn't all winning or losing. There is a category, especially in more academic schools, of boys who manage to avoid the system. They are generally quite clever, intellectual without showing obvious signs of sucking up or swotting, and having proved in a public showdown that they are perfectly capable of defending themselves successfully they are avoided by the bullies and themselves avoid most other sources of conflict, by not joining in the one-up-manship, the challenges, and if necessary taking another route home if they see trouble ahead of them. This ignoring of the system is, however, not so easy to achieve if the school, or the class, is a particularly rough one. Generally, then, you get picked on and are forced to pick on others, because some kind of revenge, even on a safer target, is vital for your honour, your self-esteem. One boy was rewarded with a bag of chips from his father, when he bloodied the nose of the bully next door, who'd been terrorising him for weeks. Many boys are in this sense forced into a struggle for power, simply in order to survive, avoid the things they fear most—failure, public humiliation and defeat. And, as Anthony Storr says, in *The Integrity of the Personality*,[15] 'A compulsive striving for power is one characteristic of emotional immaturity'.

The peer group is supposed to be the opportunity to relate to one's equals, but for boys much more than girls, it becomes a system of sharply defined hierarchies and statuses, with bonds and allegiances but no real trust. Girls form cliques based on likes and dislikes, but although some have more status than others, they are not part of a hierarchical system, nor a culture based on crude combat and competition. Girls tend to avoid competition and conflict, by publicising their failure and playing down their success. It is the submission technique used by animals, which induces an aggressor to walk away. It is a function of girls' fear of separateness, the difficulties they have as a result of not discovering confidence in a close but different relationship with their fathers, and becomes the cause of their troubles later on. But it does give girls the opportunity to form confiding, trusting, close relationships with one another.

Boys, on the other hand, grow up associating the expression of affection with femininity, something to avoid for fear of being branded a cissy. Rarely cuddled by their fathers, they do not learn to cuddle, and associate such behaviour with sexuality, proof of being a poof, which is another reason for avoiding it. It becomes dangerous as well as taboo, to express your real feelings. If you cry, you are not a man, if you tell your weakness, you are revealing your Achilles' heel, for your 'friend' to turn and use against you.

Boys constantly rely on bluff and bravado, on mutual back-slapping and positive encouragement, which is supportive in a sense, but only in a limited sense. Because they never mention their fears they grow up hiding a part of themselves, restricting their opportunities for intimacy—because intimacy is dependent upon self-disclosure—and therefore, also, their opportunities for self-knowledge, which comes through revealing oneself to others. They grow up with a distance reinforcing their separateness and yet, as Anthony Storr infers, more susceptible to group influences than the strength of their own individuality:

> In the absence of relationship with others, men become more alike, not more individual; and isolation leads ultimately to a loss of the distinguishing features of personality, not, as might be supposed, to their intensification.

Males need to bond together in packs because they have no underlying sense of mutuality. Much of their supposedly highly self-assertive, non-conformative behaviour in classroom situations is conformity of another kind, conformity to the peer group, beneath which the individual response gets lost, a kind of parrot Pavlov response, like the instance one man gave of 'standing up and shouting "Now!" and everyone laughing at Scabbie Hobbs'. A boy recently interviewed after his father had been murdered by the IRA agreed with his friend that he wanted revenge. It was only when he was alone that he was able to admit that he saw no sense in more killing, it wouldn't bring his father back. But he couldn't have said that in front of his mates.

Boys do develop a very supportive kind of camaraderie, in which they can be very free and spontaneous. But it operates within tight controls—an outward show of bravado to defend an increasingly vulnerable and neglected inner self. They may learn how to handle aggression, but they neglect other emotions and needs.

What happens is that in concentrating on positive

appearance and action the inner self with its ambivalence and fears is ignored and neglected almost to the point at which it doesn't appear to be there. Like the Daleks in *Dr Who*, boys have a fierce and impressive outward appearance, but inside is a rather primitive, unformed and unidentifiable defenceless blob. In his study[16] of grammar and public schoolboys, Liam Hudson found that some boys, generally on the arts side, had a much more free-ranging, lateral-thinking imagination than others, generally scientists, whose practical commitment to the use of objects precluded anything other than their 'right' use. He concluded that boys who were dedicated to the control of their environment were least likely to think about it in anything but conventional terms; that boys seemed to divide into thinkers or doers, divergers or convergers; and the divergers showed themselves more capable than the convergers of expressing strong or violent feelings, even when they conflicted, whereas the convergers seemed to compartmentalise moral topics, so that they avoided any internal paradoxes or conflicts. He claimed he also sensed an 'elaborate screen' between these boys' private feelings and the outside world and that this screen seemed to consist not so much of 'explicit defensiveness, more of bewildering, boring detail'. In other words they used factual detail about themselves as a defence.

They also, as John Berger's quotation at the beginning of the first chapter suggested, use factual detail as a substitute as well as a defence, a substitute for the intimate detail they do not feel trusting enough to share. Boys seem perfectly happy with such imperfect expressions of fellow feeling, resorting to teasing and mock hostility, cuffing and clapping one another on the back, as if the only safe way to express positive feeling is by a gesture which could always be interpreted as its opposite. Boys desperately need an outlet for their emotions, so they displace them, so that they are directed not towards other people, their friends, but into the objects, the games and interests, which they share. As McGuinness[5] pointed out, boys seem predisposed to relate to objects, and whatever that predisposition indicates, they use it to disarm the threat of exposure, ridicule and punishment which a more direct expression of emotion might reveal.

This seems to work perfectly as a kind of satellite communication, whereby feelings reach one another from the enthusiasms boys share. They will spend time looking at a friend's stamp book, even if it is not their own hobby, in the way girls will enter into one another's passions and crushes. And as Berger says, the minutiae, the factual detail which appeared to Hudson as a screen, become a symbol of intimacy. This is how much I know about this subject, how much I care about it, and because you care about it too, how much I care about you.

The extent of emotion males invest in their games and pastimes is most noticeable in sport. Nowhere do men express themselves so passionately—or allow themselves to unrestrainedly hug one another (because of the goal, of course). Men share a great deal in this deeply symbolic way which is partly why they appear to women like children, because of their emotional investment in their childhood pastimes. So the balsa wood model of an aeroplane becomes a plastic scale model of a US Starfighter F104C, complete with instrument panel touched in with a single hair brush; and the bent pin and piece of string transmute into the expensive tackle lugged about for weekend fishing competitions; and also, more tragically, the war-games become war.

Through their shared activities boys cement their relationships without the need to share secrets and fears, but there are several drawbacks to this approach, the main being that it becomes inadequate to resolve conflicts or difficulties in the relationship itself.

Some interesting research has been carried out at the University of Denver, Colorado, by two psychologists, Drs Wyndol Furman and Howard Markman. In order to study the acquaintanceship process in middle childhood, forty pairs of acquainted and unacquainted same-sex eight to nine year olds, both boys and girls, were observed by a hidden camera while left alone to play, and then given a written questionnaire. Observation showed that unacquainted boys demonstrated little interest in getting to know one another, restricting their conversation to what was necessary to the game rather than disclosing anything about themselves. In fact, unacquainted girls shared more than three times as much information about themselves, whereas boys were more likely to assert their status with one another. This confirms similar findings from various studies over the past ten years, of the difference between adolescent and adult men and women, which have found, among other things, that women are more self-disclosing than men and emphasise emotional sharing and talking with friends, while men prefer to do things together, regarding the sharing of day-to-day activities as more important than the sharing of abstract values.

When Piaget noted how boys become increasingly fascinated with the elaboration of rules in their games, and the development of fair procedures, he concluded (agreeing with Freud's opinion that women show less sense of justice than men) that this was the process by which boys developed the 'legal sense' necessary to moral development. American sociologist Janet Lever[17] came to similar conclusions. Studying the games of nearly 200 ten and eleven year olds, she found that boys played outdoors more often, in larger, more age-heterogeneous groups than girls, that they played more competitive games and that their games lasted longer. She observed that boys' games lasted longer not only because they were more highly skilled and less likely to become boring, but also that when disputes arose boys seemed better able to resolve them effectively. In fact, although boys were seen quarrelling most of the time, it never signalled the end of the game.

They always decided to start again, have another go. In fact, they seemed to enjoy the legal debates as much as the game, whereas disputes among girls tended to end the game. Lever concluded that the male model was better, because it suited the requirements for survival at work (which of course it does) since boys learn independence, organising skills and, more importantly, how to deal with competitive situations, how to play with enemies and compete with friends. Girls, on the other hand, develop far less experience of taking the role of the 'generalised other'. They learn the empathy and sensitivity necessary for taking the part of the 'particular other' (meaning that they respond to one another as individuals) and, rather than elaborating a system of rules, girls will subordinate the continuation of the game to the continuation of harmonious relationships.

This for girls often means that they do not confront their differences, avoid competition by underplaying their advantages, and sacrifice a winning situation for the goodwill of their friends. But what Carol Gilligan[18] discovered, when she explored these differences even further, was that boys and girls develop two different ways of describing relationships, which reflect a totally different approach, each of which has advantages and disadvantages, rather than, as Piaget implied, one being a less advanced version of the other.

She listened for ten years to people talking about morality, and after five years began to discern 'two ways of speaking about moral problems, two modes of describing the relationship between other and self' which reflected the different lines along which the sexes are encouraged to develop.

Boys see moral problems in rational, logical ways, but girls imagine the ramifications of the actual situation, failing to see the dilemma as a self-contained problem in moral logic. In other words, women see a world that 'coheres through human connection rather than systems of rules', and this response appears naive and immature. However, she deduced that posing children with the same moral problem revealed that boys and girls see two very different problems: the male child sees 'a conflict between life and property, that can be resolved by logical deduction'; the female 'a fracture of human relationship that must be mended with its own thread'.

While a girl has developed a more sophisticated understanding of the nature of choice, a boy has developed a more sophisticated understanding of the logical and rational justification, ie boys defuse interpersonal conflict by impersonal claims which ignore subjective considerations. They set up a hierarchical order to resolve conflict between desire and duty—while he thinks about what comes first, she thinks about who will be left out. The more children talk about morality, the more clearly it emerges that boys describe themselves through separation, defining self, name, place etc, and girls through connection. Boys define responsibility to others and to yourself by saying 'You go about one quarter to others and three-quarters to yourself'. For boys, responsibility spells restraint of aggression and selfishness, for girls it is an act of care. Whereas boys are concerned with limiting interference, girls have a need for response. A girl, 'assuming connection, begins to explore the parameters of separation', while a boy, 'assuming separation, begins to explore the parameters of connection'. Thus the primacy of either separation or connection leads to different images of self and relationships.

It is not surprising, considering what goes on in the separate playgrounds, that a boy depicts a world of dangerous confrontation and explosive connection where a girl sees a world of care and protection. To a boy, responsibility is not doing what one wants for the sake of others; to a girl it is doing what others want, regardless of self. He sees hurt arising from expression of aggression, she sees it from failure of response, lack of feeling, replacing the imagery of explosive connection with that of dangerous separation.

Although boys have more experience in dealing with conflict, they do not learn how to cope with it on a personal level. While girls are taking a mutual course in human relations and co-counselling techniques, boys are learning how to conduct business deals, settle union disputes and win legal cases. The upbringing of boys does not prepare them for tackling problems in close relationships, nor for examining their own feelings or absorbing and being affected by the feelings of others whom they have entrusted with an understanding of themselves. Male development is a process of differentiation, of independence, but it is a shoring-up process, during which it becomes increasingly difficult to reach the person behind the barrier, or for them to perceive subtleties conveyed to them in the form of signals from other people. The channels for interaction on a close level have not been dug. Instead, boys overlook personality differences, reinforcing the bonds between them, regarding the content of much female in-depth psychological character analysis as so much boring gossip. They pretend their inner feelings are not there and, having hidden them so well, fail to recognise their own pretence.

One defence mechanism not yet mentioned is intellectualisation, which involves separating a thought from its associated affective charge, speaking and thinking in a detached way about a recent traumatic event. Boys learn this defence through concentrating upon factual detail and logic, standing back, rationalising because they know no other way, except violence, of dealing with feelings.

So, although boys' friendships appear in a very positive light, they remain really only as deep as their mutual interests, and in the absence of a functional basis to the relationship, the friendship itself is likely to disappear— witness the failure of many men to keep in touch with one another once they have moved on.

So girls and boys grow up with very different approaches to relationships, very different methods of handling people, very different ways of expressing emotion, affection and resolving relationship problems. That the male approach is more appropriate to the world of work and the female approach to home and the family is immaterial, not just because traditional sex roles are changing. For the majority of the population, the most important adult relationship we make is that with the member of the opposite sex with whom we choose to share our lives, and yet the tragedy of this idealised, romanticised fusion of twin souls is that when boys are attracted to girls, and vice versa, neither side, when they meet, is emotionally able to speak the other's language.

All children, when they first become interested in sex, and the opposite sex, want to appear sophisticated and grown-up, in the know. They fix on 'dirty' words which are bandied about over school dinner or on the bus home, and try to trick their more knowledgeable friends into betraying their meaning, while not giving away their own ignorance. Girls, like boys, scrutinise biology books and become fascinated by nudity. But girls also freely express their self-consciousness about exposing their own changing bodies to one another, whereas boys become caught up in yet another competition to prove how cocky they are, confident and unabashed about anything. So boys make a virtue of coarse and earthy conversation, make overt anatomical comparisons in the changing rooms, flip towels at other boys' genitals, gather round the back of the bike sheds to practise masturbation, what one ex-public schoolboy described as 'fiddling about', in the same way as they used to have contests on how far they could spit or pee. But this time the prowess has to go one step further, out of the charmed circle of competing among your mates.

The need to appear knowledgeable is quickly superseded by the need to appear experienced, because a new criterion of masculinity has been added to the list. You need to be able to win with women to qualify as a real man. And adolescence is the moment of transformation, the treacherous bridge from child to man. For some boys it represents a second chance. They didn't make the football team but maybe they can make up lost points with the girls. Many boys of my generation were at this point still extremely ignorant, sex education not having been considered necessary for them. Others had been enlightened by coarse jokes from older men. Only half a dozen had been told by their parents. Many still believed that babies were born through a woman's belly button. The trouble was that in actually getting to grips with it all you had to go out with a real live girl.

Society dictated then (and little has changed) that the boy take the initiative, make the first move, ask a girl for a date. Unfortunately this goes against all the defensive strategies the boy has built up around his emotions. Here he is, laying his cards on the table. He cannot pretend he simply wants someone to play a game of chess with, or go out catching fish. And he risks everything in that one move, total rejection, total humiliation, worst of all if it takes place in front of his mates. Whatever happens, he has got to save face. Most girls, approached by a hideously spotty specimen masquerading as their fantasy lover, turn their backs, or flatly refuse, when asked to go and dance, because of the damage it would do to their image. That boy then has to rejoin his friends. One man confessed that he always positioned himself so that the girl was in line with the gents, so that if she refused he could pretend he had simply gone for a pee. Other men mentioned playing games designed to reduce the threatening tension, like competing to ask the ugliest girl in the room to dance, which is a way of hiding the fact that you daren't ask the one you really fancy, in front of whom, in one man's words, he became a 'bumbling fool'. Or you wait until you are blind drunk before you impulsively lurch forward. Meanwhile all the girls are dancing with one another and all the boys are standing at the edge, making out they'll make their move in all good time, they're really just eyeing up the talent.

At this period of his school career, my brother wrote an essay, the last page of which has somehow survived. It was about telephoning a girl to ask for a first date. 'Somehow the words managed to stumble forwards. "Yes!" she would come— ecstasy!!!' But even after she's agreed to come out with you, your troubles are not quite over. After you've met her at the bus-stop, where do you take her and what do you talk to her about? Boys were expected to pay, and feel at ease in surroundings which were probably just as new and awkward to them as to the girl, but they weren't supposed to show it. It's not surprising that the agony columns advised girls to gen up on football or politics, whatever his interest happened to be; any other way of trying to get to know him, especially the direct route girls are wont to take, would be far too dangerous. Boys often find what girls see as harmless talk about people and relationships very threatening, far too deep water for someone who's used to swimming on the surface of life.

Girls and boys tend to go out together with rather different thoughts uppermost in their minds, but both revolving around what they are going to tell their friends at school on Monday morning. For boys the pressure is on proving how far you got, if possible in the minutest detail. The admission of failure in any respect is unthinkable, so the boy usually has to exaggerate or simply invent. He'll claim she let him undo her bra and fondle her breasts (when in actual fact she pushed his hand away) so that in the end he comes to believe it himself, or else rationalises his failure—she was a frigid bitch anyway. Boys boast because it is expected, because they need to impress the group, to compete, to cover over their feelings of anxiety, to rewrite the script. And because all of them do it, most of them are perfectly aware, although it's never mentioned, that most of it isn't true.

However for some men it still seems important to believe that two boys *did* get the English mistress to strip in the back of a car, though it was actually the boys who kept quiet who were more likely to be really up to what the others were so loudly claiming, because they were in a loyal long-term relationship. Boys tend to betray their relationships with girls because at this age the peer group means more to them or at best, their loyalties are divided. Girls go through a similar kind of split loyalty, but the confidential inform-ation they reveal to their friends tends to be of an emotional rather than a physical nature. Things he has said to them, letters he has written to them, will be passed round the group—to his absolute horror if he knew. But girls, not being so competitive, tend not to feel the same pressure to boast when seeking to impress their friends. They are much more interested in pooling interpretations of what he really might have meant.

Girls have long felt themselves the victims, not just of cavalier and non-caring boyfriends, but the way in which boys exploit and abuse them sexually. A recent research study based on interviews with fifteen-year-old girls in London comprehensive schools shows that this practice still goes on.[19] They complained that they get called a 'slag' if they don't fancy a boy, yet end up with the same label if they've been out with more than two of a group of boys:

> You're known as the crisp that they're passing around. The boy's all right, but the girl's a bit of scum.

Few girls attacked the unfairness of the double standard, but they complained most about the unfairness of fabricated boasts:

> If boys don't get what they want, they lie about it anyway. That's the worst.

What boys are expressing, in this ambivalent way, are the conflicts and confusions they feel as a result of the specific role pressures they are under and their underlying lack of confidence about handling relationships with girls. Sexually, boys may be aware of a conflict in attitudes between their parents, which is never openly discussed. Sexual experience may signify congratulation and initiation into manhood as much to a boy's father as to his friends. Yet at the same time he will be aware of having disappointed his mother. One boy, who had stayed out all night at a party, came home to find his mother telling him his father was very upset about it, yet when his father finally appeared his only comment was 'Well, did you get it last night then?' Another boy's father found a packet of Durex. 'I don't mind,' he said, 'but what would your mother think?'

Similarly, boys have few opportunities to express any ambivalence they may feel about sexual intimacy. Whatever they think privately, from the moment they discover what 'it' is all about, they must never appear reluctant or unwilling to indulge once given the opportunity. Any distaste or inhibitions must be repressed. Thus one boy, enlightened by a gentle and motherly au pair who took him to bed one day in the holidays and explained the mechanics of what you did, felt free to admit he was horrified by the whole idea. But a boy who was initiated at the age of thirteen by a rather manipulative neighbour in her mid-twenties projected all the humiliation and shock of the experience into a desire to get his own back, to humiliate and exploit girls he met with his newfound sexual prowess.

Boys also find themselves caught between their attraction for girls and the guilt of their own distasteful boasting. This resolves itself into the madonna/whore split thinking of the double standard, whereby girls who have been (however innocently) victims of the boasting become tarnished, and the boy pursues in fantasy the image of the pure desirable object not yet spoiled by all these sordid boasts. They may entertain the fantasy, also, of a totally uninhibited sexual encounter with a girl while at the same time feeling completely threatened by the prospect of trying to appear in control of a situation where the girl is more experienced. They cannot discuss such fears among themselves, so they express them by denouncing such women as 'slags'. One man mentioned boys who claimed that they would 'knee any girl in the face who "went down on" them', which he privately considered a very brutal thing to say, yet publicly endorsed, 'yeah, yeah'.

And on top of all this is the threat that girls present emotionally. Theodore Lidz presents one of the tasks of adolescence, and mature personality development, as that of *daring* to make a relationship. Girls don't have to dare to make relationships. No matter how much they get hurt, they are always ready to leap in at the deep-end again and again, for they take the risk *within* their sense of self-in-relationship. Inner space is the territory they are accustomed to exploring. But boys, unused to any kind of close, direct relationship (except the one they once had with their mothers) feel despite their established independence and difference a sense of danger, a fear of the engulfment that regressive dependence represents.

With girls you can't use the safe satellite communication that works among your friends; you can't deflect all those dangerous undeveloped feelings into your shared stamp-collecting or train-spotting, or any other safe neutral object, as a barrier against hurt. The solution therefore for many boys at this difficult stage of development is to distance themselves from the girl by finding an object to project their feelings on to, that object being the girl herself. You go out with her not because she is a person with responses which may affect you because you have feelings for her yourself, but because she is a sex object and that safe ulterior motive protects you, as well as establishing another bond with your mates.

How else are you going to be brave enough to be seen going round holding hands? And so many other things encourage boys to regard girls as sex objects, from the safe fantasies splayed out in men's magazines to the advertisements which harp on women as visual images of sexuality rather than people. Mild sexual arousal also apparently reduces aggression, another way of reinforcing boys' safe relationships with one another.

It may take some years before a boy actually risks engaging his emotions in a relationship with a girl, rediscovering the feminine in himself buried so long ago. Particularly in the mid '60s when my generation was growing up, with the confusing overlap of the old repressions and the new freedom, a sex object was a fairly topical thing to be. Fortunately most men do ultimately allow themselves to be affected by women, but often only because women make it safe for them to do so. And the boy's first real relationship, where he finds something positive to do with the neglected side of himself by projecting it into the one that he loves, is also the one he never forgets. First love never dies is equally true for both sexes, and many men still hold a candle for the previously forbidden feeling as much as for the person they first fell in love with, so long ago.

The mid '60s also witnessed an upsurge of commercial pop music as well as commercial sex. The music was a focal point for both sexes, but it had a special significance for boys. Boys are especially drawn to music, for several reasons. Susanne Langer[20] states that:

> The tonal structures we call music bear a close logical similarity to the forms of human feeling ... Music is a tonal analogue of emotive life.

Music also has the capacity to appeal to different levels of our personality simultaneously, restating unconscious and forgotten events, which accounts for the 'mysterious moving quality of music and the difficulty many people have of putting it into words.'[21] Lacking any adequate verbal emotional language, music becomes for a boy the expression of inner feeling and thought. Terence McLaughlin argues that:

> Some of the unconscious appeal of music will be to the levels of the personal unconscious or individual unconscious (feelings and emotions which have been forgotten or repressed from the conscious mind), but some of the appeal will be to deeper levels, the ... common human experience and innate emotions which some writers would call instinct and which Jung called the collective unconscious ...

He adds that we therefore experience a sense of unity which arises from 'cessation of conflict between the conscious and unconscious' becoming aware of our unity with the rest of mankind and quotes Shelley:

A man to be greatly good must imagine intensely and comprehensively; he must put himself in the place of another and of many others; the pains and pleasures of his species must become his own.

This may seem a rather highflown way of interpreting the effect of the Kinks, the Beatles or the Rolling Stones, but for boys music does act in this way as the crucial link with expression of feeling, both between one another and within themselves. It may be the first legitimate experience of empathy, of mature identification, they have been allowed. And verbally, songs also allow boys to admit to, sing about, what they cannot say. There are so many songs about male heartbreak and tears. Elvis could sing about never feeling more like crying all night, the Searchers and the Everly Brothers describe the tears they had to hide, by doing their crying in the rain, the Beatles could admit they needed Help!, and the Hollies could proclaim they had suddenly emotionally come alive—freed from cold and lonely heartlessness, they could breathe, see, touch, feel. But it was Eden Kane, in 1964, singing how 'Boys Cry' where they can't be seen or heard, and pretend to act tough, who summed up how it all still had to be.

In the late 1950s and early 1960s there was a bestselling American novel (reprinted in Britain every year between 1958 and 1966), written by J. D. Salinger and called *The Catcher in the Rye*.[22] It was a novel ahead of its time, which tried to express some of the confusions of growing up male. Its hero, Holden Caulfield, a comfortably-off middle class child, is nevertheless a crazy mixed up kid, who can't stand the hypocrisy of the world he sees around him. He quits school on impulse and arrives in New York, waiting for Wednesday so that he can come home as if he had left at the end of term. He'd left early partly because he felt plagued by one spotty character invading his room:

> All he did was keep talking in this very monotonous voice about some babe he was supposed to have had sexual intercourse with the summer before. He'd already told me about it a hundred times. Every time he told it, it was different. One minute he'd be giving it to her in his cousin's Buick, the next minute he'd be giving it to her under some boardwalk. It was all a lot of crap,

naturally. He was a virgin if ever I saw one. I doubt if he ever even gave anybody a feel.

Nevertheless, Caulfield feels obliged to play the suave seducer, failing miserably, although his pride won't let him see it, at chatting up some older girls. Then he gets the chance of initiation with a prostitute but ducks out. What he seems to lack is the ability to feel connected, involved with anyone or anything; yet despite himself, this cynicism begins to be eroded, when it begins to be disclosed:

> D.B. asked me what I thought about all this stuff I just finished telling you about—I didn't know what the hell to say. If you want to know the truth, I don't *know* what I think about it. I'm sorry I told so many people about it. About all I know is, I sort of *miss* everybody I told about. Even old Stradlater and Ackley, for instance. Don't ever tell anybody anything. If you do, you start missing everybody.

There seemed to be a whole generation of Holden Caulfields in the mid 1960s trying to work some of their confusions out, by trying to change the system that supported so much of male role playing. It began, in Britain, to be noticed in the schools, where public schoolboys voted to abolish fagging and grammar schoolchildren agitated for the abolition of prefects. Halfway through the 1964 academic year (when those members of my generation who had stayed on were doing their first year in the sixth form), a report was published by the Advisory Centre on Education. Drawn up by John Wakeford, an educational psychologist, it announced that:[23]

> A sixth form rebellion is taking place in Britain's public schools... The rebellion is demonstrated among boys who are declining to become prefects, preferring to associate with other members of the school on equal terms.

In America the professional educationalists were also showing concern. When professor of sociology and education at New York University, Patricia Cayo Sexton, published her theories in *The Feminized Male*,[24] she claimed her enquiry began with the hunch that:

Boys who rise to the top in school often resemble girls in many important ways... It is the baby fat that usually floats and the muscle that sinks. Scholastic honor and masculinity, in other words, too often seem incompatible.

She claimed that school concentration upon academic success rewards feminine behaviour in boys, which encourages a wild delinquent reaction among the less able misfits. She mentioned in support of this that boy delinquents outnumber girls by five to one, and that gangs of boys are about 300 times as common as gangs of girls. Boys overreact because they have no real positive masculine role models, either at home or at school:

What does it mean to be masculine? It means, obviously, holding male values... such as courage, inner direction, certain forms of aggression, autonomy, mastery, technological skill, group solidarity, adventure, and... toughness in mind and body... the words 'manhood' and 'independence' seem almost synonymous in the minds of many boys. A man must be autonomous... without leaning on others too much or asking for too much help and guidance. This is a code that is well known to males, but not to females or feminized men.

She called this 'drive for independence... the backbone of Anglo culture and the essence of the Western hero as deified in boy culture'.

However, she noted that bright ten to eleven year olds are more feminine than the other boys, and in English more than half of the most masculine boys got grade D or F on their report cards, while boys who did well at school tended to be 'fearful, isolated, and'—worst crime of all—'incompetent in athletics':

Athletic competence is one of the trio of traits—courage, independence and athletic prowess—that defines the culture's version of the ideal American male. The boy who is identified with this idealised role tends to reject the passivity and non pragmatic character associated with the acquisition of knowledge.

Too much forced listening is passive and unmanly.

While others were noticing similar phenomena, and interpreting it rather differently, back in 1964, young men were making their own sort of statement about what was going on. They too weren't quite sure what it was, although it definitely involved a rejection of traditionally accepted outward indices of masculinity. They were doing it by wearing high-heeled boots, caring about their looks, growing their hair past their ears and over their collars, martyrs to taunts about looking just like girls. In 1964, one seventeen year old, a certain David Jones (who later changed his name to Bowie) formed a Society for the Prevention of Cruelty to Long-haired Men. For some, this defiance of what was generally seen as manly was the beginning of a sea change in their lives—but only for a few.

## NOTES

1  Thomas Hinde, *Sir Henry and Sons* (Macmillan, 1980)
2  Seventy-three per cent of eleven year old girls admitted liking love stories, against 12 per cent of boys of the same age; see 'Language performance in schools', Secondary Survey Report No 2, Assessment of Performance Unit (HMSO, 1983)
3  Erik Erikson, *Identity, Youth and Crisis* (Faber & Faber, 1968)
4  Caroline St John-Brooks 'Must girls always be girls?' (*New Society*, 1 April 1982)
5  These research findings are cited in an essay by Diane McGuinness, who believes that boys' early practice at manipulation of objects and the skill they develop may enable them to develop a higher degree of spatial imagery. She also quotes research that males show greater 'field independence', picking out visual objects more readily, and that males show more vergence movements of the eyes towards understanding and predicting the relationships of objects in space. They search 'spatially' and have a narrower field of vision with greater depth than females. Women, it seems, get distracted from what they may be seeing out of the corner of their eye. Diane McGuinness, 'Sex differences in the organisation of perception and cognition', in (eds) Barbara Lloyd & John Archer, *Exploring Sex Differences* (Academic Press, New York and London, 1976)

6 B. W. & R. G. Eakins, *Sex Differences in Human Communication* (Houghton Mifflin, Mass and London, 1978)

7 David Hargreaves, 'What are little boys and girls made of?' (*New Society*, 9 September 1976); see also *New Society*, 'Findings', 10 March 1983

8 Theodore Lidz (Professor of Psychology, Yale), *The Person: His and Her Development through the Life Cycle* (Basic Books, New York, 1976)

9 Richard S. Lazarus & Alan Monat, *Personality* (Prentice-Hall, New Jersey, 1963; 2nd edn, 1971, 3rd edn 1979)

10 Barbara Lloyd, 'Social responsibility and research on sex differences,' in Lloyd & Archer, op cit

11 One study of parental dominance (Hetherington, 1965), quoted as an example, dropped one third of its sample of 336 families from its research because neither parent was found to be dominant. Another (1972) study found that in 92 per cent of research studies based solely on males, no mention was made of their sex in the discussions or conclusions.

12 Although male and female babies show similar rates of early babbling, a much higher vocal interaction develops between mothers and daughters. Girls appear to communicate vocally and respond to emotion in speech, developing greater clarity and quality of speech and better high-frequency hearing with greater sensitivity to volume.

13 Julius Segal & Herbert Yahraes, *A Child's Journey* (McGraw-Hill, New York and London, 1978)

14 Hargreaves, see note 7

15 Anthony Storr, *The Integrity of the Personality* (Heinemann Medical Books, 1960)

16 Liam Hudson, *Contrary Imaginations* (Methuen, 1966)

17 Janet Lever, 'Sex differences in the complexity of children's play' (*American Sociological Review*, 43, pp 471–483, 1978)

18 Carol Gilligan, *In a Different Voice: Psychological Theory and Women's Development* (Harvard University Press, Mass and London, 1982)

19 Sue Lees, 'How boys slag off girls' (*New Society*, 13 October 1983)

20 Susanne Langer, *Feeling and Form* (a theory of art developed from *Philosophy in a New Key*) (Routledge & Kegan Paul, 1953)

21 Terence McLaughlin, *Music and Communication*, (Faber, 1970)

22 J. D. Salinger, *The Catcher in the Rye* (Hamish Hamilton, 1951)

23 'Rebellion in the sixth form' (*Sunday Times*, 16 February 1964)
24 Patricia Cayo Sexton, *The Feminized Male: Classrooms, White Collars, and the Decline of Manliness* (Random House, New York, 1969; Pitman, 1970)

*Chapter Six*

# THE SIGNIFICANCE OF THE SIXTIES

*There is a revolution coming... It will not require
violence to succeed, and it cannot be successfully
resisted by violence... Its ultimate creation will be a
new and enduring wholeness and beauty—a renewed
relationship of man to himself, to other men, to society,
to nature, and to the land.*

*This is the revolution of the new generation. Their
protest and rebellion, their culture, clothes, music,
drugs, ways of thought, and liberated life-style are not a
passing fad or a form of dissent. The whole emerging
pattern, from ideals to campus demonstrations to beads
and bell bottoms to the Woodstock Festival, makes
sense and is part of a consistent philosophy. It is both
necessary and inevitable, and in time it will include not
only youth, but all people in America.*

(Charles A. Reich)[1]

A GREAT deal of crap has been written and spoken about the
'60s. Even so, if it wasn't for the '60s, this small four-letter
word would not now be so easily bandied about. That
swinging decade may be looked back on as an era of
excitement, freaked-out hippies wearing headbands, in the
same way that Charlestoning flappers in fringed skirts
stylised the roaring '20s, yet most of the daring innovations
of the 1960s would not turn a hair in the sophisticated, if
cynically depressive, 1980s. The avant-garde of twenty years
ago has inevitably become the status quo of today, its ageing
groovers part of the establishment. The real impact of the
'60s can only be felt by regressing to the '50s, and from that

vantage point appreciating how much of a breakthrough the following decade was, the real start of the modern era, of the cultural Western world we know today. The '60s only really swung in relation to what went before.

However, a closer examination of the '40s and '50s tends to show that much of what went on in the '60s *had* happened before. Pop art began during the '50s, as did the Campaign for Nuclear Disarmament in Britain, and the folk protest music on both sides of the Atlantic that went with it. Jack Kerouac took his mother on the road in the '50s, when other writers of the beat generation were also producing their most influential works. Even student protest had begun in America in the '50s, with campaigning for civil rights and against the colonising influence of Uncle Sam, and student demonstrations against compulsory reserve army training. Sixties beat music and R 'n' B had its roots even before that, back with the black blues singers of the depression and all sorts of pre-war influences. Smoking cannabis was nothing new either. It was taken up in the '20s by poor Mexican labourers and other immigrant workers (hemp, unlike alcohol, grew wild and free across the USA), and was adopted within a coterie of bohemian intellectuals long before the drug-busting '60s.

Anti-consumerism, anti-materialism and self-sufficiency had all been done 150 years before the hippies by their spiritual ancestor, Henry Thoreau, in Concord, Massachusetts, in 1817. Phenomenology, the fashionable philosophical movement of the '60s, was first conceived at the turn of the century by Edmund Husserl. Karl Popper had sought to discredit empiricism in the '30s, and the New Left movement had also been gradually growing since then. Sartre, the most influential existential philosopher, had turned pro-communist during the war. Although he spent the rest of his life struggling to rationalise his political and philosophical positions, his epitomised the search for personal meaning linked with left-wing politics which hallmarked the late '60s. True, Timothy Leary[2] did take his first trip in August 1960 (and never stopped talking about it for the rest of the '60s), but even LSD (or rather, lysergic acid diethylamide 25) was first synthesised in 1938, by a Swiss biochemist in search of a pain-killer for migraine headaches.

It was not until 1943, however, that Dr Albert Hoffman of Sandoz laboratory in Switzerland accidentally swallowed the drug himself (thus, to use a sixties-ism, blowing his mind). Timothy Leary later wildly asserted that all those born after 1943, effectively into the nuclear and psychedelic age, after the secrets of the atom and of LSD had been revealed, were a special generation. Despite the fact that in so doing he was counting himself out, it was in this crazy notion that Leary grasped the true significance of the sixties.

The '60s could be said to be about what they brought to many of the population—but fitted carpets, central heating, colour TV, cars, HP and high-rise apartment blocks could not possibly convey it. Because what the '60s was truly about, who the '60s really happened to, the people who truly created the '60s by patronising and idolising those who became rich and famous, were the post-war bulge generation, the millions all over Europe and America who lived and played out their adolescent identity crises during the '60s, becoming adults as the decade reached its close.

It also seemed to be the coming of age of the post-war society itself, with all the upheaval and unrest symptomatic of its own growing pains. My generation turned teenagers around 1960. When Lenny Bruce was shocking audiences and being prosecuted for obscenity, we were discovering sex and dirty words and starting to answer our parents back. The pop music scene regenerated itself while we were starting going out and falling in love. The Beatles owe the stir they created all over the world as much to so many young girls in need of a fantasy lover and so many young boys a fantasy hero as to any raw talent they then had. It's no accident, either, that Bob Dylan rose to superstardom in the mid '60s also, when we were beginning to criticise our parents and wanting to put the world to rights; fifteen is apparently the age at which boys feel most concerned about the bomb and political injustice, and girls most concerned about 'human' social problems.

In Britain, in the mid '60s, David Bowie's generation were fighting a battle with parents, headmasters and retired brigadiers, who accused them of looking like girls. Bowie's protest struck the first blow for unisex, for androgyny, for a blurring of the superficial boundaries between the sexes, against the constriction of custom, the holy writ of what was appropriate for the male sex. This was a new generation, who had had an earful of middle class aspirations and respectability, the quiet, neat and tidy post-war garden of security and conformity their parents had tended. They felt impelled to assert their own special identity, cultivating the shadowy and the mysterious, covering spots with curtains of hair to disguise faces parents thought they knew so well; slouching round in jeans and leather jackets when their fathers wanted them to get a decent job, a better start in life than they had had.

The young, now with a bit of pocket money, wanting to assert their individuality among their own anonymous masses, dictated the fashions of the '60s. British teenagers indulged the naive materialism of the middle of the decade, with little interest in the conflicts which were beginning to divide American society, particularly with the onset of bombing over North Vietnam. It may be sheer coincidence that 1965, the year the young men of our generation became eligible for the draft, brought the first burnings of draft cards, and retaliation—a la classification from the Selective Services Commission—for those who persisted. In Britain we knew nothing of military service, we were coasting on cheap meat and butter from the Commonwealth, believing we were still one of the Big Powers and that being snubbed by de Gaulle didn't matter.

Even where no public issue cried out for their attention, the young seemed to need to protest for its own sake. The stolid Dutch weren't afflicted by race problems or colonial wars, yet it was in Amsterdam in the mid '60s that some young 'rebels without a cause' organised for the first time into a political movement, calling themselves the 'Provos'.[3] Even without the irritants of the escalating war in Vietnam, poverty, social injustice, there were millions of teenagers all over the Western world who were passing through that phase known as adolescence, and acting out the syndrome coined by Erik Erikson,[4] since become a ubiquitous catchphrase, the 'identity crisis'.

Erikson maintained that it is not until adolescence that the individual passes through the real crisis of identity, of becoming a person who has attained physical and mental maturity and is required to be socially responsible. Each stage of growth involves vulnerability and anxiety, but Erikson described the 'latency stage' before adolescence as the 'lull before the storm', the storm being the pull between the urge for experimentation and self-discovery and the vulnerability felt by the adolescent in the face of this draughty and dangerous independence. While adolescents are trying to find out who they are as individuals, they are also faced with the struggle and choice of the search for an occupational identity, and tangled urges towards sexual intimacy. They need to reject their parents in order to find themselves, yet this is the time they appear most in need of parental guidance. The intolerance and critical idealism of the young is part of their urge to resist this need, to separate themselves from their parents by amplifying the faults of the adult generation, finding solidarity in shared 'causes'. For Erikson, adolescence was the 'vital regenerator in the process of social evolution'—and in the context of the 1960s he was certainly right.

The most blatant demonstration of moody, recalcitrant adolescents biting the hand which fed them came shortly after the demise of the Provos, as if they had been some sort of scouting party for the way ahead. All over Europe and America, new colleges and universities had been built to accommodate the post-war baby boom, the ultimate investment of the forward looking society, spending much of what it had never had so good on educating its children. It didn't realise what that education would give them. In America, college campuses were becoming centres of dissident demonstration, sit-ins, statement by force of numbers. The anti-Vietnam-war movement spread to Britain and Europe, where the issue seemed to devolve into a parent/child clash, students objecting to files kept on them by the repressive governing bodies *in loco parentis*. It was in France, where the highly structured and rigid school education system gave way to inadequate universities where students crammed into overflowing lecture halls, that the situation exploded, in May 1968.

It began with the Movement of 22 March at the University

of Nanterre, where students felt strongly anti-Vietnam, anti-university, anti-bureaucracy, and oppressed by the representatives of a society which they saw as screwed up and corrupt. After the arrest of a number of student members of the National Vietnam Committee, occupations of the university buildings were organised and students prepared to boycott examinations. Tension escalated and in Paris on 3 May, the Sorbonne authorities called police to arrest the organisers of student meetings. Large numbers then gathered, demanding their release, and were attacked by police with teargas and batons. Their brutal defeat, on the Night of the Barricades, when students resisted police attempts to clear the area, earned the students a moral and tactical victory.

At this point the union movement entered the fray, linking the student demands with those of the workers against the repressive Gaullist regime. By 24 May, approximately 10 million workers were on strike, more than in the 1930s. De Gaulle was forced to call a general election. But, partly because the students had gone back to their studies suddenly worried about their final exams, partly because the May Movement had simply been too spontaneous and too extreme, in the absence of a practical political manifesto, not to burn itself out, the Gaullists were returned with a massive majority and everything slunk back to normal.

Except that nothing could quite be as normal as it had been before. Alain Touraine,[5] professor at Nanterre, concluded that although the May Movement appeared in every respect just a flash in the pan, it somehow destroyed the 'illusion of a society united through growth and prosperity...' and therefore paved the way towards an alternative, as yet without a capital A.

By 1969, campus unrest was deemed in an opinion poll to be America's number one problem. By 1970 the clash between the National Guard and large numbers of student protesters in the US had resulted in deaths. Though 1968 could be said to be the year when the younger generation seriously turned against its elders, it was 1967 around which most of the events of the 1960s seemed to pivot and which more than any other year in that decade brought into focus the effect the 1960s would subsequently have on the world, the end of the post-war world of the '50s and the beginning of the era of the global village. It was, more specifically, the summer of 1967.

Summer 1967 was the season of flower power, but also, with the organising of the anti-war movement in America and the drug busting of the Rolling Stones in Britain, it marked the beginning of the real generational rift, a confrontation between the values of the old and those of the young. Young men who had no intention of risking their necks for a cause they didn't believe in dodged the draft, sneaking over the Canadian border, coming across to London, and suddenly found themselves rebels, fugitives from the law. Sitting around listening to pop records became a much more serious business, not just a hallowed silence while your new stereo record player vibrated to the tones of Cream, Pink Floyd, Jefferson Airplane and everything that was now being described as progressive rock, but a conspiracy of tightly closed curtains, carefully emptied ashtrays and joss sticks burning to mask the strange sickly smell which now tended to waft round at rock concerts and in the cinema after the lights went down.

But something other than a smouldering joint was being passed around, from the summer of '67 onwards. Now the trouble-makers were not simply kicking against authority, like the mods and rockers, before settling down to conform. They weren't interested in smashing telephone kiosks, holding running battles on holiday beaches. Both actively and passively, their aim was to upend the establishment, the anonymous father figure expecting them to follow meekly in his footsteps when he should have been getting out of the old road, because the times were a' changin'. It was natural that students should feel disaffected, unable to get credit in the consumer society, envied and distrusted by those who saw themselves footing the bill for this idle, aristocratic existence. But as American sociologist Kenneth Keniston pointed out, this was also the age of the non-student, the school-leaver who didn't get into college, but hung around the campus and the summer vacation lifestyle, supported on the dole instead of on a grant.

They reflected, more than anything else, the changing

attitude towards careers, of which the summer of '67 somehow became the turning point. A former drama student remembers:

> When I graduated in 1965, your final year was spent making plans for your career and applying for jobs. I went straight into teaching. But when the students I was teaching reached their final year, in '67, suddenly everything had changed. The last thing you would dream of asking them was what career they had in mind. They were all on an inner search for the meaning of life, to understand themselves, which involved taking time off and travelling, trekking off to Istanbul or Marrakesh or treading barefoot round Brighton beach reciting poems on Sunday mornings.

In Britain, 1967 marked the passing of certain Parliamentary reforms concerning the legislation of abortion and homosexuality. In America social reform had to be celebrated more informally, in the sunny climes of California. Summer '67 was the beginning of the quest for 'peace and love' rather than 'work and love', the fascination for Eastern religion, the concern for ecology, recoiling against the damaging effect of what had previously been seen as civilisation and 'progress'. The generation which had grown up under the shadow of the Bomb began harking back, in dress and demeanour, to a more peaceful, pastoral age. But although they personified the identity crisis of the latter half of the twentieth century, it was only a small band, a tiny minority, who actually gave the '60s the indelible image it has today. (See note.[6])

For 90 odd per cent, the vast majority of those growing up during the '60s, the Summer of Love had no greater immediate relevance than the title of a song playing on the juke box after work. To be strictly accurate, the song which reached number one that summer was called 'San Francisco (be sure to wear some flowers in your hair)' sung by Scott McKenzie and played by thousands of people who had no intention of going to San Francisco or wearing flowers in' their hair. While the one or two black sheep from their year at school were dressing in embroidered crushed velvet, getting stoned out of their heads, laid back, knew where it was at, enjoyed whatever was too much, and developed the irritating habit of raising one hand either in a Winston Churchill V-sign or a red Indian salute, with the most patronisingly hollow greeting ever invented—'Peace, man' —huge armies of people who'd sat next to them at school hadn't the slightest idea that another popular song 'Let's go to San Francisco, where the grass grows so very high' meant anything other than that the place hadn't lost its rural charm.

Most of the '60s generation absorbed little more than early adolescent Beatles and the beat scene, and would never have dreamed of joining a demonstration or a sit-in, let alone a love-in or a be-in. Most people, rather than prolong the battle with parents, resolved the adolescent identity crisis by seeking financial independence through work and the adult status that went with it. According to Theodore Lidz,[7] identity crises are more severe in those who reject familiar patterns. He gave the example of women pursuing careers or putting off marriage, but it could just as well have been bearded hippies contemplating their navels, cross-legged, palms up, while the rest of their age group were articled clerks, travelling salesmen and the like.

The majority of men in the sample I interviewed got stuck into earning a living, straight from school, and even those who went to university subsequently settled down into a career. A few had vague dreams of pop stardom, but realised their education was too important to waste. Tony, who had been the singer with a local group but gave up to concentrate upon 'A' levels, had to take his medicine for betraying the group, being beaten up by the bass guitarist, in front of his girlfriend, as he was walking her home. One or two others had the urge to travel, even got as far as buying an old VW van, but most lacked the courage that comes from feeling in good company ('Nobody around me was doing anything like that'), let alone the ready cash.

Consequently by the time they reached their early twenties most had found their 'niche', set on future tramlines by serving an apprenticeship or following some kind of training. The counter culture, by contrast, beckoned those who had all or nothing. It is no accident that the big names

were either milkmen like Joe Cocker, ex-art students like
Brian Eno, or those like Mick Jagger, who left LSE with a
place open if he ever wanted to go back . . .

However better their career prospects compared with
women, the men I interviewed left school largely without
ambition. Going to grammar school had somehow shot
many of them off course, since the education itself was
geared towards academia and the gentlemen's professions.
Consequently many drifted into the first vacancy that came
along, the interview their dad fixed up, the advert in the
newspaper, without any real idea of where that would land
them in ten years' time, let alone forty.

What made it so natural and easy for most young men to
opt for the narrow, alienating path of working life was the
way they took to it, like ducks to water. It was tailor-made for
them, because it was a continuation not of the education they
had received at school, but of the peer group set-up of which
they had become a part. School might not have prepared
them for the world of work, but the peer group had. At work,
they slotted into a similar sort of world of controlled
relationships, bound by set rules, an accepted hierarchical
structure, where you won status by playing the game. They
walked into an all-male atmosphere, where the company
product replaced allegiance to the local football team as the
mutual object of interest and concern and where the skills of
competing with friends and cultivating enemies, of con-
cealing true feelings as well as failings, boasting success and
boosting self-confidence, exactly matched the operational
basis of the commercial world. And the functional necessity
of your role at work finally gave you that sense of security, of
identity, of being something, which had always somehow
ultimately eluded you. Added to that you were safe, you were
expected to be self-defensive, to cultivate relationships
which never came too close, to exchange facts and figures
rather than feelings.

What, though, of the other goal of mature personality
development, the attainment of intimacy, the capacity for
loving and intimate relationships with others? This was not
to be found in the controlled atmosphere of the office. Nor,
although men who joined the forces speak nostalgically of

the camaraderie with their 'oppo' and with the 'lads', was it to be found among the other men at work. Of course most personality theorists indissolubly and exclusively link intimacy with a genital relationship with a member of the opposite sex.

For many men this is a fact which is true, and sad. Their most (and often sole) intimate relationship following that with their mother is the relationship with the first girl they fall in love with, and/or the one they eventually marry. Young men are not constantly seeking out intimacy and relatedness in the way in which young women focus their lives around romance and social links with people they care about. For young men, the ultimate resolution of the Oedipus complex happens almost against their will. The differing attitudes of the sexes towards falling in love reflect their differing fears. Theodore Lidz[7] describes a 'fortress' approach to making an intimate relationship, implying virtually a 'siege mentality', in which he is almost certainly referring to the male experience:

> Now that problems of dependency and symbiotic strivings have been worked through, the boundaries of the self are secure enough for young adults no longer unconsciously to fear losing their identities when they seek after intimacy. They do not fear that a needed person will devour, engulf or annihilate them, or that the loss of the self in orgasm will lead to obliteration . . .

Although the reality of female experience of intimacy has often, in the absence of a valid experience of self-as-other, father-daughter relationship, meant loss of identity, girls will allow this to happen without *fearing* it; the fear of engulfment is a male characteristic, just as seeing all dependency as 'problems' to be worked through is a male approach to intimacy.

Girls will fantasise about the future possibilities of a relationship while they are still getting to know the boy. This is not necessarily a symptom of their dependent status; rather, their dependent status arises in part from their capacity to allow themselves to feel dependent. Young men may fall in love in spite of themselves, yet once it has happened, it is surprising how many men virtually canonise their first love. She was the woman with whom they were at last able to resolve their dilemma, to re-contact early feelings of identification and merger without threat to their own identity, because they were projecting the feminine part of themselves—the part which identifies—on to this person, this other being, this love *object*, and they were thus able to cherish that part of themselves not as something dangerous and threatening within themselves but something which could be valuable because it was apart. For most men this is a tremendously personal experience, not just because they lack the vocabulary to express it, but because loyalty to the peer group demands that they overtly disown it.

Depending very much upon social class, and your particular gang of friends, the mates of mid-teens modify into the 'lads' of late teens and early twenties. With much of the anxiety of adolescence overcome, peer-group confrontations transmute into horseplay, rough and tumble more reminiscent of father-son games than the pushing and shoving of the latency period. The lads gather on neutral territory over a number of pints and indulge in an orgy of backslapping repartee, guaranteed to raise the lowest spirits—but God forbid that anyone mention, other than as a joke, that something is actually getting them down. Problems are voiced with the same glib and hearty bravado that alcohol is consumed; managing to contain drink is as much a ritual initiation into the world of the grown-up male as is containing the emotions which alcohol is likely to release. It is as important for a young man to be able to withstand the tendency of drink to release feelings as it is for him to prove he can withstand its physically incapacitating effects. The crucial concept is control.

Alcohol helps (and is often necessary) to oil the wheels of social intercourse, but emotions must never run out of control, except of course along acceptable lines of expression, meaning anger and violence. One man described how his duffle coat, unknown to him, knocked over another bloke's pint of beer as he was pushing his way out of a pub. For the price of a pint, he was collared outside and had his nose broken. Many men who avoided fights for most of their school career bring out similar late-teens anecdotes, in

which for the sake of your own status you were forced to fight
as a result of a slight (or supposed slight) on someone else's
honour. Luckily your mates usually did their bit by
'restraining' you:

> I don't think I had a fight after I was about eleven, but yes,
> actually, I did have a fight at university. One punch each and
> that was it, before all the rest pulled you apart and you thought
> thank Christ for that. It was one of those visits from the local
> university competing in sporting activities. He was a bit of a
> loud mouth and I'd had a few drinks, and we had words and
> then the shoving started. Yes, I had been in three or four fights
> around that age, now I think about it, one over a girl where I got
> duffed up by a dancehall bouncer who seemed to think she
> belonged to him. I think it's to my credit that I didn't bloody
> well run, I stood and took my medicine.

Socialising with the lads may not always be quite so
blatantly stereotyped, but most young men enter all-male
working worlds which encourage it. And men who work in
totally male establishments seem to continue to indulge the
nudge-and-wink page-three mentality rather more than men
who come into contact with women at work, even though
these women are usually, as one man put it, 'underlings'.
Men who prefer the company of other men explain that you
can't be coarse in front of a woman, or talk about football,
and therefore you can't be yourself; probably in the same way
that women feel they can't share intimate personal
confidences in the presence of a man, although they might be
less likely to refer to it as not being yourself. Other men will
maintain that those who continue to indulge in sexual
innuendo and boasting are juvenile and to be frowned upon.
A real man keeps his feelings to himself.

Gradually the ties with the lads are likely to weaken, as
young men start becoming involved in 'serious' relationships and getting engaged. But rather than a goal of mature
personality development, this is treated as a betrayal of the
group. The lads will joke that marriage is the final
capitulation, loss of freedom. She dragged you into it, sank
her claws in you, you didn't have a chance. The symbolism
of the 'stag' night is the final celebration of freedom, and a

last attempt by the boys to sabotage the wedding, snatch back the defector by showing him what he'll be missing, or making sure he's too ill to be there. Only a hangover is the proper state for the supposedly reluctant bridegroom. All this ritual serves to mask the very real threat that intimacy poses to men, that the bridegroom comes to his wedding day as fearful and naive emotionally as his bride may hitherto have been innocent sexually. Carol Gilligan[8] explains that the world of intimacy appears so mysterious and dangerous to men because their hierarchical ordering of relationships dissolves the interconnecting network of relationships whereby women sustain safe connection to others. This difference in structuring relationships means that one defines as dangerous that which the other defines as safe. Women fear damage to the web of interconnectedness, being abandoned, left, 'stranded', whereas men fear entanglement in the web, being trapped, stifled, 'caught'.

Male fear of commitment in relationships stems from men's very early and unresolved fear of engulfment by the female, by their primary identification figure. One man explained that he grew up vowing he would never marry because of 'fear of the vestry'. As a boy he noticed that after the ceremony the couple would disappear together into the vestry. He had no idea why, but whatever went on in there, he really didn't fancy it.

Recent research by American psychiatrists at Duke University, North Carolina, concentrated upon three prospective bridegrooms who played the Space Invaders computer game four times more than usual (up to fifteen times a week) in the weeks preceding the ceremony. One man delayed his honeymoon by an hour in order to get in a few more games and another man always had a game before seeing the psychiatrist because he knew he would have to talk about his impending marriage. Space Invaders necessitates shooting down aliens invading one's own planet, but however many are destroyed, more appear and eventually overwhelm the player. Dr Donald Ross and his team[9] felt that having to compulsively re-enact being taken over by an alien force, was highly significant:

> We believe that each man's obsession with playing Space

Invaders was a means of handling his anger over the recent commitment to marriage. The disintegration of invading aliens who were trying to overrun the 'home base' took on symbolic significance.

While continuing all practical arrangements they were trying to repel the threat of invasion. The fiction that men sustain in front of 'the boys' because they cannot bring themselves to admit personal vulnerability, real feeling, and have no language for it, is reinforced by the very real fear which harks back to their inadequately resolved gender identity crisis.

The film, *A Kind of Loving*, taken from Stan Barstow's novel and released in 1962, caricatured the state of play between the sexes for much of the decade to come. Vic and Ingrid are physically attracted to one another, but feel most at home with their same-sex friends, although Ingrid is sure that she is in love with Vic. Horsing around with the other lads in the office, ogling the talent in pin-up magazines, Vic keeps in mind the idea of marrying someone sympathetic, sensible, intelligent, a friend, just like his sister.

Ingrid, by implication, comes into the category of the kinds of girls you go to bed with but never marry. While Vic lusts after Ingrid, his feelings fluctuate. Sometimes he thinks he loves her; at other times he cannot stand the sight of her. His mates call her the 'preying mantis', because she runs after him when he tries not to see her, unable, in her direct, female way, to understand his hot-and-cold behaviour. After sleeping with her, Vic suddenly withdraws into the company of his mates, cuts her dead, leaving Ingrid feeling hurt and rejected. Having exorcised his desire through conquest, satisfied his passions, Vic now makes up his mind he wants to travel, find more in life than his mum and dad settled for, in true '60s style. At which point, at a dance, Ingrid corners him to whisper, also in true '60s style, that 'Something which should have happened, hasn't'. 'Well, you've got me now,' he remarks bitterly, and settles down to married life in the home of his mother-in-law. Both women seem to side against him, expecting him to share their fireside TV quiz domesticity when he still wants to get out and about. Even when Vic and Ingrid start afresh with a flat of their own, you are left with the suspicion that he will still be stumbling in drunk at night, to her disapproving gaze. Neither is to blame, they are simply handcuffed by the start of sexual liberation yet pulled apart by their separate sex role upbringing.

*A Kind of Loving* paints a gloomy picture of the relationship between the sexes in the early part of the '60s. Most of the men in my sample married in their mid-twenties, about a decade later, when things had perhaps changed slightly. One or two men did seem to have a rather exploitative attitude towards women, marrying when they seemed in need of a housekeeper/mother figure rather than a meaningful relationship, and quite a few couples' lives seemed set on a path of polarisation, each with their own interests and their own friends. However, an equally significant number of men described their wife as their best friend and indicated their preference for 'mixed company', although this often meant socialising with the husbands of their wives' friends or not having any real friends at all, outside the family circle. The myth of the battle between the sexes seems hard to eradicate. Men would comment, almost in passing, 'You tend to run your wife down in front of your friends'; men who were happily family-centred described dropping occasionally into the local to be greeted by 'She let you out, then, did she?'

Most men, however much they had left behind the 'night out with the lads', carried on playing similar games at work. Contrary to what many people think, most men aren't very ambitious. Only a small number of the men I met claimed they were playing to win, to get to the top. And some of these men pointed out that they weren't *really* ambitious, otherwise they would be the MD by now. Most men were working their way up the ladder because it was expected, because, in one man's words, they needed the status among other men: 'It's nice to introduce yourself to strangers as a *manager*.' Status, because of the hierarchy, matters a great deal. Family life becomes secondary, a back-up support system to *real* life, the wheeler-dealer games played at work. Family life is still life: clean never crying children, beaming, immobilised wife, quick frozen in the photographs so many men have beside them on the desk. Is this how they prefer it, neatly, safely, parcelled into compartments?

Men who have opted to remain at a working level they enjoy (usually it means more contact with people) begin to feel the pressures of loss of status. They express them in jokes, in the relief they show on finding a subordinate who is actually older than they are. They explain defensively their reasons for preferring personal satisfaction to power, salary and status. Only a tiny handful of men had dared take the risk of losing status by switching careers. What moved them to do it? Some described feeling like a 'round peg in a square hole', like Graham who followed his rejecting father into the police force. As a child, it had been the image of his father he had tried to emulate, pedalling round in his little car, and he joined the force with little other thought than that he would get a squad car of his own. A series of events led to him dropping out to become a social work trainee, going back home:

> The final straw was over a statement about some kid I'd nobbled for housebreaking. I can remember expressing all sorts of opinions about why he'd done it, reasons back in the home, and I can remember my inspector chucking it back at me and saying he wanted it totally rewriting, he just wanted the facts that he'd done it proved. But I just thought no, I can't tolerate this any longer. If I can see a reason I want to be able to talk about it and try and tackle it. You've got to start asking why ... I did find it, and still do, very difficult to be authoritarian, much rather just have a chat to somebody and say on your way, now. But as a young policeman there is so much pressure, they have this chart of arrests called top of the pops and if you didn't appear on this they wanted to know why. I left the force at the end of the '60s. My mother subsidised me at home and all my friends changed then. Going into social work, as far as the police is concerned, is joining the other side.

Other men were supported for a time, while they retrained, by working wives, but Geoff, who changed careers at twenty-six did it all with a wife and two children to support. He'd been a successful accountant, second only to the finance director and with a staff of thirty, at the age of twenty-four:

But I would look at myself, take the roof off the company and see myself sitting in my office, paper flying round the firm, attending meetings, and I really didn't see this as what I was going to do for the rest of my life. I felt I wanted to be more involved with people than figures. So I took an incremental view of it, because I had a family to support: what are the options, given my qualifications, and are any of them appealing?

Geoff had done a bit of teaching, saw a job advertised at a provincial polytechnic and applied for it. He'd meanwhile been headhunted for another accounting job, so the salary, when he started as a business studies lecturer, meant an 18 per cent drop:

The biggest bonus of my time is the flexibility, the freedom. I could get more money, but at the end of the day I wouldn't be a satisfied person. It's improved the intellectual muscles considerably, but also my perspectives have changed; no, wrong word, developed. For that I'm eternally grateful. I've been able to address myself to more important issues for me, self-development, rather than worrying about whether the figures will be got out on time this week. I have more time for the family and working with people has made me more able to cope with people. I'm more open, more tolerant, and I can understand the kids' quirks a bit better than if I hadn't had everyday contact with people.

You dress how you want to dress. Most days I ride in on my bike. I would say I'm as close to being myself as I could be in any position. I'm very ambitious, but not for status or self-aggrandisement, for personal development.

Interestingly, all the men who had switched careers moved into people-oriented, traditionally female occupations, like social work, community relations, and teaching. They all talked about self-development and the need for personal honesty, as opposed to material ambition and tough reliability. They all stressed the need for empathy and the ability to examine one's personal weaknesses. As Graham put it:

I can express a great deal of myself at work. I've always had a great fondness for the human race. I like people, they fascinate me. In this job you need tolerance, kindness, understanding and patience, those sorts of things. That's why I left the police force, because I couldn't express them.

These men may be pioneers, but the move they have made, largely within a conventional lifestyle, was made possible by the real pioneers, the small number of young men during the late '60s who opted for no career at all.

Although the two most widespread movements which have grown out of the counter culture have been the ecology movement and the modern women's movement, the most significant aspect of '67 was the way it seemed to mark rejection of the male role in all its aspects—protector, provider, active aggressive ambitious go-getter. It was a rejection of repressive and alienating hierarchies, of deference to authority and power, of exploitation of others for the purposes of self-aggrandisement, and of unnecessary restrictions of personal freedom, such as being at someone else's beck and call eight hours a day, five days a week, fifty weeks a year. Having tasted the freedom of the long summer vacation, travelling with a backpack on the savings of a few weeks' casual labour, who wanted to sit in an office all day waiting to grow old?

A few young men deduced that the cost of success simply did not measure up to the rewards it offered, and the corruption it entailed, because winning the game meant the defeat and oppression of others. The counter culture began to emphasise traditionally female preoccupations, nurturing and caring attitudes towards others, and female preserves, hanging around the house rather than going out to work, even if it didn't encourage much in the way of domesticity.

But who were the drop-outs of the late '60s, the ones who turned their backs on male privilege, the male role? Essentially they were the increasing numbers of sixth formers who left home to become students, persuaded that they were the *crème de la crème*, that with a degree the world would be at their feet, or else already seduced by the glamorous image of the bohemian student lifestyle. Patricia Cayo Sexton bemoaned in *The Feminized Male*[10] that middle class education had a feminising effect upon those who conformed to its goals. The longer, therefore, that young men were exposed to its influence, the greater one would presume would be the feminising effect. In the UK, between the mid '50s and the mid '60s, the total number of male students in fulltime higher education doubled from 55 000 to 112 000. In the USA, between 1900 and 1970, the average length of education increased by more than six years.[11] This elongation of the education process not only subjected a sizeable proportion of the male student population to further 'feminising influence'; it created, as far as the identity crisis was concerned, a hiatus, rather than a clean resolution of the dilemma by wading into the adult world of work.

The male undergraduate had been promised that the world would be at his feet (this was before inflation of numbers reduced the market value of the degree certificate). As a student he became an independent adult yet remained with the inferior status of a child in many respects, labelled as shiftless and irresponsible. In a sense this was the perfect solution to the identity crisis. The vagaries, dependencies and restrictions of childhood were left behind, yet the responsibilities and risks of adulthood were still around the corner. The peer group was alive and kicking rather than dispersed on to the bottom rungs of separate hierarchical structures. Student life was a reprieve, a breathing space and the longer it lasted the more, for some, it encouraged the desire to put off the terrible choices of facing up to the responsibility of becoming an adult.

Students may have been their parents' pride and joy, but landladies didn't trust them. They were a class apart, the privileged and yet also the disaffected, the alienated, the outsiders. Outwardly they were at odds with the society that had sponsored them. Inwardly, psychically, they were in suspended animation. Although Theodore Lidz[7] was very much more concerned with the tribulations of the female adolescent, he made a telling point about such a hold-up in the resolution of the identity crisis: 'When the forward flow of the stream is halted, much old debris can float to the surface.'

For young men, this 'old debris' was the remains of their inadequate resolution of the early gender identity crisis.

As the clever ones, academic high achievers were more likely to have gone through school avoiding the hierarchy of physical intimidation or failing to find status within it. They found themselves expressing the long-buried conflicts and needs of their earlier identity crisis, without the convenient displacement of directing their energies into the conventional work-oriented persona, in the way that most young men of their generation were doing. Much of the late '60s rebellion can be seen as an expression of the conflict between the image of their own fathers and the public expression of masculinity.

Although most personality development theorists pass over the specific problems of young men, Kenneth Keniston (who made his reputation as a sociologist by charting the progress of the American '60s generation) identified different types of adherents to the counter culture, depending on the personalities and involvement of their fathers. (See note.[12]) His analysis differentiated between the alienated personality, drawn to the drug culture and the 'peace and love' ideology, and the protest-prone personality, dabbling in left-wing politics, minority-group rights and against the Vietnam war. He also studied, in 1966, a category which would subsequently never have quite the same meaning— the college drop-outs. He found these young men agitated about a 'spoiled' identification with their fathers. In their search for a new self, they were constantly either praising or criticising their fathers, to whom they had once felt close. Or else they were struggling to come to terms with a father they had only recently realised was inadequate, weak or otherwise unacceptable as a masculine role model. The protest-prone personalities also frequently portrayed their fathers as weak and unsuccessful, and expressed what Keniston describes as a 'schism' in the paternal image—the desire to reconcile 'nice' father with the 'tough' public image of masculinity (although some of the protest-prone young men claimed idyllic relationships with their fathers). The alienated personality, on the other hand, complained of an ineffectual, absent father, rather than a soft caring one. All the young men described their deepest ties as with their mothers. What Keniston failed to analyse, while he was about it, was the gender role identification of these young men and how well, during their school years, they had fitted the norm of masculine role preference and adoption. If he had, he might have discovered that the men with the caring fathers felt torn between the personal and the public, whereas the young men whose fathers had been ineffectual and absent felt themselves lost within the public image of masculinity. (See p. 121 note 21.)

The counter culture offered a resolution of these conflicts, by allowing repressed anger against inadequate fathers to surface. The counter culture, by siding with the indians, created a powerful ideological contradiction to the patriarchal male and the kind of masculinity which grew out of what Charles Reich, in *The Greening of America*[1] called Consciousness II. (See note.[13]) And as Reich pointed out, its adherents didn't need to mug up on this kind of enlightenment but simply join forces with it, and get carried along. For the stream was now moving, debris and all.

Although there was no need to study for enlightenment, just as there was no need to question anyone with long hair, the disaffection of students was no doubt encouraged by the tendency of college education to foster the questioning of established values and attitudes. In 1968 William G. Perry Jr[14] felt the time was right to publish a late '50s/early '60s study of students' attitudes. The questioning that is encouraged by a liberal arts education because of the need to consider a variety of points of view, colours the student's whole frame of reference. One student listened to the first lecture as if it was the word of God, until someone said 'Well, so what?' Another student described the first year as 'the tearing away of a lot of beliefs in what has been imposed by convention... I'm (laughs) not trying to drum it up into an emotional issue...' But it was an emotional issue.

The counter culture seemed to be allied to a growing realisation among some of the establishment of the inadequacy of the disciplines on which the male psyche prided itself: the logical, the empirical, the objective, the detached. Back when Perry's students were at college, C. P. Snow[15] had described the growing schism between the separate worlds of the scientist and the literary intelligentsia, warning of the dangers of this splitting and specialising which often began at the tender age of twelve or thirteen.

In his follow-up to *Contrary Imaginations*, in 1968, Liam Hudson[16] took issue with Snow (and to a certain extent with his own previous work) by challenging the two categories of 'arts' man and 'scientist', the one the guardian of sensibility, imagination and artistic appreciation, the other rational and devoid of moral conscience, dedicated to the pursuit of objectivity. Hudson felt the split to be more between technologists (those applying scientific principles and therefore like 'convergers', concerned with practical action) and intellectuals, freer in thought not tied to deed, whether studying literature or physics. Hudson did however acknowledge that 'convergers' were more likely to be attracted into the sciences and 'divergers' into arts subjects.

His most interesting discovery, however, was that although scientists as a group embodied, in Angus Wilson's phrase, that 'masculinity demanded conventionally in our own day of those who call themselves men', they were less and less attractive as models of masculinity. His study, concurring with early '60s American research, showed that students saw scientists as materialistic, shallow, dull and decidedly unsuccessful with the opposite sex. Hudson's seventeen-year-old schoolboys were attracted to an ideal self which was 'warm, exciting, imaginative, manly, dependable, intelligent'. Scientists were manly all right, but arts graduates much more sophisticated and successful with the opposite sex. (Today, attitudes may well have veered back towards the scientist. Since J. D. Watson (see note[17]) reestablished the image of the scientist as glamorous explorer, the rapid developments in computer science have conjured up brilliant young magician whizz kids, out there on the outer limits of technology making lots of money producing miracle new machines.)

Back in the '60s Hudson saw an opposition between pleasure and value, that conventional masculinity was becoming a minor puritan virtue while 'femininity' looked more attractive. He noticed that his 'divergers' were more prone to *feelings* of depression or guilt, whereas 'convergers' tended towards *symptoms* of touchiness and restlessness, indicating too much emotional control. And he remarked that instructions seemed to set the 'converger' at ease:

> He cannot proceed, especially into areas of emotional expres-
> sion, without clear and authoritative route signs [which] not
> only allow [him] to plan his journey they also shift the
> responsibility for travelling in the first place.

He remarked that the swing from science in favour of
psychology and sociology, noticed in England, West
Germany, the Netherlands and Australia during the late
'60s, reflected the increase in affluence, the relaxation of
censorship and public prudery, an increasing concern with
self-determination, and the relaxation of sex roles.

While Hudson was persuading his 'convergers' to think
like 'divergers', Edward de Bono was exploring the
limitations of rational analytical deductive reasoning in
favour of what he described as lateral thinking, a free
associative problem-solving technique. A certain Professor
Kazimierz Dabrowski[18] at the University of Alberta, was
advocating personality shaping through what he called
Positive Disintegration, arguing that much mental illness
was actually a symptom of healthy development. Similarly,
R. D. Laing was in the process of questioning accepted
diagnoses and treatment of mental illness. And continental
philosophy remained critical of the objective approach,
claiming it was simply a rather restricted illusion.

All these arguments came to a head within the trendy new
departments of psychology and sociology. At my own
university, Liverpool, it became a successful takeover, the
existential phenomenologists banishing the structural
functionalists to the department of economics. Whereupon
we were confidently informed that everything we had learnt
in the previous year was a load of rubbish. There is, of
course, no greater way of sharpening the critical faculties
than to have one respected authority denounce another. And
as Charles Hampden-Turner confidently asserted in *Radical
Man*, it was within the social science departments that the
protest-prone personality was encouraged to develop. (See
note.[19]) Theodore Roszack, who wrote about *The Making of
a Counter Culture*,[20] and concluded that the student lifestyle
itself created the radical alternative because youth had
become such a 'long-term career', endorsed this theory:

In England, Germany, and France, the most troublesome students are those who have swelled the numbers in the humanities and social studies, only to discover that what society really wants out of its schools is technicians, not philosophers.

Hampden-Turner's *Radical Man* is an interesting, if somewhat indigestible, manifesto of the rebellion against scientific method. He explained that although scientists argued that only objectivity can be validated, most existentialists regarded objectivity as nothing more than a consensus among investigators as to how a phenomenon is to be regarded and measured. He denounced the safe compartmentalisation of science, which, by dissecting, kills that which it seeks to understand. *Radical Man* claimed to attempt a reconciliation between formal disciplines and human relevance, by cutting across the division between arts and science. Its title may now seem sexist, but it was advisedly so, for with his highflown language Hampden-Turner was saying something particularly relevant to men. He proposed a model of psychosocial development, including the quality, in his radical man, of 'suspending his cognitive structures and *risking* himself in trying to *bridge the distance* to the others...' They are his italics. He proposed that:

> The existential knower cannot by definition practise the traditional scientific detachment. He is studying relational facts, the attempt to detach himself could destroy these. Even where he is observing the mutuality of others, the source of his insight will run dry with the source of his concern, since his own feelings and powers of identification are important clues to the shared human condition...

But a certain kind of detachment *was* necessary:

> In order to understand others one must achieve at least a momentary suspension of self-concern in order to comprehend *their* perspectives—to switch from self-involvement to other involvement. A man with the... capacity to understand why his most cherished idea is a dead duck from the perspectives of his listeners is still attached to human concerns.

Hampden-Turner was conveying the need for men to

cultivate the 'feminine', develop their capacity for empathy and reach the part of themselves which could acknowledge and utilise feeling rather than repressing or denying it. The student revolt of the late '60s and the counter-culture values represented a radical attempt among young men to rediscover themselves as whole human beings, by redefining masculinity, in the interests of personal development. (See note.[21])

Talcott Parsons, a sociological theorist influential in the '50s and '60s, extended Erikson's concept of inner and outer space to describe male self-expression as 'instrumental', meaning directed towards the manipulation of objects, and female self-expression as 'expressive', meaning more concerned with feelings, opinions, relationships and decorative self-expression. Hippie culture rejected work, the traditional instrumental male expression of self, and embraced expressivity to the ultimate degree, as Fred Davis noticed:[22]

> One has only to encounter the lurid *art nouveau* contortions of the hippie posters and their Beardsleyan exoticism, or the mad mélange of hippie street costume—Greek sandalled feet peeking beneath harem pantaloons encased in a fringed American Indian suede jacket, topped by pastel floral decorations about the face—or the sitar whining cacophony of the folk rock band, to know immediately that one is in the presence of *expressiveness* for its own sake.

In *An Essay on Liberation*,[23] Herbert Marcuse extolled the growing opposition to the 'repressive continuum' he had outlined in the earlier *One Dimensional Man* as 'the ascent of life instincts over aggressiveness and guilt', expressed in the sensuousness of long hair, and the release of libidinal energy. He saw co-operation, the hippie ideal, as the social expression of the liberated work instinct.

Becoming a whole person, however, was not just a matter of eating wholefoods, and contacting and expressing the hitherto neglected and denigrated, repressed and stunted feminine side of yourself, was not as simple as letting your hair grow.

Richard Neville, in *Playpower*,[24] talks about the relationship between the sexes being free and easy and uncomplicated, purely physical pleasure, and if anything else grows out of that, fine; if not, also fine. The rest of his book is devoted to extolling the superiority of young people over their fucked-up, repressed, inhibited and hypocritical elders. As one young man admitted to Kenneth Keniston, the worst possible sin for the young was having to admit to a hang-up. You were not supposed to betray anything that implied lack of confident control and easy acceptance of the actions of others. All that was necessary was peace, love and long hair, and everyone would get on 'beautifully'. There would be no need for discord or uncomfortable difficulties in relationships; people either wanted to be together because they dug one another, or they didn't dig, so they moved on.

In *Woman's Consciousness, Man's World*,[25] Sheila Rowbotham explains how she sensed something very complicated going on in the heads of young men around her in the late '60s. How there seemed a split in their minds between their ideals of equality and their actual treatment of women, how playing it cool really stood for being selfish and condescending. She also noticed the odd way in which young men split women into sex objects, the fanciable and the fuckable, or comrades, women who were ersatz men, as if they couldn't conceive of women as whole sexual and intellectual human beings. Yet at the same time their songs showed they were very scared of the threat the new women's movement posed to the old way of being one of the boys. Here the sexes were mixing more, with looser, less role-defined relations with one another. But women glided more easily through the familiar territory of peace and love and personal honesty.

These young women of the '60s generation found that sexual liberation often meant a disturbing tendency among young men to leap out of bed soon after they had leapt into it. What the young women had felt was a promising beginning to a potential relationship and the fascination of getting to know one another in the process, became 'See you around' in the cold light of morning, when last night's lover couldn't wait to get out of the door. This disappointment on the part of the women could simply be interpreted as female dependence, the inability to recognise a no-go area in a relationship, an emotional cul-de-sac, but one man who had been on the edge of all that sexual freedom described it in a different way:

> With me, I know exactly what it was. I used to get that awful bad taste depressed feeling after sex, as if something had been spoilt. It was very easy to connect the girl with that and decide you just had to avoid her at all cost, in case she started getting clingy. But, for me at any rate, I reckon it was to do with the fear of letting anyone really close, of somebody really knowing you. Because you had exposed yourself totally physically, you had to shut yourself off mentally and emotionally. It was an automatic reaction to women—screw them, but don't let them come near you because they just cause complications and bring out messy feelings, screw things up. Of course, now it's all turned round the other way. It's easy to make friends with women and much harder to make a move towards them physically, so I'm now experiencing the problem from the other way round. It took me a bloody long time to realise it was a problem. I think it was only when all my mates, the men around me, were getting into steady relationships that I began to think perhaps it was *me* that was wrong, not them. I think men swallowed all that West Side Story romantic crap of seeing the girl of your dreams across a dance floor, just that they never admitted it. And instead of, like girls, thinking every man was going to be Mr Right, as a bloke, you made sure every girl wasn't the One, the perfect woman.

It took the young men a long time to realise they might be making mistakes in relationships. They were so used to playing the game to win, getting their kicks from conquests rather than real fulfilment. Some men of the '60s generation still haven't realised it. I talked to a musician living in a chenille- and velvet-draped time warp, who had had plenty of one-night-stands but never a committed relationship with a woman 'because the right one hasn't turned up yet'. He would know her when he saw her, he assured me, 'because I've been in love once and I know how it feels. I was fifteen, I fell in love with a girl I met on holiday. We never saw one another again.'

No wonder many women of my acquaintance, including myself, wasted their energies battering themselves like mesmerised moths against the emotional plate glass wrapped around so many of the young men they met, wondering why they couldn't reach the light they saw inside. They complained constantly of the power games it seemed necessary to play with men, not realising that games were the only relationship skills they had been taught. Regardless of how much they mouthed about honesty and openness and cooperation, they sat inside a protective layer—not so much of glass, perhaps, as of toughened steel. And, as in the motto Richard Nixon had on his desk in the late '60s ('When the going gets tough, the tough get going') their protection meant that they could always move on, when they hit a rough spot in a relationship. It was the other person, nothing to do with themselves.

Erik Erikson[26] correctly surmised that

> ... the youth who is not sure of his identity shies away from interpersonal intimacy or throws himself into acts of intimacy which are 'promiscuous' without true fusion or real self-abandon.

However, promiscuity is mostly dealt with as a problem for girls, a desperate search for affection. Its far more frequent occurrence among young men, for opposite reasons (escaping from intimacy), is usually interpreted as normal acting out of the male role.

The concern for promiscuous girls reflects the risks that they are likely to run. For girls of the '60s generation, this was a fear with which they lived constantly, before the pill was widely available, and often had to keep to themselves, because of the no-strings basis upon which many of their liaisons were built. It wasn't fashionable to want to trap your man; nor did you particularly want to be trapped yourself. More than any other moral issue, the decision to have an abortion reflected a highly significant turning point for women, a personal dilemma which they often could not resolve without going against the traditional female moral stance of denying oneself and thinking of the hurt to others. The unwanted invasion of their bodies, the unthinkable prospect of having to face the consequences of having an illegitimate baby, propelled more and more girls into the self-protective expediency of an abortion, against all the 'feminine' values they had grown up with. More than anything else, it created an unbridgeable rift between mothers and daughters; the one secret you never told.

The equivalent dilemma which alienated young men from their fathers and everything that conventional masculinity represented, mainly faced young Americans. (See note.[27]) The 'protest-prone' personalities studied by Kenneth Keniston,[12] in 1967, were those taking part in a plan of campaign called 'Vietnam Summer'. With the bombing and the escalation of the war in all its brutality visible in people's living rooms, student anti-war groups had gradually been growing. At a Vietnam teach-in, televised at the University of Virginia in February 1967, one student confessed:

> I have the problem of realising the attitude of my parents, especially my father. I am certain that he would consider any refusal of mine to participate as nothing but cowardice, lack of patriotism, and it's a dilemma I just hope I don't have to face. And there's a possibility I won't have to face it, because I will be in school until I'm twenty-six.

Despite increasing draft calls, college students could avoid military service while they remained in school. Most who were drafted obeyed the call, although some fled the country and others engineered failing the medical. Others stayed to fight, burning their draft cards or joining an organisation called the Resistance. (See note.[28])

As the war escalated, 5000 protestors clashed with troops at the Pentagon, but by late 1967, for the first time, a poll indicated that the majority of Americans considered the war a mistake. Jerry Rubin, of the Youth International (Yippie) Party described the struggle as between young people and the menopausal middle-aged men running the country, but after the riots at the Democratic Convention in Chicago, in 1968, attempts were made to move the protest away from its campus base and out into the community, more moderately, so that ordinary people would feel they could align themselves to it. In November 1969 President Nixon appeared on television to make his famous reference to 'the great silent majority, my fellow Americans', but the war continued to be discredited, with the trial of those held responsible for the My Lai massacre, when a company of eighteen to twenty-year-old Americans, newly arrived in Vietnam, gave in to what Erik Erikson later described as 'an easy pattern of violence', killing innocent civilians when they couldn't find an enemy. (See note.[29])

The American population at large continued to regard the student protestors as unpatriotic cowards, but an increasing number of GIs were returning, decorated and disabled, from their tour of duty, to denounce the macho game they had willingly played.

Many young GIs in Vietnam resorted to drugs to numb their sensibilities, but there was also a stereotypically male defensive denial of danger, particularly among helicopter ambulance crews who were often exposed to great danger, yet commented 'I do not see what stress we are under...'[30] Other men reacted to the opposite extreme, exaggerating the danger of every sortie and therefore creating a myth of their own invincibility, turning their fear into its opposite, since they actually did perform great acts of heroism. The denial of stress, which transformed sensitive men into insensitive technicians, was medically substantiated by testing the release of stress hormones which actually decreased as men began to adapt to danger. It was like World War II all over again, fostering the belief that dependence on others was a sign of weakness, that aggression should be used to deal with any threat, including the displaced aggression of flaring up at one's own comrades.

However, the loss of life during the longest war in America's history was not entirely in vain. Three things emerged from the Vietnam war, which were to have a positive effect upon the more lethal aspects of the male role. A considerable number of young men, regardless of those who answered the call, denounced personal glory at the expense of human life, struggled to develop adult self-respect without resorting to a trial by fire initiation to *prove* that they were men. Secondly, as commentaries from medical teams show,[30] official recognition was growing that war was not the ultimate test of manhood, but a severe psychological stress situation, to be catered for by attempting to relieve and reduce the stress long enough for it to be tolerable. In most other wars, the only (honourable) way out was death, injury or the end of the war. Vietnam introduced the 'tour of duty' in which young men were persuaded to stick it out, knowing that at the end of a year or so they could go back home. Improved communications (telephone calls home), also dispelled the idea which had been emphasised during World War II, that men rallied round their 'buddies' for emotional support. The men in Vietnam looked 'back home' for emotional support.

Lastly, the war exposed the unacceptable face of Reich's Consciousness II—which dealt with any threat by denial and aggression—hastening the arrival of the more humane and gentle Consciousness III, the much publicised dawning of the Age of Aquarius.

In 1969 the musical *Hair* celebrated every aspect of the younger generation's creed, from drugs and long hair to guerrilla warfare and racial harmony. It included a pop lament called 'Easy to be hard', in which a young woman bemoans the fact that the man she fancies only cares about the 'bleeding crowd', because it's easier. Men were pouring all the emotion and expressive care they were rediscovering in themselves into a safe repository, the Generalised Other, rather than risk expressing it in close relationships. The counter culture became for some just another alibi, as perfect as the working environment behind which other men hid their emotions. The principle that you shouldn't express any needs which were likely to conflict with another person (ie might create explosive contact) effectively stifled any expression of need. By playing it cool you played it down and the apparent spontaneity was in fact tremendously controlled, superficial and self-centred, a means of getting along with others, just as living communally meant safety in numbers.

Young men also faced the disturbing prospect of honestly encountering themselves through intimacy with a woman, rather than bolstering bluff confidence as they did with their mates. One man remembered telling his girlfriend of two years (whom he was leaving for someone he had just met) that he hated her because she knew him too well, meaning that he hated and couldn't face himself. Erik Erikson made the point that intimacy is difficult to achieve if there is too little or too much of its counterpoint, which he called 'repudiation'. Between the sexes in the late '60s, one side had too little of this ingredient, the other side had too much. The identity-hungry person, according to Erikson, in reaching out for an intimate relationship is actually not ready for it but is simply looking for narcissistic reassurance, trying to reach themselves and in the process indulging in genital combat in order to defend themselves. Having successfully repudiated one relationship, the sufferer simply carries on to the next, in the naive assumption that all will work out well this time. Sometimes it did, if the woman made no demands. (See note.[31])

Growth entails stepping outside one's defences and becoming vulnerable. But young men were scared to step out of their depth emotionally, and young women, accustomed to diving in at the deep end, could not recognise a fear they themselves did not feel, because the male would never admit it even to himself. Derek Bowskill and Anthea Linacre[32] describe men as trapped behind a mask of arrogance and the effort needed to keep up a pretence of invulnerability, particularly where sex is concerned:

> Scalphunters live and die lonely; isolated in a network of false relationships they neither meet nor know another person, and their world is peopled by the crippled objects of their sexist thinking, kept alive by those who make their money from the commercial products of a culture dominated by titillating, sexy chauvinism.

They quote Anna Raeburn as saying:

> For most people it's a damned sight easier to take their clothes off and get into bed with someone than it is to take their mental clothes off and reveal themselves as a person.

All the joyful and eloquent idealism of radical man could not make it any easier to cast off the pretence and defence they had grown up with. Yet they were being moved to try, and many a PhD thesis at many an American university concerned itself with the question why. Why should young men wish to throw away their power and privilege? A research project in Philadelphia, with a grant from the National Institute of Mental Health, studied commune-dwellers, between 1966 and 1969, as if they were some rare South American tribe.[33] It had started life as a study of drug-takers, but, as these middle class kids moved away from hassle from their parents, into pads and communes, the researchers followed.

Not only were communes predominantly male (a ratio of three or four to one), but 'chicks' weren't officially counted as commune members. So the researchers had to ask 'And how many chicks?' Given the intrusion, often late at night, of a psychiatrist, a social worker, a psychologist and an anthropologist, one should perhaps view what they observed with a pinch of salt. But they maintained that while little was done in the way of cleaning or cooking (unless some 'chick' took it upon herself to dispense tea or boiled brown rice for breakfast), a great deal of time was devoted to the playing of games. These games were virtually compulsive, excluded chicks and involved competitive sport and rough and tumble which was taken very seriously... *Plus ça change*, one might conclude. The researchers commented that although girls appeared to be accepted as intellectual equals and there was no bragging or boasting about sexual conquests, nevertheless the status of commune women was that conjured up by their nickname, something between an object and a pet animal, which conveniently provided food. Ultimately, surrounded at 1am by stoned heads swaying to rock music, feeling slightly *de trop*, the researchers record calling it a day and thankfully going home.

The attraction of cannabis, rather than alcohol or speed, testified to the desire of these young men, the alienated of Keniston's analysis, to escape from the macho, dominant, aggressive male culture into the shared fusion inspired by music. The striking thing also about marijuana is that its effects include intensity of sensual experience, almost as if its smokers were desperately trying to dissolve that thick layer of defensiveness which muffled their sensitivity. Similarly, the effects of LSD and mescalin include loss of the boundaries of the self, a synthetic means of achieving the ego boundary merger which young men found so difficult. The trouble with the drug culture was that it was a short cut to the kind of maturity which has to be hard won in the fray of real experience of life.

The young latched on to drugs, partly out of the need to shock and rebel against parents, partly out of the desire to transcend the dullness of suburban life, partly because it was a passport to sophistication, partly because they were simply young and eager to experiment and this was what society had left lying around, and partly because they wanted to heal the open wound of their difficulties in coming to terms with the twin goals of mature personality development—love and work. So they searched and found meaning in the distortion of perception which appeared to lift them on to a higher plane of awareness. Interestingly, included among the ravings of those who propounded drug-taking as a spiritual panacea, is Timothy Leary's attack (*The Politics of Ecstasy*[2]) on the expression of emotion. He extols serene self-composure through pill-popping; meaning, by self-composure, confident self-control, the closing of the cast-iron gates of defensiveness yet again.

Essentially this sort of prescription was the same old superficial hearty macho positivism (a naive recognition of where most men had left off, aged three), but Leary's recipe for self-development was to let go, achieve harmony through chemistry, through the mind. In *The Pop Process*,[34] Richard Mabey points out that most pop songs of the late '60s sang about the 'mind' in the way that previous singers had sung about their hearts. Whereas girls fastened on to the myth of perfect romantic ecstasy, still in touch with the bliss of that first fusion of connectedness, the primary relationship, the boy is loose in a dark maze where he imagines the minotaur to be lurking. He reaches for the weapon he knows he has, his rationality, and looks for ecstasy through his mind. Leary condemned emotions as the lowest form of con-sciousness because they were all, according to him, based upon fear. He was right, as far as males were concerned, because male stability is based on self-control, seeing emotions as rendering you vulnerable, and therefore unavoidably linked with fear. (See note.[35])

In 1967, Fred Davis predicted that the hippies were

'rehearsing *in vivo* a number of possible cultural solutions to central life problems posed by the emerging society of the future.' What *has* come out of it all? A great deal, for women, for the peace movement, the ecology movement, alternative medicine. These 'fringe' activities have gradually been percolating through so that those who would never have dreamed of going to the Isle of Wight, feel a part of something expressed by Schumacher in the early '70s, a more close-focused, caring approach to life. But as far as men are concerned, more headway appears to have been made in producing real ale than real people...

There has, however, been a lessening of formality in the workplace, first name terms, more casual dress and with it more friendly relations. Numerous men mention wearing coloured shirts and leaving their jacket in the car on hot summer days, when they would previously have sat and suffered in a stuffy uniform. And there is much greater tolerance of stress-related illness. Ten or fifteen years ago, a man having a nervous breakdown or any kind of psycho-somatic illness faced dismissal, forced resignation, a mark for life. It is acceptable now for a man to crack, although the strain itself has not lessened a great deal.

The present game of musical chairs in the job market means that the working population is trapped on a treadmill while millions of the unemployed sit twiddling their thumbs. Work sharing is not seen as a realistic practical alternative yet, because it runs against male dependence for identity upon work. In this respect, as in many others, the graduates of the late '60s remain the pioneers, having moved into areas traditionally dominated by women—community and social work, teaching and the crafts movement. What seems to have been happening is a strengthening of the numbers of men who, for various reasons, never really felt part of traditional maleness. Gay men have been coming out, particularly in cities, and a small number of men have been joining men's consciousness-raising groups, becoming a part of something as yet difficult to define but loosely described as the 'men's movement'.

None of the men in my sample had been anywhere near a men's group. The movement in Britain has only grown very gradually since the early '70s. Men who join are those who are already converted in principle to the idea of change, because they have begun to question their own lack of sensitivity or awareness. They are often moved to join because, although they intellectually support the women's movement, the shift between the sexes has yanked them off balance emotionally, from the well defended male position. They come to the group because of some problem in their relationships with women, some gulf between what they believe in and how they behave . . . And they stay because they recognise that the real problem is between themselves.

## NOTES

1  Charles A. Reich, *The Greening of America* (Random House, New York, 1970; Penguin, 1971)
2  See Timothy Leary, *The Politics of Ecstasy* (Putnam's & Sons, New York, 1968; MacGibbon & Kee, 1970); also *Flashbacks*, an autobiography (Heinemann, 1983)
3  In 1966 the Provos actually won a seat on the city council, with 13 000 votes; thereby, because of their anarchistic ideals, having to disband themselves, since they had become a part of the establishment.
4  Erik Erikson, *Identity, Youth and Crisis* (Faber & Faber, 1968)
5  Alain Touraine, *The May Movement: Revolt or Reform* (trs. Leonard Mayhew) (Random House, New York, 1971)
6  Frank Musgrove estimated from studying a sample in the urban north-west of England, that out of a population of 500 000 probably between 500 and 1000 were sympathetic to the 'counter culture' as the youth movement came to be called. They were predominantly male, roughly 2 per cent of the 40 000 or so males in their twenties at the time (1971-3). Although acknowledging this as a rough estimate, Musgrove linked it with the 150 000 people who attended the Isle of Wight pop festival in 1970—some 2 per cent of the 8 million or so people in the relevant age group. I would say that his is probably, on that basis, quite a conservative estimate; since there were many of us who couldn't afford the time, the ticket or the high-priced hamburgers, or couldn't face the overflowing loos, and missed out, regretfully, on something to tell our grandchildren.
   Frank Musgrove, *Ecstasy and Holiness: Counterculture and the*

*Open Society* (Methuen, 1974)

7  Theodore Lidz, *The Person: His and Her Development through the Life Cycle* (Basic Books, New York, 1976)

8  Carol Gilligan, *In a Different Voice: Psychological Theory and Women's Development* (Harvard University Press, Mass and London, 1982)

9  Dr Donald Ross, *Journal of the American Medical Association*, *248*, no. 10, 'Letters' p 1177 10 September 1982

10  Patricia Cayo Sexton, *The Feminized Male: Classrooms, White Collars and the Decline of Manliness* (Random House, New York, 1969; Pitman, 1970)

11  Eighty per cent completed high school in 1970 (compared with 6.4 per cent in 1900), and more than 50 per cent began college. From 238 000 in 1900, the college population had risen to 2.3 million in 1950 and then more than doubled, to 5 million in 1964, reaching more than 7 million in 1970. UNESCO figures give a massive increase in France, also, from 140 000 in 1950 to 455 000 in 1964, and almost as big an increase in West Germany, from 123 000 to 343 000.

12  Most of Keniston's work is summarised in a collection of essays entitled *Youth and Dissent: The Rise of a New Opposition* (Harcourt Brace Jovanovich, New York, 1971)

13  Reich sought to emphasise that the new generation of the '60s had emerged with a new consciousness, not Consciousness I, the every-man-for-himself, *laissez-faire* of the originators of the American Dream; nor Consciousness II, the bureaucratised, more brutally dehumanised facelessness of the advanced industrial consumer society, but a new caring image stressing co-operation rather than competition, and giving a new spiritual rather than material meaning to life.

14  William G. Perry Jr, *Forms of Intellectual and Ethical Development in the College Years* (Holt, Rinehart & Winston, New York, 1968, 1970)

15  C. P. Snow, *The Two Cultures and the Scientific Revolution: The Rede Lecture* (Cambridge University Press, 1959); *The Two Cultures and a Second Look* (Cambridge University Press, 1964)

16  Liam Hudson, *Frames of Mind* (Methuen, 1968)

17  See the account of the discovery of the molecular structure of DNA, in J.D. Watson, *The Double Helix: A Personal Account of the Discovery of the Structure of DNA* (Weidenfeld & Nicolson, 1968)

18  Dr Kazimierz Dabrowski, *Personality Shaping through Postive Disintegration* (Little, Brown & Co., Boston and

London, 1967)
19  The campus revolt at Berkeley, according to Hampden-Turner began in a university where nearly 49 per cent of the students were studying the social sciences and over 50 per cent of the Free Speech Movement majored in this area. May '68, in France, began in a sociology department. Early in the Columbia University revolt, social science students occupied a hall, and at Harvard students of social relations outnumbered those from other faculties among the arrested in the spring of 1969. At this time the most popular course in the entire university was Social Relations 149, a breakaway student-run course, with over 800 attending.
    Charles Hampden-Turner, *Radical Man* (Schenkman Publishing, Mass, 1970; Duckworth, 1971)
20  Theodore Roszack, *The Making of a Counter Culture: Reflections on the Technocratic Society and its Youthful Opposition* (Faber, 1970)
21  Hampden-Turner dated his own conversion to the counter culture from the collision, in 1963, between his liberal (presumably feminising) British education and the full force of the Harvard Business School, then advocating ultra macho, self-seeking, exploitative, inhuman business methods.
22  F. Davis, 'Why all of us may be hippies someday' (*Transaction*, 5, December 1967, p 14)
23  Herbert Marcuse, *One Dimensional Man* (Routledge & Kegan Paul, 1964); *An Essay on Liberation* (Allen Lane, 1969)
24  Richard Neville, *Playpower*, (Jonathan Cape, 1970)
25  Sheila Rowbotham, *Woman's Consciousness, Man's World* (Penguin (Pelican) Books, 1973)
26  Erik Erikson, op cit
27  Australians also faced it, and Canadians were made very aware of it, but young men in Britain and Europe, especially countries with no military service, never had to cross this moral threshold.
28  The date set for the first national draft card return, the outcome of all the planning that summer to organise resistance to the war, was 16 October 1967. Demonstrations took place in eighteen different cities, the largest in San Francisco, where 2000 gathered on the steps to the federal building while a basket was passed round, in which draft cards were thrown. The aim was to get the young men who were against the war to stand up for their principles, rather than simply take the easy way out.
29  In *Toys and Reasons*, Erikson explored the significance of game playing—an attempt to ritualise and therefore create

boundaries around experience. He called My Lai an example of 'catastrophic deritualisation', 'the deadlines that takes over when all gamesmanship has gone from an adult scenario'. He was referring to the male need to fall back on rules and principles of 'fair play', rather than the sympathetic sense of humanity which would prevent, should prevent, any normal human being from 'deadliness', with or without the element of the game.
Erik Erikson, *Toys and Reasons: Stages in the Ritualisation of Experience* (W. W. Norton & Co, New York, 1977; Marion Boyars, 1978)

30 Peter G. Bourne, MD, *Men, Stress and Vietnam* (Little, Brown & Co, Boston, Mass, 1970)

31 Erikson also made the point that only through the attempt at intimacy are weaknesses in character truly revealed, hence the propensity for so many people to seek counselling for relationship (rather than work) problems. Again, here we find a male commentator generalising about something peculiar to male development by referring to a young person's caution in commitment, when he really means male caution in commitment.

32 Derek Bowskill & Anthea Linacre, *Men, The Sensitive Sex* (Frederick Muller, 1977)

33 Ross V. Speck, *The New Families* (Tavistock, 1972; Basic Books, New York, 1972)

34 Richard Mabey, *The Pop Process* (Hutchinson, 1969)

35 It was Leary who also announced, following the idea that independence preceded interdependence, that you 'can't make it with a woman unless you have made it with yourself...' In a sense he was right, except that all the self-help and therapy groups that sprang up amid the loneliness of single people living the city life prospered on the inability of young people actually to commit themselves to mutually supportive painful growth *within* a relationship.

*Chapter Seven*

# MEN AND WOMEN, WOMEN AND MEN

*I support the women's movement, I really do, because I just put myself in a woman's position, having the frustrations of what society expects them to do. We're just human beings with different reproductive systems. I do everything I can to give them a fair crack. My attitude to women has changed over the past ten years. I've become more aware of the women's movement. Ten years ago, I paid lip service to lots of those things, over cups of coffee at college, but if someone had sat me down and asked me, I would probably have come out with the same old answers—it really is their place to stay at home, and we can't have babies, can we, dammit. They've got breasts, it's all biological. But I do think men and women are different, emotionally women are more honest and they can get their minds around one person quite comfortably, whereas men shrink from the commitment. They make it, but they don't remind themselves too often that they have . . .*

(Tony)

*I prefer to retain my individuality, so I never get too close to anyone, except Jane.*

(Andrew[1])

THERE IS a saying that women hope men will change after marriage, but they don't; men hope women won't change, but they do. The same could perhaps be said about the women's movement, in the aftermath of which many women have been changing. But many men haven't, and they seem particularly resistant to the idea of changing in response to the changing role of women. Most of the men I interviewed firmly denied that the changing role of women had affected their lives, even some of the men whose wives worked full time. A few men spoke of noticing women at work becoming more self-assertive; that women were expanding their activities beyond the domestic sphere of their mothers' generation; that women were becoming more visible in the world of work. But it was very rare for a man to admit that his own life had been touched by the changes happening to women.

It wasn't that they disagreed with the notion of equal pay, or refused to believe in the equality of the sexes. Far from it. Most men claimed that they had grown up believing in sexual equality, just as they had been brought up to open doors and walk on the outside of the pavement, as a sign of good manners. Most men described themselves as chivalrous towards women, often because they like to feel protective towards them. There has been one slight change though, in that few would now offer their seat to a woman, either because they feel in the light of women's demands for equal rights that it's every man for himself, or because at some point they have met with an embarrassing rebuff. They also described situations in which a woman retaliated against a door being held open for her. For them, the gesture does not bear heavy repressive symbolism and they react defensively against such hostility, while other men complain, thereby accepting the symbolism, that women still expect all these social niceties of deference to the weaker sex, while at the same time demanding to be treated equally.

Most men believed in equal pay; they believed that women should be free to do whatever work they want (although some couldn't understand why they should want to do dirty manual work), that they should be able to earn as much as men, that married women are just as entitled to look for work, even in an economic recession, and that, theoretically, it didn't matter which partner went out to work and which stayed at home to look after the children. But they also, almost unanimously, believed that the sexes are different; equal, but different, and in defining these differences they ended up by defending conventional roles.

It's not that they think that women aren't competent in most walks of life. Very few men voiced any objection to female newsreaders or politicians, although one man reckoned a robot would make the best politician. Many men are ardent devotees of Margaret Thatcher, it would seem, and several men mentioned that it was 'ludicrous' that there were only a handful of women MPs when half the population are female. However, many men still appear critical of women drivers, although there is not the same amount of derision and contempt as there might have been in the past. They simply feel that, although good women drivers are probably better than most men drivers, the majority of women do not make very good drivers, and a bad women driver is worse than any man. Some men did feel that women were safer drivers, because they drive '10 per cent within their capacity, whereas men take risks and drive 10 per cent outside it', but most men felt that women were not decisive enough, and that hesitation is what causes accidents. Several men also mentioned that a woman driver is likely to look at her passenger while she is talking, while a man doesn't feel the need to do anything but look straight ahead at the road, even while he is talking.

Numerous men regarded women as less good at organising and less adaptable to being organised than men, and one man mentioned that women were less able, in his opinion, to carry off an authoritarian role without resorting to distance or officiousness, because the 'maternal' role does not readily translate to the work hierarchy in the way the 'paternal' role does. Most men described women as more sensitive, compassionate, patient, caring and gentle than men, and therefore much more suited to nurturing roles, to jobs that involve dealing with people. Women are soft and understanding. Women are different.

Yet men actually seem to know very few women, aside from women to whom they are related, or women with whom they are involved, ie women in a particular kind of role relationship towards them—mother, sister, wife. Few men had ever worked with women as colleagues, on a level with them, and most men regarded the suggestion that they might have 'female friends' as an attempt to discover whether they had ever been unfaithful to their wives. Perhaps because the male is always supposed to be on the look-out for sex, most men regarded the idea of close friendship with a woman as unthinkable, almost an infidelity in itself. A great many men knew men they would describe as 'chauvinists', but very few men knew anyone whom they would call a feminist, although only one man didn't know what the word meant. Hardly any men had ever read anything about women's rights, which might account for the fact that many men expressed rather rigid and contradictory attitudes towards the subject, and few showed any kind of understanding of the more subtle difficulties which might prevent women from participating fully as equals with men.

A number of men freely admitted that they hadn't 'given the subject much thought', although very many men had strong views about it. Generally, they tended to express sympathy towards the aims of the women's movement but criticism of its methods, which was often very vehement, even from men who were informed and understanding about women's rights. Comments ranged from 'They go about it sometimes in the wrong way, but good luck to them' to:

> I support equality of the sexes, I've got sympathy with the women's movement. But I'm not sure they're doing things the right way round. I think they probably might antagonise people more than win their co-operation.

Gerry, a local government officer, had definitely been antagonised:

> I'm for equal opportunity. What really niggles me is women bleating on about not having equal opportunities when if they got on with what they were doing they probably would find they have. I ripped up a questionnaire we had at work about women's rights, because it was so stupid.

So had Ray, an advertising consultant:

At the moment, the women's movement gets up my nose a bit. It's amusing that suddenly there are all these *women* that are doing things, not people that do things. Women aren't doing themselves justice. The things they're talking about aren't worth all the shouting. I don't believe that things are quite as frustrating as they sometimes make out. They put people's backs up and do damage to their cause.

Ian, a photographer, who was very interested and informed about women's rights, also questioned the methods used by feminists to try to end the oppression of women:

They're far too bigoted, too much blame thrown round and out of hand damnation.

And Geoff, a lecturer, felt:

There's male chauvinism and male bias running through most walks of life, I really find it crazy. But I don't necessarily go along with all the moans of opposition.

However, Mick, a computer project leader, felt it was understandable:

I think the women's movement probably had to go too far. They're pushing too hard, trying to be too unfeminine, but in all walks of life if you don't get what you want you tend to go too far, ask for more just to get what you want, like in union bargaining.

Numerous men mentioned that feminism made women unfeminine, like Brian, an environmental health officer:

I believe in women's lib for the sake of equality, but not the butchness that goes with it. I like a woman to be the 'little lady'.

And Nick, an office manager, felt:

Women should be soft and in need of a man's protection and care. They're quite welcome to do their own thing, but they're not making themselves feminine in my eyes.

Chris, a financial director, felt the women's movement itself had achieved very little:

> All this women's lib and Germaine Greer doesn't do a lot for me;
> I don't think it really did a lot for women, anyway. I think it's
> civilisation realising that women have an equal part to play.
> The women's movement has died, hasn't it?

The majority of men felt that the women's movement was
very much alive, and echoed the fire station officer's
comment, 'I'm fed up with women's lib.' They were almost
unanimous in feeling that feminism made women unfeminine and although its ideals were right it was going
completely the wrong way about realising them. Most men
felt that the right way was for women to prove themselves,
and then they would be accepted. Real headway had not been
made because women themselves weren't taking action. As
one man put it:

> Steps have been taken whereby they can advance themselves, but
> it hasn't been followed up. It's the fault of the women, they
> haven't pursued it...

Naturally, I have no idea how far men's comments were
tailored to suit my ears. Certainly, some men seemed to be
modifying their opinions on their feet, but perhaps this was
because, in one man's words, 'I've not given the subject
much thought, as you'll see from my answers.' And some of
the things men said appeared totally self-contradictory. Bob,
an assistant manager, for example, was all for the women's
movement:

> The women's movement hasn't advanced yet on a broad enough
> wave. There's an awful lot of untapped talent that could be used
> for the nation's good, and for the individual's self-enjoyment...
> I would like to see a situation where women could develop as
> human beings and not get forced into an artificial role...

However, when asked whether he knew any feminists, he
replied that his wife 'collects them', one in particular whose
'poor husband lives the life of a slave, he does just what he's
told'. Chauvinists he knew at work, on the other hand, really

only said things in a 'semi-joking way', and he'd be very
wary before employing a girl:

> I'd want to know a lot about her, that she was going to stick at
> the job and not go off for six months or two years and have a
> baby. So that's chauvinism, in that way, but governed by
> practicalities.

Bob's own wife kept him for several years while he 'went off'
and did a university degree.

Another man, Dick, a quantity surveyor, conceded that:

> If you could spread the jobs around so that every family had a
> breadwinner it doesn't matter to me if it's a man or a woman.
> But I can see a problem. My sister, for example, who will be
> married in five years. Yet she's done A levels, gone off to training
> college, works somewhere for the civil service and I think well,
> it's crazy, that surely isn't what women are fighting for? I don't
> understand. There's a whole waste of assistance to educate her,
> give her that training, she knows she's going to get married,
> she's quite pretty. And she'll probably give up work for ten
> years. It all seems daft to me...

And Alec, an office manager, was adamant that the women's
movement should:

> ... get on with living life rather than being a pain in the neck. I
> don't run round as a bloke, saying treat me the same. They want
> to stop trying to set themselves up as different. There's a free
> choice, you discriminate against somebody every time you don't
> give them a job, so discrimination is just a function of
> selection, which should be on ability, rather than anything
> else.

However he then added:

> Although given the choice I wouldn't have any women working
> in industry at all, because they spend more time talking, more
> time away, more time having babies and looking after husbands
> and children when they're ill. You don't get a full day's work out
> of them. Having said that I don't think people should be
> discriminated against, I wouldn't have a woman working in the
> office if I could help it, but they're a necessary evil and blokes

don't like typing and filing... terrible attitude, I've got, haven't I darling?

These two last speakers were in fact among the small number of men who said that they couldn't see how people who were so different could possibly be equal. It's understandable that men should feel critical and defensive about a movement which is, after all, highly critical of them as a sex. But apart from a certain amount of straightforward ignorance of the finer points of the issues involved, there did seem to be a strange intransigence and blindness about their reactions, which pointed to something more complex and less straightforward than 'sour grapes'.

Time and again, men would criticise the methods of the women's movement and suggest that all women need do to gain equality is 'prove themselves'. This attitude is in fact something that women complain about, as part of the reason they are not treated equally, arguing that men accept one another as competent, but expect women to prove themselves first. What women don't realise is that men don't just accept one another. They spend their whole lives trying to prove themselves, in the power and status games which they play. And their whole moral ethos is based on the idea of proving yourself. If you win the game, you're entitled to the prize. If someone helps you on your way (as in the old boy network), then that's just part of team spirit. As Carol Gilligan[2] pointed out, male morality refers to rules and fair practices rather than compassion for the worthiness of the individual case. Implicit in male morality is that each person largely looks out for himself ('You go about one quarter to the others and three quarters to yourself') rather than showing caring concern about others. Men who have grown up with these rules regard the attempt of women to bypass them in some way as cheating or asking for favouritism, wanting the same handicap as everyone else, without having proved that they can play the game.

The rules by which men are brought up, especially in relation to work, do not include responding to the *needs* of others. So why should the rules be bent to accommodate the needs of women to be treated as equals? Women, from their totally different moral stance of care and concern for others, cannot understand why men do not respond to their needs, and become angry about it. Which serves to alienate men even further, because men instinctively respond to attack not by questioning themselves, rethinking their attitude, but by becoming defensive. So men don't listen to 'bleating', 'shouting', 'those butch radicals', and each position becomes more entrenched.

Men judge life as sport—if the cap fits, wear it, and may the better man win, aware that it is more likely to be a man, but unable to modify the rules ('You can't legislate people's attitudes. Things are progressing, but it's got to be slow.'). The male moral code does not readily allow for sympathy for the underdog. At school, if you were no good at games, you suffered accordingly. This external rule of thumb stems, as has been seen, from the male lack of ability to enter imaginatively into another person's situation and understand it from their point of view, to empathise. Cut off from their capacity to develop empathy through mature identification, men judge from the outside, and this also conspires to render them relatively insensitive to the arguments of feminism. How can they possibly understand sexual harassment or discrimination if it is not expressed overtly and they cannot project themselves into such a situation to observe it as a woman might. The problems women face are nothing like the problems men face, so it doesn't exist, or women exaggerate. They may observe both a male comment and a female reaction, but they will not readily be able to interpret that comment and that reaction from a female point of view. Thus one man, Glyn, a telephone engineer, felt that it was stupid to make a fuss about sexist things, because he didn't think they were spoken or written intentionally. He quoted an advertisement for a car, which was captioned 'Don't show your wife this advert because she wouldn't understand it'—to his mind it was silly, but not worth making a fuss about. Similarly, he continued:

> Those sorts of things, like instead of saying salesman you've got to say salesperson and draughtswoman, that's bloody rubbish, nitpicking. It's not important.

But when I asked him whether he would apply for a job asking for a saleswoman, he said:

> No, I wouldn't apply for it. I suppose, when you think about it, it probably could do, put women off.

Men can understand another person's point of view, but they don't automatically do it, because it isn't in their psychological make-up to do so, in the same way that it may not be in a woman's psychological make-up to assert herself, though she has that capacity for self-assertion in herself, even though it may not be as developed, as finely tuned as men's self-assertiveness. At the root of many men's lack of understanding of the effects of sexual harassment on women is the fact that it is a form of 'personal attack' they have rarely experienced themselves. And the defensive bravado developed to toughen them against the pain of rejection when they were teenage also renders them insensitive to signals that women do not welcome this behaviour. I only heard one or two men spontaneously remark that they modified how they acted 'because some women get annoyed, don't like it', with regard to 'protective' or chivalrous behaviour. Most men simply did it, and then felt defensive if it wasn't well received. And it was also noticeable that the men who were aware of the effect of sexual harassment were among those who had been sexually harassed themselves and hadn't reacted violently:

> I didn't know how to handle it. The guy was quite persistent. He kept asking me to go home with him and as many times as I took his hand off my knee, the hand just kept coming back, he wouldn't take no for an answer. I didn't know how to get out of the situation, because I didn't want to do anything to hurt him. In the end I grabbed the car keys and ran out and locked myself in. It was very embarrassing. I think that five-minute encounter with that bloke did make me think what it must be like for a woman in the same situation, whereas before I would have taken it for granted that it was quite OK to pressurise a woman. But now I notice good-looking women being touched, talked to, and about, stared at...

Most women, at some time or another, run the gauntlet of

jeers and catcalled compliments from gangs of workmen. It is the hazard of walking past any building site or roadworks. A long time ago, in the early '70s, I came home to find the road where I lived being dug up. For a woman, a great deal depends upon how far away they are, the tone of the comments, and your prevailing mood. Sometimes you smile because you can't help it, at other times because you feel you have to. You never speak, because you sense that anything you say would somehow be inappropriate. Only the smile or the feigned indifference can guard your self-esteem. On this particular morning, armed with some spurt of indignation, probably from the gathering arsenal of the women's movement, I rounded after passing the labourers and demanded:

> How would you like comments made about your anatomy in your hearing? I don't walk past you, passing personal remarks, and I think it's very rude.

They all burst out laughing and I stormed up the road. It was only when I reached the house that I realised I would have to walk past them again, confront their derision, as I was going away for the weekend and had to catch a train. But although they made jokey comments about my suitcase, 'Don't leave home because of us, love', one of them actually approached me and apologised. 'We're very sorry,' he said, and I could tell by the tone that it was genuine. 'We honestly didn't mean to offend you.' I don't believe it had ever crossed their minds that it could possibly be offensive, simply because they had never been, and could never imagine themselves, upon the receiving end.

Coupled with their tendency not to empathise, is men's tendency to differentiate. The whole process of their identity formation is based upon reassuring themselves of the boundaries around them and others, the things that separate us rather than the things we have in common. It is from this that the male urge to bond into groups stems, because men have cut the cord of common humanity which links all of us, because they find the connection dangerous. Whereas men will tend, therefore, to see the differences between the sexes, women will see their similarities. Women will fail to see the boundaries as sharply defined, often because of their lack of a close relationship with their opposite-sex parent, with their father. And men will see only the boundary, because of their lack of a close relationship with their same-sex parent, their father.

Added to this is the in-built defence against identifying with a woman, as this identification threatens the bedrock of male identity which has been built upon turning against the female, rejecting primary identification with a woman. This is reflected, generally, in men's need for women to be 'feminine' in many more ways than women need men to be 'masculine', because men need to project their own femininity into the women they are attracted to. Thus one man, who worked with women and had shortlisted a woman for a boiler worker/handyman job (in the face of his male colleagues' prejudice against her), nevertheless commented, about feminists:

> I wouldn't want to be married to one. I wouldn't want a complete role change because women are women, for their beauty or whatever. I wouldn't want my wife with overalls on underneath a car. Men and women should be different, have got to be different.

Research[3] carried out in the '60s found that sex-typed identification among adult males was associated with low self-acceptance, high anxiety and neuroticism. And it seemed significant, in my research sample, that the most chauvinistic attitudes were to be found among men who talked about a particularly problematic relationship with their fathers, which seemed to result in almost total dependence upon external sex role preference and adoption, rather than inner security of sex role orientation, for confirmation of their gender identity. (See p. 121 note 21.)

Only a couple of men were prepared to come out as self-confessed chauvinists who believed that a woman's place is in the home and that women are in no way the equals of men. Frank, a sales representative, made his views on the subject very clear:

> I don't believe in equal pay, I don't think women should be

given the vote, because I don't think they understand what they're doing with it, and if they want equal pay—this is very old male chauvinist pig stuff coming out now—then they should be down mines, up chimneys, etc. Women vote for personalities, not policies. I believe women should be in the subservient role, the kitchen sink and the bedroom and that's about it. I think for every intelligent woman there are ten thick ones. Women drivers are worse than I am, and I'm the world's worst driver. I'll probably die at the wheel of a car, because if I see a car in front of me, I've got to overtake it. I just don't like being beaten.

The other man said basically much the same, that women shouldn't have the vote because they're too emotional, and were therefore only fit to be wives and mothers. Interestingly, both men described a violent and aggressive father, who in Frank's case came home drunk every night, particularly when he was younger, and a saintly, long-suffering mother to whom they were particularly attached. (See note.[4]) Other men with punitive, authoritarian and highly rejecting fathers paid lip service to the notion of equality (perhaps for my benefit or because intellectually they believed in it), but then began to voice their antipathy towards women, either expressing hostility directly, 'I've never liked women particularly', or indirectly, through putdown jokes, particularly in front of other men, about their wives, 'The last thing I would do, I keep telling her, is if I got rid of one wife, to find another one.' These men had grown up totally absorbed in the peer-group world, often seeming only to remember being rewarded by their fathers when they won a fight, and they appeared more likely to resort to fights at junior school with their friends ('You'd be best of mates afterwards'), although often avoiding fights later on at secondary school, either because they didn't feel confident they could defend themselves, or because they felt they might defend themselves too well:

I knew I would hurt someone, possibly kill them.

Some men who expressed patronising attitudes about women described an ineffectual father, dominated by their mother, a father for whom they felt pity or contempt. These men were more likely to pick fights with other boys, sometimes to the extent of bullying. All of them claimed that they much preferred the company of other men, 'You can't be yourself with a woman', and exhibited very rigid attitudes towards the sexes, defending conventional roles to varying degrees and particularly emphasising that they liked 'a man to be a man', whereas 'Women shouldn't get sweaty and hot and bothered and walk round unladylike and unfeminine.' Although many men expressed their preference for women to appear feminine, it was most marked among these men, especially those who at other points in their conversation described themselves as 'soft, really', or 'very emotional', 'I can cry, I can almost turn it on'. It is as if they never really resolved their identification with their mothers and need desperately to disown it, to play up what they hold in common with other men, because they need to reassure themselves about it. They are constantly bolstering their image of themselves as men, and this affects the way they see women.

As Pete, an electrical contractor, put it:

> I don't think women should be eligible to fight, because you feel protective towards women, so you'd get yourself shot trying to look after some bird that shouldn't be there.

These men's lives revolve totally around the things they do with their male friends, yet these friendships seem almost deliberately held at arm's length:

> We tend to go down to the local, across the road. Socialising doesn't really interest me. We have a laugh and a joke, but I like to be at home on my own, I wouldn't invite people round. Nor do I like going to other people's houses for some reason. I feel very uncomfortable.

Socialising has to take place on neutral territory.

Although virtually all the men I spoke to found difficulty articulating their feelings, most of them (bar those who had retained an identification with their mothers, in spite of themselves) were aware of and emphasised this difficulty, either in the way they answered questions about themselves, 'I don't know what my personality is like; other people know

you best, because they observe you,' or in a direct admission,
like Alec's:

> I find it difficult to express feelings about things, because it's
> very difficult to understand what your feelings are about
> something because you're not sure what's going through your
> mind, whether it's a conscious or a subconscious thought you're
> having. It's a very twisted thing that goes on in your head. I can
> articulate about anything, apart from what I feel, because you
> have to think so hard about what you've felt...

In this respect, men who perceive women as more emotional,
more sensitive and more compassionate than men are
actually reflecting a more or less basic truth. The fact that
they do not question themselves as not emotional enough,
not compassionate enough and not sensitive enough, simply
reflects the current drift of accepting the male as the norm,
male development as normal development, and conventional sex roles which confirm and encourage the separate areas
in which the sexes appear, naturally, to excel.

One or two men exhibited an attitude which irritates
feminists as much as chivalry, because they see it as masking
the contempt men really feel for women and the way in
which they dominate them. These men said that they
considered women superior to men. One of the men, who
counted among the chauvinists, expressed this in a rather
negative way:

> Oh dear, if they haven't caught on yet, they've been ruling the
> man for years. If they've got to prove it in the lib movement, well
> the less said the better. There's nothing more wounding than a
> woman's tongue. Nothing more devastating than the power of
> the spoken word, better than a bunch of fives.

Nigel, an insurance broker, voiced similar feelings, although
slightly less abrasively:

> I don't look upon women as equals, I look upon them as almost
> slightly above the man. That's why I open doors for them, it's
> respect. It's their guile that puts them above men. Over the years
> they've developed this ability to manipulate men and over these
> last ten years, with the women's movement, they've thrown a lot

of what they'd built up over the centuries away, of being able to psychologically control men. Men have lost a lot of respect for women as a result. I opened a door for a woman once and she said 'There's no need to do that, you know, now that we're equal,' so I turned back and said 'I'd have done the same for you if you'd been a man.'

Interestingly, both these men had joined the forces after leaving school and spent a number of years almost exclusively in the company of other men, during adolescence and early adulthood.

Many men appear confused about women, defensively adjusting their attitudes and contradicting themselves in the process because they cannot fully understand what is going on. They sense, rightly, that women *do* have power and skills they lack, yet they are accused of being dominant and victimising women. Many men find female articulateness very threatening. Men may have a good training in rational thought and defensive logic but they cannot, in the way women do, argue from a deep understanding of the core of the human issue involved. As one man pointed out, the only real superiority men have over women, face to face, is their greater physical strength. Yet society and morality dictate that men should not resolve conflict with women in the normal way they have learned to resolve it between themselves, so any man in an argument is at a disadvantage confronting a woman.

Because they do not work alongside women and have no real women friends, most men's experience of women is of people who exist in a peculiar and potentially powerful role relationship with them. You can't be yourself with a woman because any approach towards a woman is loaded, usually with sexual significance. Since a real man has to be looking for sex wherever he can find it, every woman has to become a target, fair game. One man said he couldn't even bring himself to have a conversation with ugly women.

Most men knew someone, or several men, they would describe as chauvinist, like the man next door, who expected his wife to do everything in the home and would think it all right for him to have an affair, but not for her. Or the bar-room big-mouth, the kind of bloke you meet in a pub who starts shouting his mouth off. Most men let this kind of thing go, pass it off as part of his ebullient character, because the man in question is often popular and entertaining, good company, 'a man's man', and they feel he is probably putting up a front to other men about women, when his personal views would be no different from their own:

> I know one who professes to be a chauvinist, makes a big thing of saying he's one, even to the point of wearing his MCP tie with a pig on it. I'm sure it's a front more than anything else. He wasn't married at the time. I'm sure he was probably as much for equality as anyone.
>
> I think most of my friends are chauvinists. In their heart of hearts, though, they probably have slightly different attitudes. I think men are inclined in men's company to front the chauvinist point of view, whereas in relationships they are probably less so.

It's interesting the different ways men define chauvinism, the different things they notice. Usually it's the attitude towards the man's wife. That he leaps to his feet at the suggestion of going to the pub without asking if she minds or if she wants to come along. That his attitude is 'Get in there and cook my dinner, woman,' ordering her about. That he expects her to do everything in the house and takes no interest in the children's lives, never visits the school on open day, so that she stops bothering to tell him when it is. It was rather less often that they noticed men making actual derogatory remarks about women. Their reaction is usually to pass it over. They see no point in arguing, either because the man doesn't really mean what he's saying, or because whatever you say will be water off a duck's back. Besides, chauvinist men are good company, good sports, a good laugh.

One man reckoned probably one in ten men are still chauvinist, expect to come home and find the tea ready, that sort of thing. A few men actually do challenge them. Mick, a computer project leader works:

> ... with quite a load of them. They know my ideas and they tend to apologise to me, tailor what they say, because they know what my reaction's going to be. I'll probably ignore it completely, or tell them not to be so stupid, or something.

Nick, an office manager, says he has a couple of friends who behave chauvinistically towards their wives, but they don't actually say anything chauvinistic. 'We would disagree if they did.' Dick, a quantity surveyor, also meets MCPs at work:

> It's the way they talk, their attitudes really. I can't remember specific things, but I've thought to myself, you male chauvinist pig—because of their attitude, really. It's the way they talk about women behind their backs. There's this fellow at the tennis club who has lots of girlfriends—good luck to him—but he's really cold and sometimes I think I'm quite friendly with him, but sometimes I stand there when we're talking and think blimey, I can't see that point of view. And he's really sort of nasty, in his attitudes to women, the way he treats them without any compassion, or any feeling. I tell him he's a chauvinist pig. He just thinks you're joking. He'll laugh it off as being the clever person he is, he probably feels good because he thinks that's the way men should feel.

Nigel also confronts men about their sexist views:

> I think they tend to make a point of it, I'll show her, put her in her place. They do it to impress, show they've got control. It comes back to the old schooldays, of what I did and didn't do with my girlfriend last night stuff. Some people don't grow out of it, I think. I usually give my argument as you chauvinist pig and that normally shuts them up, or they laugh and go on to another subject.

Frank, the self-confessed MCP, had this to say about his views:

> Most of my friends disagree with me. I can't deny that women are definitely justified in feeling disgruntled. People like me shouldn't be allowed to speak as openly as I do, as often as I do. I shouldn't be saying it, but there again these are just personal feelings and I know a lot of people do agree with me. A lot of my friends disagree with me. I don't think it's right, you rarely hear women knocking men. Women don't tend to be *against* men as males are against females. You don't hear women saying that men are bad drivers, but you hear a hell of a lot of men saying

that women are dreadful drivers.

Chauvinists know that their attitudes are no longer socially acceptable, yet the need to denounce the feminine within oneself, which is present to some degree in most men, gives the chauvinist tacit support, and bolsters the compartment-alising of women, whereby if they become too like you they cease to be women and become 'almost like a bloke'. These ideas of what a woman should be, partly defensive, and partly handed down from father to son, as Evelyn Goodenough[5] noticed, must remain entrenched because so few men have female friends, mix with women on a truly equal basis. Most men appear to prefer the idea of mixed company and see spending a night out with the boys as some kind of hang-up, a problem; but even when they socialise with other couples, they actually gravitate more towards men and find women's company difficult. It is not hard to see why; there is so little common ground, because, as various research studies have shown, men connect through shared activities, and swop facts and related opinions, whereas women talk, for the sake of talking, exploring inner avenues of thought, seeking some kind of truth about personal relationships.

B.W. and R.G. Eakins' *Sex Differences in Human Communication*[6] suggests that men talk mainly about sex, sports, politics, work and other men. An American researcher in the 1920s analysed fragments of conversation overheard walking down Broadway in the early evening, and deduced that between themselves, men talked shop 50 per cent of the time, about sport 14 per cent of the time and about other men 13 per cent of the time. Whereas women talked about men 44 per cent of the time, clothes 23 per cent of the time and other women 16 per cent of the time. Other studies during the same period confirmed these findings, showing that 37 per cent of women against 16 per cent of men talked about people, and that men talked to women about themselves 17 per cent more than when they were talking to other men.

The kind of communication that the sexes share between themselves, reflects the different meanings and functions they ascribe to friendship. Just as men do things and help one another, while women exchange confidences and support one another, a friend to a man means someone he could call on for help, whereas to a woman, a friend is someone you can trust.[7]

Men tend to have fewer friends than women, and less interest in friendship, according to Argyle and Furnham. And because men's friendships are based on shared activities, they will more easily lose touch if they stop seeing one another. When asked how close his male friends were, Gary said 'very close', elaborating:

> I'd lend them money, go to their aid at three in the morning, fight for them.

Whereas a woman would be inclined to define close friendship in terms of love, trust and shared confidence. Gary felt that any conversation with a woman was likely to be pretentious 'because you are putting on a front, trying to impress or whatever'. Male conversation, on the other hand, is 'factual, deep and true'. But Brian had this to say:

> I find it difficult to talk to people. It's easy to talk to men inconsequentially. Very rarely do I have a meaningful discussion with them. I always think it's a failing in me, but I suppose it works both ways. There are three of us at the office who regularly stay behind, get a few drinks in and talk about work, cars. Occasionally it develops into quite a personal discussion. And I find that stimulating. It's something that I find lacking in most relationships. My best friend, Mick, I've known him since I was four. I can't remember ever having a meaningful discussion with him about anything other than music, which is sad, really.

Brian, an environmental health officer, was one of the few men who worked in a field where meeting people, and to a certain extent sorting out disputes between people, was a fundamental part of the job. He was not, however, the only man who described himself as basically a shy person, needing an alibi, a functional excuse to talk to other people, and male conversation often remains on this superficial level. Men rarely disclose, or confide in their male friends.

Over 95 per cent of the men I interviewed claimed they never confided in friends. They would turn to their wife if they wanted to confide, but many men said they often kept things to themselves.

Research[8] during the '70s generally confirms the impression that men are more intimate with women than other men, but that women are more self-disclosing than men. Thus, although men tend to have no female friends, their best friend tends to be a female. This makes men extremely emotionally dependent upon women, which feminism has pointed out. (See note.[9]) However, they suppress much of what they are feeling, because they find it hard to articulate their feelings and in talking to their wives have to overcome this barrier. Alan, who works as a fire station officer, suffers a great deal of stress in the course of his work:

> You get a technique of dealing with distraught people, they react very differently. Some people you can talk to very quietly and calmly, others you've got to shout at, or even get physically violent with. At the same time, you've got to keep in mind their feelings, what's happening to them, their family, their property, dog . . . I do get upset at times, I must admit. But I try not to show it. I'm very much the sort of person to keep my feelings to myself anyway, but I do get upset, especially if I see children badly burned, or killed in a fire. But you keep it to yourself, you come back to the station and you all sit round this table. You know all the rest of the blokes are feeling exactly the same as you are, but no one will show it. It's a funny situation and sometimes, the most horrific thing you may have just seen, and everyone is making the most sick jokes you can imagine. All they're doing is releasing their feelings, that's what it's all about. I can only speak personally, but I've had things happen to me which have given me nightmares a week later, I've woken up in the night quite literally screaming. It has affected me that way but not during waking hours, always when I'm asleep. And these nightmares are totally unrelated to what's happening. You might get a terrible road accident, and three nights later I wake up screaming. I haven't been dreaming about the accident, but I can relate it back to that, because it always happens after something like that.

So although a man may feel that he is most himself in male

company, it is the woman in his life who knows him in the deeper sense, and in the deepest sense he is often hidden, even to himself. As Sidney Jourard put it, in *The Transpersonal Self*:[10]

> Self-disclosure is a symptom of personality health *and* a means of ultimately achieving a healthy personality... People's selves stop growing when they repress them... Every maladjusted person is a person who has not made himself known to another human being and in consequence does not know himself. Nor can he be himself. More than that, he struggles actively to avoid becoming known by another human being.

And as Martin Buber put it in *Between Man and Man*:[11]

> ... the possible and inevitable meeting of man with himself is able to take place only as the meeting of the individual with his fellow man—and this is how it must take place. Only when the individual knows the other in all his otherness as himself, as man, and from there breaks through to the other, has he broken through his solitude in a strict and transforming meeting.

Buber speaks of the third dimension of a relationship, that which exists in the space between those who relate to one another, 'on the narrow ridge where I and Thou meet'. Yet all too often, because the man does not reach out from himself through a relationship, it is the woman who takes the risk of negotiating the narrow ridge, who comes to him.

Male emotional dependence upon women is shown by the higher frequency of depression, mental illness, death and suicide among recently widowed or divorced men. The relaxation of divorce laws was heralded, in the mid '70s, as a 'Casanova's Charter', yet out of the one marriage in three which ends in divorce in Britain (the statistics in America are even higher—half of all marriages end in divorce) seven out of ten are sued by women. As one of my interviewees put it, 'We've stayed together because we talk about things.' Too many men don't want to change or develop after marriage. Just as men are less sensitive to ordinary non-verbal cues in the course of communication, so they fail to see when communication is needed, when something is going wrong for their partner. And behind that failure to see it, is a real fear of having to see it, of being compelled to question themselves. Men may be the first to jaywalk,[12] risk their lives daring to cross the road, but they are rarely the first to risk stepping into heavy traffic in their relationships. Jane Jackson, a TV director making a documentary on men, commented[13] that 'Men don't like home truths about themselves,' nor opening up and talking about themselves, because their security is invested in their public image, rather than a bedrock of inner truth and honesty.

Men find their confidence through self-assertion; their bravery comes to them through whistling a happy tune, their fighting spirit through making a noise, to frighten their inner enemies away as much as outward ones. The act of stopping in one's tracks and listening to another person's point of view threatens that kind of confidence. As Charles Hampden-Turner put it, in *Radical Man*:[14]

> Suppose that I am trying to convey to a friend the value I see in a new social policy. In order to comprehend how it is impinging upon his needs and interests I must temporarily suspend the structure of meanings that it has for me and imagine myself in his place. I must do this in spite of the frightening consequences for myself. The risk I undertake is permitting my structure to crumble, with the knowledge that a new element supplied by him may prevent the logical restructuring of my beloved ideas. I risk being ridiculed by him at a moment when my competence is not firmly in my grasp... I tell him something which shows that I value his judgement but leave him free to disconfirm and devalue my judgement and so alter the definition of our relationship.

If the communication of ideas and receptivity to the responses to one's ideas by others can be so threatening, what of an emotive subject like the relationship between the sexes, and what of emotions themselves? Men appear to have such large, yet fragile, egos, because they grow up needing to be self-contained, to defend themselves against one another. Writing about brothers, Phyllis Chesler[15] uses a Paul Cadmus painting (*To the Lynching!*) and comments:

> Cadmus' swirls of violence show us how hard it is for men to act gently, lovingly, with a sure sense that every fellow creature is

'brother' and not 'stranger'... for a man to 'understand' too much, or to ask too many questions, leads to slow and painful castration by other men—and men would rather settle the matter quickly... Last year, a young man told me that he felt uncontrollably vulnerable whenever he experienced empathy for the suffering of others. 'It tears me apart. I feel castrated,' he said. 'I'd rather have a group of guys coming at me with knives, than feel this awful feeling.'

Men have hitherto managed to get by without developing the skills necessary for intimate relationship because marriage involved a kind of bartering, each providing for the dependence needs of the other, rather than sharing in mutual interdependence. Husbands financially and economically supported wives, while wives emotionally, psychologically and socially supported husbands. However, couples now expect much more from marriage in terms of companionship and mutual compatibility and at the same time women have been becoming more independent of men, able and desirous of supporting themselves. They are no longer satisfied with the traditional bargain. Research studies have shown that women rate their husbands highly as breadwinners, but are much less satisfied with them as communicators or in expressing their feelings. They find husbands inept as confidants and unsatisfactory as companions, partly because men do not indulge in the kind of soul-baring talk which women accept as part of making a bond. Research now appears to show that husbands and wives have different needs from marriage which don't slot neatly into one another. Women are more concerned with love and understanding, while all men appear to want is a well-run house and a wife who impresses their friends. However, this is simply another symptom of male lack of self-awareness. Their emotional dependence upon marriage has been shown to be greater than women's, because of the greater stress men suffer after the marriage has broken down.

The fact that divorce upsets men and damages their health and resilience points to hidden needs in marriage which they don't express. Not only do they stand to lose their confidante and counsellor (whereas women have numerous confidantes, among their female friends) but they are also likely to lose their social circle, since their wife is the one who maintains social contacts. Similarly, kinship bonds (which represent 50 per cent of ties outside the home) are kept up by women. Men simply slot into these networks women create; remembering birthdays, ringing up and keeping in touch are things they rarely bother to do, because women do them.

Women are beginning, however, to resent their continuing support of men. Without perhaps fully appreciating male lack of skill, both verbally and empathetically, women are expecting men to give the same emotional input into relationships that they do. They are no longer quite so willing to lose themselves in men, to give up their identities, merge themselves in men because men refuse to shift their own ego boundaries, lose a part of themselves in women.

Problems are therefore beginning to emerge in man/woman relationships which men are finding very difficult to face. Despite (indeed, because of) their dependence on women, men are not very good at coping with and resolving difficulties in relationships, in saving the relationships for which their need is so great. Sixty-five per cent of the social meaning of a situation is apparently conveyed non-verbally. Not only do women indulge in more eye contact than men, but they are more prone to reveal their emotions openly, in their facial expressions. A psychologist's experiments in the mid '70s, showing pictures designed to elicit emotion, revealed that while the men's heartbeats increased and they sweated more during the experiment than the women, they were much less likely to betray emotion expressively. The researcher concluded that men are 'internalisers' who tend to keep their emotions to themselves. They are also less likely to notice non-verbal signals from others, and are especially insensitive, apparently, to signals from a partner with whom they are not getting on.[16] Men will fight to preserve the status quo in a relationship. When something begins to threaten the easy passage of the relationship, they often instinctively 'tune out', 'switch off'. They will ignore the warning signals and if their partner demands that they recognise something is wrong, they will treat the problem as hers, not theirs. In *Marriages in Trouble*,[17] Julia Brannen and Jean Collard interviewed many couples who had approached marriage guidance counsellors, and found that most initial help-seekers were women. 'It was clear that, especially for the men in the study, this kind of disclosure was either a totally new or a rare occurrence.'

Of the 22 men and 26 women interviewed, 18 men but only 7 women had a negative attitude towards disclosure. Most of the men apparently 'couched their reluctance in normative and moral terms', and for 'many of them, non disclosure constituted an unchanging, central and even fervent part of their identities'. The authors observed that the men's reluctance, unwillingness and lack of regard for the need to communicate personal problems was sustained by a 'sense of inner precariousness or insecurity about the possible consequences of their weaknesses and failings becoming known to others'—understandably, since men grow up in a world in which vulnerability signals weakness and invites attack. Men feared loss of control over the information they would disclose (much as confidences could be used to taunt and make fun of you, when you were at school), and for some men it was noticeable that the problem was only allowed to exist when a solution had become available.

Male perspectives on problem-solving were apparently frequently expressed in mechanistic terms, as if the men were unable to grasp the idea of emotional problems—or perhaps felt a need to disguise them. Women have been able to admit that they feel external constraints, lack of confidence, which inhibit them outwardly. Men find it hard to admit the internal constraints they feel, against inner exploration. The authors of this study noticed that husbands would try to use the counsellor relationship to maintain the status quo in the marriage, in much the same way that men show resistance to development or change once they have made a commitment. A typical response from one man, when asked when he first noticed something was wrong, was, 'I suppose I didn't really notice it until she told me. I mean, it's not something one really notices.'

Often when communication, and the relationship, is breaking down, a woman will try to confront the man with the evidence, and an argument ensues. The man will feel extremely threatened, frightened by this kind of verbal aggression, where it will lead, far less able than his partner to acquit himself effectively in it. One man, interviewed on a television programme about divorce,[18] said that it would get to a pitch of arguing when neither one would back down and the only way to stop it was through violence:

> At one time, I almost strangled her... Everything was boiling up that much, it was just a case of shutting her up. It wasn't a case of violence meaning harm, it was I want to stop this arguing and this is the only way I know how.

In an article on battered wives, Ros Coward[19] asks 'Why do men express frustration with physical blows rather than speech?' and then supplies her own answer:

> Any close sensual relationship is a form of acting out primary relationships of dependency... Domestic relations sometimes appear like the coupling of two alien species with utterly different traditions of oral and physical expression. Women are often able to use speech but sometimes only critically or negatively because our society does not encourage women to make demands positively and without guilt. Men, on the other hand, are often inarticulate. They have no practice in their male friendships which teaches them that the process of communication might help individuals understand each other.

They grow up with a lot of practice, on the other hand, of resolving differences through a trial of strength, proffering threats and blows. Intimate conflict threatens men, because they lack women's verbal skills and psychological insights. Conflict between men consists of a lot of flailing at limbs, but women have a tendency to strike at the heart, piercing male armour with painful self-revelation. Men react defensively, in the only way they know, to ward off attack. The majority of men have been brought up to comply with the admonition 'That's a girl, don't hit her', so instead they will close up, retreat or escape in some way, either physically or psychologically. Men try to block out problems in relationships, not understanding that if conflicts are worked through, the relationship can grow stronger.

According to a recent study,[20] divorced and separated

women become more radical after the break-up of their relationship. But what of the radical effect upon men? Another recent study, *Surviving Divorce*, revealed that 56 per cent of a sample of divorced men reported that their networks of friends had suffered badly or collapsed, and 75 per cent trusted women less than before.[21] So where did they now turn for emotional support? Significantly, the authors suggested work-based counselling schemes, because work was said to be the only 'safe' place to talk. The survey covered ninety-two divorced men and was carried out in the spring of 1981. The authors reported that they found it difficult to track down men who would be willing to talk about the experience of divorce.

I too tended to find that men in the process of divorce or the break-down of their relationship were unwilling to be interviewed. The divorced men who did talk to me were those who had entered into another relationship (ie found a solution to the problem, and were therefore able to talk about the problem), although I did talk to two or three men who had lost wife and children, and were feeling very bitter and isolated, distrustful of women ('I don't want to get hurt all over again'), yet finding little meaning, with no emotional life, in their work.

Previous research has apparently shown that divorced men have about 60 per cent more time off work for health reasons than married men. In the *Surviving Divorce* study, men who had previously never suffered any kind of 'psychiatric' problems were breaking down, unable to sleep, losing all interest in work, some spending a lot of time in tears—alone, of course. Nearly two out of three men felt that the effect on their career at the time of the divorce was either 'serious' or 'disastrous', because of the deterioration of their living conditions and their health. But many men also admitted that the loss of their role affected their motivation:[22]

'I kept asking myself why I was bothering to build up a business.'
But, ironically, the same man had given 'my total involvement in my business' as the main reason for the failure of his marriage.

However, as for learning from experience, one typical

response was:

> I am sadder but really no wiser... I feel more isolated and more incapable of initiating and/or maintaining a mutually good relationship than before... There seem to be rules of the game I never suspected... I am much less naive.

Many divorced men remarry, although at the time of this survey, 65 of the sample of 92 were still un-remarried. The divorced men in my sample who had remarried, or were living with someone, reported a distinct improvement in the quality of their relationship. The pattern in each case was very similar. They had married fairly young, their first wife had given up work to start a family and they had become more involved in their own work. Gradually the relationship became more and more polarised, an empty shell. They talked of having nothing in common with their wives, little real relationship with their children (who seemed to belong exclusively to their wives), and often stayed late at work because they felt uncomfortable in their own homes:

> When I first came to this job, there was an awful lot of work to be done. I used to work in the office till nine, ten at night, go in Saturdays and Sundays. And that became a way of life for me and when things got a bit easier, I had no need to stay late or go in at weekends, I used to anyway, because I felt happier there. What came first, I don't know. Whether it was the work that alienated me towards her, or whether that process had begun, so I turned to work... She could put new curtains up at home and I wouldn't notice for weeks. But now, I like going home. It's the best part of the day, the end of the afternoon when I can go home. I am very interested in what I call our home, which is a bedsit for a maximum sixteen-week let...

When the marital relationship was at its lowest ebb, they became closer and closer to a female friend at work. This relationship was much more real, cemented by shared interests rather than polarised roles. And after the divorce, these men are financially on a much more equal footing with their new partners. Life is a struggle, because of the maintenance payments, but what they cannot invest materially they now put in emotionally, and feel much greater and closer communication.

Divorced men still feel protective towards women, how-ever, and don't seem to see a connection between this attitude and their exclusion from family life before the breakdown of the marriage and the financial burden they have to carry after it. But they are beginning to discover the drawbacks to the conventional male role. Women have already learnt that male protection does not adequately prepare them to face life; men are only just beginning to discover this in relation to their dependence upon women. It is to be hoped that men can begin to learn the skills of maintaining relationships, without the painful process of their breakdown and the disruption of family bonds caused by divorce.

Just as women express more non-verbally, they use more expressive intonation in their voices, which may be why some people find it disturbing to listen to a woman reading the news. Conversely, men don't communicate their feel-ings very well through their tone of voice. Eakins and Eakins[6] say:

> Some men find it difficult to verbally show feelings of tenderness or strong emotions. Many men are not adept at managing their vocal apparatus so that it is responsive to various shades and types of feelings. They may find themselves misunderstood or they may not really communicate what they intend as they growl out endearments, mutter their compliments, or bellow their apologies.

In America, couples in marriages under stress seek guidance which may include training in communication skills for husbands and training in 'contracts', for example, the husband taking the wife out for the evening, in exchange for her sexual responsiveness one night a week.[23] This seems to me to be too much like the kind of bartering which goes on in the traditional relationship, obscuring real communica-tion and the expression of real needs. Some schemes even include 'tokens' to be earned by a non-communicative husband. Each conversation earns him a token, and when he has enough he is rewarded with a kiss!

This approach seems to me to deal with the symptoms of non-communication rather than its cause. Psychologist Ted Hoasten, at the University of Pennsylvania, has been directing a much more promising programme of research into marital adjustment. He has come to believe that intimacy will develop if each spouse allows for the individuality of the other and develops shared goals and interests with the other. They also need to communicate effectively, to listen to one another and to learn one another's language, because men and women do subtly speak two very different languages.

In this respect, women appear to have made a head start. They have become much more involved in the 'men's world' of work, sport, current affairs, have even started invading men's clubs. And they retain the advantage of having grown up in the woman's world, learning to express themselves honestly and directly. Only a very small number of men have been making the effort to move in the opposite direction. One such man, Martin Stone,[24] who gave up work to stay at home and look after his children, noticed that his first sense of dissatisfaction stemmed from his contact with other parents, all of them women. He was left feeling that they hadn't really talked about anything, and decided that something was being withheld because he was a man:

> One of the legacies of twelve years at work is a familiarity with... a particular kind of communication. From football to sex, from politics to literature, talk had one thing in common: it knew where it was going... it wasn't speculative. It knew and went for the heart of the matter... As a rule, these conversations were gladiatorial, a contest in language with a familiar topic the arena.

Continuing to miss the battle of 'wit against wit', Stone found no 'rite of passage'. But he began to appreciate a different kind of language, based on trust, listening to what people said:

> ... this ease of access to an area where personal feelings and reactions can be exposed without fear of criticism, without the bland response of someone showing gratuitous 'interest'...

And he began to see a different perspective of life:

> ... behind the offers or requests for help, behind the almost

confessional revelations of anger or despair... a need to co-operate rather than compete... affirm the process of growth and change rather than a need to analyse and dissect, a willingness to accept confusion and speculation as an end rather than rely on the dogma of formulae.

Stone also mentions, with poignant significance for men, how the process of the growing relationship with the child brings with it a reawakening of emotion and sensitivity:

One's emotional centre wells up like the Kraken disturbed from years of slumber, and is so sensitised that it forces its presence on all your responses.

He remarks that were he still at work he would probably, as one of my interviewees did, dismiss the Greenham Common women as achieving nothing except to obscure the real political issues. Now he feels he has moved closer to understanding this as the only opposition to the bomb. And although childcare has its own drawbacks, it offers

... a potential which, unrecognised in the unreasoned praise of work, has value far beyond the limits of the domestic universe.

## NOTES

1 Comments from two of the author's interviewees.
2 Carol Gilligan, *In a Different Voice: Psychological Theory and Women's Development* (Harvard University Press, Mass and London, 1982)
3 T. C. Harford et al, 'Personality Correlates of Masculinity-Femininity', *Psychological Reports* (1967, *21*, pp 881-884)
4 The character in Claude Chabrol's film *Le Boucher*, who brutally murdered women, detested a violent father and worshipped a saintly mother. And Nicole Ward Jouve's book about the Yorkshire Ripper describes 'an effeminate man out of place in a macho world, feeling threatened by his own femininity'. *Guardian*, 'Guardian Women', 15 April, 1983; N. W. Jouve, *Un Homme Nommé Zapolski* (Editions des Femmes, Paris, 1983)
5 Evelyn W. Goodenough, 'Interest in persons as an aspect of sex differences in the early years' (*Genetic Psychology Mono-*

*graphs*, 55, pp 287-323)

6 B. W. and R. G. Eakins, *Sex Differences in Human Communication* (Houghton Mifflin, Mass and London, 1978)

7 Michael Argyle, 'A friend in need' (*New Society*, 2 June 1983), based on research by Argyle, Adrian Furnham & Monica Henderson

8 M. Komarovsky, 'Patterns of self disclosure in male undergraduates' (*Journal of Marriage and the Family*, 1974, *36*, pp 677-686); M. A. Caldwell & L. A. Peplau, 'Sex differences in same sex friendship' (*Sex Roles*, 1982, *8*, pp 721-733); P. C. Cozby, 'Self disclosure: a literature review' (*Psychological Bulletin*, 1973, *79*, pp 73-91); F. L. Johnson & E. J. Aries, 'Conversational patterns among same sex pairs of late adolescent close friends' (*Journal of Genetic Psychology*, 1983, *142*, pp 225-238); W. H. Rivenbark, 'Self disclosure patterns among adolescents' (*Psychological Reports*, 1971, *28*, pp 35-42); P. H. Wright & A. C. Crawford, 'Agreement and friendship: a close look and some second thoughts' (*Representative Research in Social Psychology*, 1971, *2*, pp 52-69)

9 Male emotional dependence upon women has been particularly pointed out by: Luise Eichenbaum & Susie Orbach, *What Do Women Want?* (Michael Joseph, 1983)

10 Sidney Jourard, *The Transpersonal Self* (Van Nostrand, New Jersey, 1964; Reinhold, New York and London, 1971)

11 Martin Buber (trs. R. G. Smith), *Between Man and Man* (Routledge & Kegan Paul, 1947)

12 Liesl M. Osman, 'Conformity or Compliance? A study of sex differences in pedestrian behaviour', *British Journal of Social Psychology*, 1982, *21*, pp 19-21

13 Aidan White, 'Is there life after liberation?' (*Guardian* 'Guardian Women', 12 October 1982)

14 Charles Hampden-Turner, *Radical Man* (Schenkman Publishing, Mass, 1970; Duckworth, 1971)

15 Phyllis Chesler, *About Men* (Simon & Schuster, New York, 1978; The Women's Press, 1978)

16 Research findings quoted in Eakins & Eakins, op cit (1978)

17 Julia Brannen & Jean Collard, *Marriages in Trouble: The Process of Seeking Help* (Tavistock, 1982)

18 *Forty Minutes: Divorce, the Law ... and After*, (BBC2, Thursday 2 February 1984)

19 Ros Coward, 'Erin Pizzey adrift in a misogynist society' (*Guardian* 'Guardian Women', 2 November 1982)

20 Jenny Chapman Robinson, *The Politics of Separation and Divorce: A Study in Attitude Formation* (1983, available from

Dept of Politics, University of Strathclyde, Glasgow)
21 Peter Ambrose, John Harper & Richard Pemberton, *Surviving Divorce: Men beyond Marriage* (Wheatsheaf Books, 1983)
22 Peter Ambrose, John Harper & Richard Pemberton, 'Men after divorce' (*New Society*, 23 June 1983)
23 American research quoted in Michael Argyle, 'Why do marriages break down?' (*New Society*, 19 May 1983)
24 Martin Stone, 'Learning to say it in cup of tea language' (*Guardian*, 'Guardian Women', 19 April 1983)

*Chapter Eight*

# MEN AT HEART

WALLY: ... *You know, we do live in ludicrous ignorance of each other. I mean, we usually don't know the things we'd like to know even about our supposedly closest friends. I mean, suppose you're going through some kind of hell in your own life, well, you would love to know if your friends have experienced similar things. But we really don't dare ask each other.*

ANDRE: *No. It would be like asking your friend to drop his role.*

WALLY: *We just put no value at all on perceiving reality. On the contrary, the incredible emphasis we place now on our so-called careers automatically makes perceiving reality a very low priority, because if your life is organised around trying to be successful in a career, then it just doesn't matter what you perceive or what you experience. You're just thinking, Well, have I done the thing that I've planned? Have I performed this necessary action for my career? And so you really can sort of shut your mind off for years ahead in a way. You can sort of turn on the automatic pilot...*

(Wallace Shawn[1])

Robert Fein,[2] writing about men and young children in one of the first books to question the male role, explained that childcare can be threatening to a man *because* it awakens emotions he buried so long ago, feelings he repressed and needs he stifled:

Sometimes caring for children can trigger a bewildering and disturbing range of emotions in men who long ago blocked off parts of their childlike selves.

Men can ignore or become angry with crying children because they are reminded that at some point *they* were not allowed to cry. Fein points out that little children communicate simply, honestly and directly what they feel, and that emotional honesty, simplicity and directness are the three paths to a man's buried soul.

The potential value, therefore, that childcare has for men beyond the limits of the domestic universe, is that it can break the chain reaction of the Laius complex, whereby the father rejects the son, who, cut off from his own fathering capacities because he never came to know the father in himself, feels threatened by *his* son's expression of needs and emotions, and repeats the pattern.

All through life men have the opportunity, as everyone does, to grow through relationships. Many men achieve this in spite of the pressures of the male role and the privations of their childhood. The 'family man' is more likely, however, to have developed in himself than the 'man's man' who strives for the patina of ambition and outward strength. Increasingly, since the late '60s, it has been possible for men to escape the macho stereotype. The degree of their ego defences varies and diminishes as their relationships develop. The 'woman's man', however, prefers the company of women because he cannot find sustenance in the company of men. Many men who do develop more fully as human beings find themselves cut off from the men around them. For example, Geoff preferred women's company when he worked in the commercial world, but when he moved into teaching he found male friends with whom he felt he had something in common.

But it is through relationships with their children, particularly their sons, that men have the greatest chance of re-contacting the closed-off sides of themselves, letting down the barriers of their defences and unfreezing their emotional centres, as Martin Stone (chapter seven) discovered. Mutual regression between couples can only go so far, to the point at which the man cut off from his identification with his mother. But fathers, with sons, can rediscover the mutual symbiotic relationship, the blurring of ego boundaries, the security in sameness of their earliest identification with their mothers. This can be a healing experience, regrafting that lost sense of mutuality without the threat of losing their male identity in the process. Fathers can rediscover the small boy within themselves, but they have to go much further back in the active caring process than the train-set or the Scalextric that they couldn't resist buying for him, even though he was only two.

However, Peter Moss, quoted in chapter three, said that the choice would have to be children or power—in our society you can't have both. And whoever heard of people in power voluntarily giving that power up? The unassailable logic of this argument has become the stumbling block of the women's movement. Men won't relinquish their power simply because women want them to; they'll only do it because *they* want to, because they see something in it for them.

There are men within the men's movement who *have* seen something in it for them, the opportunity to exchange some of that outward power for a little more inward strength, to be less competitive and controlled, more warm and responsive. However, although the men's movement has been slowly growing since the early '70s (there are now apparently about 5000 men's groups in the United States and 1500 in Europe, mainly in Denmark and Holland), unlike the women's movement it has retained a rather cranky, minority group image, not something to which ordinary men would align themselves (whereas many women are now tuned to the ideals of the women's movement who would never dream of going to a consciousness-raising group).

The men's movement has one rather huge credibility problem. Men are not visibly oppressed; they seem to have no common passionate grievance to air. There is, however, the masculist movement,[3] whose founder Hugh de Garis has rightly surmised that 'Men grow up into robots, unable to communicate properly with women, other men or our own children' and is very angry about it. His tactic is aggressively demanding that women go into careers, pull more weight as breadwinners, complaining that men are victims of stress and that British men are stuck in the male feminist guilt phase. They haven't got angry yet.

In one sense, de Garis is perfectly right. Men do die earlier, not just because of the stress of their role but because they are often denied the healing, life-giving sustenance of intimate relationships. A long-term study in America has been following up the case histories of doctors who graduated in one year in the late '30s from Johns Hopkins University, in an attempt to map out the variables linked with sickness and health. Some of these subjects are already dead. And the study has found that the father-son relationship affects health, that cancer subjects had parents who tended to be ambitious, strict, cold and detached. 'Father was hard on me' could be a death sentence in itself, because lack of closeness to parents was the common denominator among those who suffered mental illness, committed suicide or died of lung cancer. A Canadian medical conference was apparently recently told that four hugs a day is an antidote for depression; eight contributes greatly to mental stability, and twelve cuddles could promote real psychological well-being because touching helps establish feelings of security and identity in the world.[4] Yet the overwhelming majority of the men I interviewed admitted they were not at all demonstratively affectionate, certainly never hugged or kissed anyone outside the immediate family. If women's health suffers because they suppress anger, men's health suffers because they suppress sadness and emotion.

This is why de Garis, in borrowing the tactics of the women's movement and inciting men to get 'angry' about their problems, is going about it in entirely the wrong way. Anger was the tool the women's movement originally used so successfully because it was the emotion women needed to release. The emotion men stifle is not anger, and therefore anger will not serve their purpose.

One long-established member of the men's movement in Britain told me that the drop out rate in men's groups is high, around 50 per cent. The groups which survive, he said, are the ones which concentrate upon men's relationships with one another, rather than their abuse of power or their attitudes towards women. These men's fumbling attempts to make honest, simple and direct relationships with one another may seem absurdly self-indulgent to many women,

for whom it comes so naturally, but women have got to
realise that this is the only way for men to begin to abandon
their embattled positions. Combating anti-sexism by simply
trying to re-educate boys and men (as some schools and
employers are now doing) only treats the symptoms of the
problem, rather than its cause, which is rooted in the way
men are forced to grow up.

John Rowan,[5] writing of the barriers he feels in relation to
women, admits to:

> ... a real distaste for certain ways of thinking, feeling and acting
> which I find in women. I don't like being submissive, I don't
> like serving others; I don't like feelings being too near the
> surface, or being at the mercy of my feelings; I don't like gossip
> about neighbours, or talking about relatives, I don't like being
> too patient... there is a long list of these things. And they all
> have one thing in common—these are all things which remind
> me of my mother and not of my father. It is as if I had at some
> time made a note of all the things that remind me of my mother
> and given myself an instruction: 'Don't be like that.'

However, being aware of the prejudice doesn't actually make
it go away. Concepts and theories about the way feelings
have become inaccessible to men are badly needed if they are
to be whole people and not 'fragmented and one sided
apologies for human beings'. Rowan's words are strong, but
he is right that men must redefine masculinity in a way that
acknowledges its drawbacks. Rowan suggests more research
into the notion of 'psychic celibacy', defined as keeping
women mentally and emotionally at arm's length...

Men who have overcome their 'psychic celibacy' in
relation to one another no longer need the controlled
aggressive defensive stance, nor do they need to confirm their
mutuality through bonding together in groups which
exclude women or depend on some external enemy to cement
the bond, often with such destructive consequences. Lionel
Tiger[6] reckoned men bond into groups because of their
mutual positive attraction for one another, but this is
something women express without needing to form gangs or
exclusive clubs. Adam Curle[7] explains that belonging (as in
belonging to a group or to a nation) is a second-class

substitute for self-awareness, and it is this territorial, patriotic consciousness, this need to 'belong', which is the greatest potential destructive force among men, since it involves seeing everything in black and white, living on the surface, denying inner life. And unfortunately those who deny their inner life are more likely to be dominated by it.

Interestingly, men who said they would have volunteered for the Falklands War saw it in might is right, black-and-white terms. Asked about his attitudes to the war, Pete simply said 'I won. We did a good job.' They described the willingness to risk their lives as 'patriotism, knowing what you're doing is right and what they're doing, the other side of the line, is wrong'. However, there were only six would-be volunteers, all of them having been in the forces themselves, and some of them expressed a certain amount of cynicism about heroism:

> By the time you get out there, and realise it's not all shrill trumpets, it's blood and guts, it's too late...

Even the official view, according to one naval psychiatrist sent out with the Task Force,[8] is that 'We have to indoctrinate them. Otherwise they wouldn't fight.' It seems that the tough hero ideal (perhaps in the absence of a military rite of passage into manhood) is modifying itself in men's own minds, along with notions of what constitutes courage.

Out of all the men interviewed, one third said they were pacifist, that war was 'insane' and they would rather go to prison than fight. As Brian put it:

> I don't know what gives men the capacity to risk their lives, but it isn't courage; it's bloody insane, patriotic jingoism, I suppose. I don't understand why people can't leave each other alone. If you could solve that problem, you could solve a lot. How can one person hurt another?

Other pacifists felt that soldiers had no choice and were scared stiff, that they fought out of 'ignorance, misguided loyalty and chauvinistic attitudes in general', or 'bravado, keeping up appearances in front of everyone else,' all

soldiers are 'duped'. While these men were talking, a
different notion of courage began to emerge. They spoke of
feeling pacifist, but not knowing if they would have the
courage to be one. One man said 'I would probably have
been a coward, and gone.'

But while a sizeable proportion of men spoke of the
Falklands War as 'disgusting', 'insane', 'a waste of life and
money, which could have been spent on poverty at home'
instead of 'a lot of young men dying for very little', the
majority of men were still in favour of the war. However
most of these men expressed criticism of the government's
handling of the situation, saying that it should never have
got to the point where force had to be used, and they also had
few illusions about heroism. They saw courage as being the
harnessing of natural aggression, the result of training in
team spirit, not so much courage as discipline and
sometimes blind stupidity:

> A lot of them were bloody frightened, but like gang fights at
> school, if you go out together you can feel quite secure.

Although some men felt it was 'probably instinctive, you
fight all your life', many mentioned the fact that men join
the army not expecting to have to go and fight and are simply
trained to take orders. One man said:

> Men are more foolhardy than women, not necessarily more
> courageous. That's what's wrong with a lot of politicians, men
> do things women would think twice about.

Most men still project their finer feelings on to women, that
it's all right, if necessary, for men to shoot one another to
pieces at a distance ('I could drop a bomb easily, but I don't
know if I could kill someone face to face') but 'seeing a
woman shooting the arse off some poor sod would shatter
too many of my illusions.'

Although, as one man pointed out, all it will take in the
next large-scale war is the capacity to die, and women can do
that as well as men. Men may be seen as more aggressive, but
at the same time aggression as one man put it 'is in us, but we
should grow out of it'. Eisenhower, in the aftermath of the

atomic bomb declared that war had become an anachronism. Men are, however, all over the world, still fighting. The Swedish Advisory Council are quoted as saying:[9]

> What the world needs today is not toughness. We don't need hunters, warriors, power hungry politicians, the world needs a capacity for involvement, a will to cooperate, human understanding, tenderness. This can only be achieved by giving a fair and equal share of the responsibilities of life to both sexes.

It is the feminine qualities of communicating, listening, responding, caring, nurturing which are urgently needed. The danger for men is not being swamped by extreme emotionality, but the cutting-off of emotion that enables men, unlike animals, to kill in cold blood. Increasingly, in the nuclear age, aggression is being questioned. It has been suggested that war is caused by upsetting the balance between aggression and fear; the brainwashing soldiers undergo; the use of long-range weapons, thereby removing appeasement and distress signals which would stop soldiers short of killing. Desmond Morris[10] claimed that the goal of aggression is domination not destruction but that this becomes blurred because of the 'vicious combination of attack remoteness and group co-operativeness'. Tinbergen,[11] who linked territorialism with imbalance between aggression and fear, said that an all-out attack was needed 'on the enemy within' . . .

Meanwhile, arguments as to the inherent (as opposed to acquired) differences between the sexes continue. Some studies argue that differences in the respective hemispheres of men's and women's brains predispose females towards verbal fluency and males towards reasoning and spatial ability. Other tests claim to show that these differences are negligible in that, with practice, girls can catch up on their disadvantage. And nicely positioned between these two points of view is the work of Rupert Sheldrake[12] and his hypothesis of formative causation.

According to this theory, an organism's shape and instinctual or hereditary behaviour depends on fields of influence called morphogenetic fields, rather than the simple transference of matter from gene to gene. Active energy of the living specimens of the organism sets up what is called morphic resonance which acts across time and space. Experiments with rats have shown that if one sample of laboratory rats are taught a new trick, rats of the same breed all over the world will then learn the trick faster. Rupert Sheldrake draws human analogies of this, whereby athletics records are constantly being broken, average IQ levels have been consistently rising, and feels that better education and nutrition do not adequately account for it. The idea, similar to Jung's concept of the collective unconscious, creates a bridge between theories of nature and nurture in that it embraces both. And it confirms the idea that while the sexes live different lives, in different ways, they will remain very different in their outlook and abilities.

However much sex is viewed as a continuum and we are reminded of our androgenous beginnings in the womb, the physiological fact of being male or female for most people creates the most insurmountable dividing line, all through life. How can anyone know what it really feels like to be a member of the opposite sex? Plato, in a famous passage from the *Symposium*, explained how humans were once complete beings, possessing the structure and quality of both sexes. But the gods, threatened by these happy and potent creatures, decided to have them cut into two. Only those who have had sex-change operations are qualified to make comparisons, and even then they usually underwent the operation because they did not feel they fully belonged to the sex to which they had been anatomically ascribed. Jan Morris was one such person. In her fascinating auto-biography, *Conundrum*,[13] she offers intriguing insights into the different sensation of inhabiting a male, as opposed to a female body.

*James* Morris' body:

> ... was lean and sinewy, never ran to fat and worked like a machine of quality, responding exuberantly to the touch of the throttle or a long haul home. Women, I think, never have quite this feeling about their bodies, and I shall never have it again.

She calls this feeling 'unfluctuating control' and reckons men respond to team spirit more than women because they have 'more rhythm than melody', their bodies can work at a more regular pace together. However, while she was still

James Morris, she began to have female hormone treatment, and felt the:

> ... stripping away of the rough hide in which the male person is clad ... a kind of unseen layer of accumulated resilience which provides a shield for the male of the species but at the same time deadens the sensations of the body. It is as though some protective substance has been sprayed on to a man ... so that he is less immediately in contact with the air and the sun ...

As a woman, she felt physically 'freer and more vulnerable. I had no armour.'

In a science fiction short story called 'Options', John Varley[14] describes a society in which people can temporarily, or permanently, switch sex. Those who do so are called 'changers', are more likely to be women, and develop closer, more understanding relationships between the sexes, from a basis of shared understanding. This may not be so far away as it seems from science fact, since Professor John Money of Johns Hopkins University claims genetic engineers are close to enabling people of uncertain sex to spend part of their time as women and part as men. The idea is for the reproductive organs to be encouraged to regress to their rudimentary bisexual origins and then regrown appropriately.[15]

Until then we are left with Plato, and also the allegory of the Third City. Jerusalem and Babylon being the symbolic good and evil cities of the philosophers, the third city, containing elements of both, is real life. It is the polarisation between opposites, the splitting which vests one sex with killing capacity and the other sex with caring qualities, which poses the greatest threat to real life. The saddest obstacles to intimacy between men are the cultural taboos against it, because any male advance is assumed to be sexual. It is not just men approaching women that is suspect, but men approaching small children and above all men approaching one another. We are all so accustomed to the separate, distanced relationships among men that any indication of intimate friendship signals homosexuality. Nearly all the men I interviewed admitted they would feel hostile and/or threatened by an approach from a homosexual. Answers ranged from 'Much as my mind tells me to be liberal about it, homosexuality is, for me, distasteful, there's a deep thing inside me which shrinks from it' to 'They wouldn't dare. Do you want it graphically? I'd end up in court.'

This seems partly because any questioning of their masculinity strikes so close to the bone, but also because of the more general fear of closeness, of 'explosive connection' which Carol Gilligan discovered. Men spend their lives out on the edge of their personal space patrolling its boundaries, having grown up to interpret most infringement of those boundaries as a personal attack. It seems highly significant that the one man who claimed he would feel no embarrassment or discomfort from an approach by a homosexual (and wasn't defensively joking, saying he would be flattered although he wasn't that way inclined) was a man who not only had friends among homosexuals but cuddled his friends and let his son run around with his teddybear in a pram, to the horror of the neighbours.

One of the more hopeful signs of the times is a father's recent description of holding his child for the first time 'It felt fantastic—the closest to being female.' One of the more hopeless is the story[16] of the man who became addicted to a computer he had programmed to tell him that it loved him:

> Although I knew what it would say, the fact that it printed it out by itself made me believe there was really a relationship between us.

His wife left him, because she thought he was having an affair with another woman.

Men have got to start questioning themselves, admitting their lack of skill in making relationships, their fear of closeness to women, to other men and in a very basic sense to themselves. They have got to shatter the myth of masculinity which stifles their expression of their real needs. They are not strong, cool and detached, but a prey to undeveloped emotions because their energy is so exteriorised, simply acting out their conflicts and frustrations, often to the detriment of others. They have got to be kinder to themselves and realise that the sort of strength they are encouraged to develop is a brittle shell, a wall cutting them off from a firmer foundation of strength based on mutual care and acceptance, which accepts weakness and vulnerability as human.

Computer compulsion is apparently a male affliction to which women are immune, perhaps because they do not learn to relate and express their emotions through the safety of objects. Not all the objects men play with and the games they set up are safe, however. Men need to tackle their fear of trust, closeness and open self-awareness not just so that they live longer. So we all live longer.

## NOTES

1 Wallace Shawn, *My Dinner with André* and *Marie and Bruce* (Methuen, London, 1983)

2 Robert A. Fein, 'Men and Young Children' in (eds) Joseph H. Pleck & Jack Sawyer, *Men and Masculinity* (Prentice-Hall, New Jersey, 1974)

3 Brigid Grauman, 'The masculists strike back' (*Guardian* 'Guardian Women', 22 February 1983)

4 John W. Pratt, 'Keep in touch' (*Observer*, 5 June 1983)

5 John Rowan, 'Psychic celibacy in men' in (eds) O. Hartnett, G. Boden & M. Fuller, *Sex Role Stereotyping* (Tavistock, 1979)

6 Lionel Tiger, *Men in Groups* (Nelson, 1969)

7 Adam Curle, *Mystics and Militants* (Tavistock, 1972)

8 Surgeon Commander Morgan O'Connell quoted in Polly Toynbee, '"Yes," says the psychiatrist, "we indoctrinate them in the forces. Otherwise they wouldn't fight"' (*Guardian* 'Guardian Women', 1 November, 1982)

9 Swedish Advisory Council, quoted in Beata Bishop with Pat McNeill, *Below the Belt* (Coventure, 1977)

10 Desmond Morris, *The Human Zoo* (Jonathan Cape, 1969)

11 Niko Tinbergen 'On War and Peace in Animals and Man' (*Science, 160*, pp 1411–1418 28 June 1968)

12 Rupert Sheldrake, *A New Science of Life: The Hypothesis of Formative Causation* (Blond & Briggs, 1981)

13 Jan Morris, *Conundrum* (Faber, 1974)

14 John Varley, 'Options' in (ed) Terry Carr, *Best SF of the Year*, (9) (Gollancz, 1980)

15 Andrew Veitch, 'Sex change "to become routine"' (*Guardian*, 14 March 1983)

16 Jane McLoughlin, 'Discreet charm of the computer' (*Guardian* 'Workface', 1 November, 1983)

# INDEX